82-1440

9.95

JEFFERSON COLLEGE

3 6021 0002

P9-DGX-817

82-1440

LC214.2
.E35   Effective school
                desegregation.

Jefferson College Library
Hillsboro, Mo.   63050

NO LONGER
PROPERTY OF
JEFFERSON
COLLEGE
LIBRARY

SAGE FOCUS EDITIONS

EFFECTIVE
SCHOOL
DESEGREGATION
EQUITY, QUALITY, AND FEASIBILITY

Edited by
Willis D. Hawley

Jefferson College Library
Hillsboro, Mo. 63050

NO LONGER
PROPERTY OF
JEFFERSON
COLLEGE
LIBRARY

 SAGE PUBLICATIONS   Beverly Hills   London

Copyright © 1981 by Sage Publications, Inc.

All rights reserved. No part of this book may be reproduced or utilized in any form or by any means, electronic or mechanical, including photo-copying, recording, or by any information storage and retrieval system, without permission in writing from the publisher.

For information address:

SAGE Publications, Inc.
275 South Beverly Drive
Beverly Hills, California 90212

SAGE Publications Ltd
28 Banner Street
London EC1Y 8QE, England

Printed in the United States of America

Library of Congress Cataloging in Publication Data

Main entry under title:

Effective school desegregation.

(Sage focus editions ; 42)
"Prepared under the auspices of the National Review Panel on School Desegrega-tion Research" —
Bibliography: p.
Contents: Brown in perspective / William L. Taylor — Reducing racial prejudice in desegregated schools / John B. McConahay — Minority achievement / Robert L. Crain and Rita E. Mahard — [etc.]
1. School integration — United States — Addresses, essays, lectures. I. Hawley, Willis D. II. National Review Panel on School Desegregation Research (U.S.)
LC214.2.E35   370.19'342   81-14484
ISBN 0-8039-1455-5   AACR2
ISBN 0-8039-1456-3 (pbk.)

FIRST PRINTING

CONTENTS

PREFACE

The chapters that make up this volume were prepared under the auspices of the National Review Panel on School Desegregation Research. The National Review Panel is a private organization which, since its inception in 1977, has sought to synthesize and interpret the empirical research and legal developments related to school desegregation and to make the findings of this scholarship available to other researchers, policy makers, and practitioners. Primary financial support for the Panel's activities has come from the Ford Foundation. Additional funds have been provided by the National Institute of Education.

The members of the National Review Panel are:

Mark A. Chesler, *University of Michigan*
Robert L. Crain, *Johns Hopkins University*
Edgar G. Epps, *University of Chicago*
Willis D. Hawley, *Vanderbilt University*
Betsy Levin, *University of Colorado*
John B. McConahay, *Duke University*
James M. McPartland, *Johns Hopkins University*
Gary Orfield, *University of Illinois*
Peter Roos, *Mexican-American Legal Defense Fund*
Christine H. Rossell, *Boston University*
William L. Taylor, *Catholic University*
Mark G. Yudof, *University of Texas*

The Panel has been cochaired by Willis D. Hawley and Betsy Levin, who, at the time the project was initiated, were on the faculty of Duke University.

The Panel's activities have centered around the preparation, discussion, and publication of scholarly papers assessing legal developments and social science research relating to the desegregation of elementary and secondary schools. Some of these papers were coauthored with collaborators chosen by the panelists. The first set of papers prepared by the Panel was published in a special two-volume issue of *Law and*

Contemporary Problems (Volume 48, Summer and Autumn, 1978). This volume presents the second set of papers prepared by members of the Panel. There were two chapters (those by Slavin and by Fernandez and Guskin) added to this collection to assure coverage of most of the significant issues affecting desegregation policy and practice.

Throughout its work, the Panel's work has benefitted from the advice and criticism of an advisory board composed of experimental researchers, practitioners, and policy makers. Members of the Advisory Committee are:

Richard D. Ashmore
Joel S. Berke
Elbert D. Brooks
Jose A. Cardenas
Norman J. Chachkin
Joseph M. Cronin
Richard P. Duran
Ricardo R. Fernández
Robert Glaser
Bruce Hare
Arthur Jefferson
Hon. William Wayne Justice
Hon. James B. McMillan
Hon. Robert R. Merhige, Jr.
Thomas K. Minter
Janet W. Schofield
Margaret Beale Spencer
Gail E. Thomas
Meyer Weinberg
Ben Williams
John B. Williams
Paul M. Wortman

The topics dealt with in this book include, as noted, most of the significant issues about which judges, policy makers at all levels of government, educators, and parents of school children are concerned when they evaluate and debate the desirability of school desegregation. The chapters presented here represent the most comprehensive existing collection of studies synthesizing research and suggesting its implications for policy. Collectively, the chapters examine more than 500 studies related directly to desegregation as well as many other books, articles, papers, and legal decisions that are relevant to assessing the possibilities of enhancing the effectiveness of school desegregation.

While the evidence presented in this volume speaks to the question of whether desegregation has worked, the purpose of the chapters is not to question the desirability of desegregation. Rather, they speak to the question of how desegregation, assuming it is to be pursued, can be carried out most effectively.

All in all, the authors of this book conclude that much could be done to enhance the benefits of desegregation and minimize its costs. Moreover, their recommendations would not, in most cases, involve substantial economic costs. They would, however, require many schools to change, both internally and in relation to the parents and the larger communities they serve. Further, the changes required would not involve the sacrifice of such values as high academic achievement for all students, the maintenance of order, or the preservation of pride in one's racial and ethnic identity.

Of course, despite the extensive scope of this book, it does not provide sure-fire answers to all of the important problems of effective desegregation. As researchers are wont to observe, more research is needed. The final chapter of the book identifies a number of policies and practices that school systems can use to enhance the effectiveness of school desegregation.

A number of people have furthered the work of the National Review Panel on School Desegregation Research. The assistance of Ralph Bohrson, Mary von Euler, Marianne Toms, Mark Smylie, and Marilyn Zlotnik has been of particular importance in the preparation of this volume. While we acknowledge assistance, we should also note that the analyses and interpretations presented in these pages do not necessarily reflect the views of the Ford Foundation or the National Institute of Education.

OUTLINE OF THIS VOLUME

In Chapter 1, William Taylor, Director of the Center for National Policy Review at the Catholic University, provides the legal context within which the policies and strategies for more effective desegregation must be developed.

Part II is concerned with the effects of desegregation on students. John McConahay, who is on the faculties of policy sciences and psychology at Duke University, identifies the conditions under which school desegregation is most likely to enhance race relations. Robert

Crain of the Rand Corporation and the Johns Hopkins University, and Rita Mahard, a graduate student of the University of Michigan, find that when minority students are desegregated in early grades, there are positive effects on their achievement. Crain and Mahard also find that white students in a given school or district almost never experience reduced rates of academic performance as a result of desegregation. Most of the research on minority students in desegregated schools has focused on black youngsters. The *Brown* decision focused attention on the psychological damage to children of racial segregation. Edgar Epps, Professor of Educational Psychology at the University of Chicago, examines the complicated literature related to this question. He notes that, in general, desegregation can produce stronger self-assessment and achievement orientations among minority children, but that this is often not what happens. He suggests some policies that seem likely to enhance the potential benefits of desegregation.

Ricardo Fernández and Judith Guskin, of the School of Education at the University of Wisconsin at Milwaukee, draw attention to the special problems of desegregating school systems in which bilingual educational programs are needed, and suggest some ways to deal with these challenges. James McPartland and Jomills Braddock of the Johns Hopkins University point out that the consequences of desegregation extend to job opportunities and experiences in postsecondary education.

Part III of the book is concerned with demographic aspects of desegregation. Christine Rossell of Boston University and I summarize what is known about white flight to suburbia and to private schools. We suggest a number of things that might be done to encourage parents to keep their children in public schools or to encourage those who have left to return. Gary Orfield of the University of Illinois at Urbana describes the relationship between desegregation and housing policy. He suggests strategies that will enhance the desegregation of residential areas and thus decrease the need for busing to achieve desegregation.

The final part of the book deals with various aspects of organizing school systems for effective desegregation. One of the things about desegregation that seems to concern parents and teachers very much is that it results in more diverse and apparently more difficult to manage student bodies. Robert Slavin of the Johns Hopkins University shows how racially and socially diverse classrooms can be structured so as to promote both better race relations and higher achievement for children of both high and low levels of academic performance.

Mark Yudof, Professor of Law at the University of Texas, examines the intrinsic difficulties of implementing desegregation policies which invariably are mandated by courts or federal and state agencies but ultimately depend for their effectiveness on the ability and commitment of educators and parents at the level of the school. James Crowfoot and Mark A. Chesler identify a number of community and school-level strategies for enhancing the positive effects of desegregation, and draw attention to the difficulties of successfully implementing these "attractive ideas."

The concluding chapter of the volume is intended to serve as an epilogue. I draw heavily on the other studies in the book to identify several key characteristics of effective desegregated schools and school systems. I also address the often-heard claim that minority students would be better served by focusing more on improving racially isolated schools than by desegregation . . . and conclude (as the title of this book suggests) that there is little, if any, contradiction among the goals of equity, excellence, and feasibility in the process of desegregating American public schools.

Willis D. Hawley
Nashville, Tennessee

PART I

**THE LEGAL CONTEXT OF
DESEGREGATION POLICY**

1

BROWN IN PERSPECTIVE

WILLIAM L. TAYLOR

The effort to make *Brown* v. *Board of Education* (1954) a reality by ending deliberate segregation in public schools across the nation has been going on for more than a quarter of a century, and it is still to be completed. In that time, *Brown* and later decisions giving content to its principles have generated conflict and controversy at every level of society.

One difficulty with the public debate is that it rarely gets to the heart of the matter. Politicians and community activists center their attacks on desegregation on the use of busing, neglecting the fact that the real concerns of parents go far more to the perceived quality of schools than to the means of transportation. Journalists focus overwhelmingly on a single moment in time — the conflict that frequently occurs when desegregation plans are first implemented — ignoring both the past and the unfolding story of how the plans work after they have been in operation for several years. Academics continue to use the *Brown* decision as a playground for theories, often highly abstract, about the role of courts and government in dealing with social problems.

The intent of this essay is to redirect attention to what I regard as basic issues:

(1) whether in outlawing deliberate segregation, the original *Brown* decision was solidly based on principles the Supreme Court has traditionally used in interpreting the Constitution;

(2) whether the comprehensive remedies that courts have imposed over the past decade depart from the principles of *Brown* or are otherwise of questionable legitimacy; and

(3) whether there is a fit between what research and practical experience tell us about the educational needs of children.

Recognizing that an issue that is central to one person may be peripheral to another, it is submitted that the critical questions that have persisted over time concern the legitimacy of court actions on desegregation and the practical impact of those actions on the education of children.

WAS THE BROWN DECISION
SOLIDLY GROUNDED IN THE CONSTITUTION?

In the years of massive resistance that followed *Brown,* part of the attack was based on the notion that the decision did not have a solid basis in the Constitution and rested, instead, on shaky sociological evidence that racial segregation caused educational harm to black children.

The charge focused on the Court's statement (*Brown* v. *Board of Education* 1954: 494) that the separation of black children "from others of similar age solely because of their race generates a feeling of inferiority as to their status in the community that may affect their hearts and minds in ways unlikely ever to be undone." The Court also quoted approvingly from a lower court opinion in the Kansas case:

> Segregation of white and colored children has a detrimental effect upon the colored children. . . . The policy of separating the races is usually interpreted as denoting inferiority of the negro group. A sense of inferiority affects the motivation of children to learn. Segregation with sanction of laws, therefore, has a tendency to [retard] the educational and mental development of negro children and deprives them of some of the benefits they would receive in a racial[ly] integrated school system [*Brown* v. *Board of Education,* 1954: 494].

In embracing this finding, the Court said it was "amply supported by modern authority," citing, in its celebrated Footnote 11, the work of Kenneth Clark and several other social scientists.

Much of the criticism that followed was based on the view that social science evidence is a flimsy foundation for constitutional decision making since the findings of social scientists may be altered by new research or may even change with the times (see, for example, Cahn, 1956).

But this criticism of *Brown* can be valid only if it is assumed that the findings of educational harm were an essential part of the decision and that without them there would have been no legitimate constitutional basis for striking down segregation laws. That assumption is unfounded. The heart of *Brown* may be found early in the *Brown* Court's opinion in which the Court quotes from an 1879 decision of the Supreme Court setting forth the central purposes of the Fourteenth Amendment:

> The words of the amendment, it is true, are prohibitory, but they contain a necessary implication of a positive immunity, or right, most valuable to the colored race, — the *right to exemption from unfriendly legislation* against them distinctively as colored, — exemption from legal discriminations, *implying inferiority* in civil society, lessening the security of their enjoyment of the rights which others enjoy, and discriminations which are steps toward reducing them to the condition of a subject race [*Strauder* v. *West Virginia*, 1879: 307-308; italics added].

Whatever else may be said of the racial segregation laws that pervaded the South and border states in 1954, it cannot be denied that they were "unfriendly legislation." Segregation statutes were adopted in the nineteenth century without the participation or consent of disenfranchised black people, and they were intended to affix second-class status on people solely by virtue of their race. In the words of one commentator, such laws were a "massive intentional disadvantaging of the Negro race" (Black, 1959).

In the companion case to *Brown*, *Bolling* v. *Sharpe* (1954), the Court employed a parallel method of legal analysis. The opinion noted that "classifications based solely on race must be scrutinized with particular care, since they are contrary to our traditions and hence constitutionally suspect" (*Bolling* v. *Sharpe*, 1954: 499). The question, then, was whether such scrutiny would yield a persuasive governmental purpose for racial segregation in the public schools. The principal justification offered had been that keeping the races separate was useful in maintaining peace and order, an unsupported argument that, if sustained, would validate repressive treatment of any unpopular group whose presence or assertion of rights might spur conflict. Accordingly, the Court concluded that "segregation in public education is not reasonably related to any proper governmental objective," and thus imposed on black children of the District of Columbia a denial of their rights to due process and equal protection of the laws (*Bolling* v. *Sharpe*, 1954: 500).

What is notable about the "unfriendly legislation" and "racial classification" analyses is that both follow traditional paths of constitutional interpretation and that neither depends upon the presentation of evidence that segregation causes psychological or educational damage to black people. Under the first analysis, the *intent* of the legislation is pivotal; parties challenging an act that has a racial purpose are not required to prove effects beyond the fact that the legislation was actually carried out. Under the second analysis, effects are also irrelevant unless state officials, in seeking to carry their burden of demonstrating a legitimate governmental purpose, are able to show that segregation practices have beneficial educational results.

The treatment of detailed evidence of harm or effect as unnecessary is hardly novel in constitutional litigation. Indigent criminal defendants, for example, are not required, in seeking to establish a right to counsel, to present evidence that defendants who have lawyers fare better in the criminal justice system than those who represent themselves. In our constitutional system, liberty and the right to fair or equal treatment at the hands of government are values entitled to respect in and of themselves; a person asserting them need not prove their practical value in order to obtain the law's protection.

While the constitutional bases of *Brown* remain open to debate, every development since 1954 reinforces the argument that the Court's citation of evidence of psychological harm to black children was not essential to its decision. In the years immediately following *Brown*, the Court summarily struck down a host of other laws requiring segregation of municipal golf courses, public parks, restaurants, and other public facilities without any suggestion at all that the plaintiffs had demonstrated, or needed to demonstrate, that such practices caused psychological harm (see, for example, *Holmes* v. *City of Atlanta*, 1955; *Mayor of Baltimore* v. *Dawson*, 1955; *Gayle* v. *Browden*, 1956). Nor has the Supreme Court (or lower courts) permitted state officials to relitigate the issue of psychological harm — a matter that would certainly be relevant if the result in *Brown* turned on the weight of "modern authority." The Court has also made it abundantly clear in decisions amplifying *Brown* that school segregation cannot be attacked successfully in federal courts without proof that it was racially motivated — a result inconsistent with the view that the Court in *Brown* was simply striking down governmental practices that have a harmful effect (see *Swann* v. *Charlotte-Mecklenburg Board of Education*, 1971: 24, 28; *Keyes* v. *School District No. 1, Denver, Colorado*, 1973: 208).

Why then did Justice Warren's opinion place such emphasis on the psychological damage done by segregation? The answer may be in the political context in which the case was decided. The Court was well aware that its decision to end a racial caste system that had been entrenched in large areas of the nation for more than a half-century, and that had been thought to be legally acceptable, would evoke strong reactions. Recognizing that the legal imperatives for the decision would be obscure to most people, the Court sought to appeal to the moral conscience of the nation (Kluger, 1976: 705ff). "Look," the opinion said in effect, "we take this major step, not only because it is legally necessary, but because the lives and careers of children are at stake."

Every important piece of research done since *Brown* has confirmed the Court's view that segregation is harmful to black children (Coleman et al., 1966). But it is ironic that, in an effort to appeal persuasively to moral conscience, the Court simply engendered more controversy about its decision.

HAVE THE COURTS GONE TOO FAR IN IMPOSING REMEDY?

ARE "SYSTEMWIDE" OR "RACIAL BALANCE" REMEDIES LEGALLY JUSTIFIED?

The original controversy over *Brown* has faded. Many critics of the role of federal courts in school desegregation cases would now concede that the *Brown* decision, in striking down laws and policies which classify people by race without justification, was solidly grounded in constitutional jurisprudence. But some do object to remedies required by lower courts and approved by the Supreme Court in the wake of *Brown* — remedies that these critics say impose racial balance on the public schools and go far beyond what is necessary to correct the wrongs committed by state legislatures or school boards. These objections are directed against plans commonly adopted by federal courts since 1971 which call for "systemwide" desegregation. Systemwide plans require that all public schools be desegregated — often using as a rough guideline that schools should reflect within 15 to 20 percentage points the racial composition of the system as a whole. Exceptions are limited to schools where such desegregation could be achieved only by having children spend an excessive amount of time on buses. School districts are often required to make whatever adjustments are required to maintain the desegregated character of the school for 3 to 5 years.

The reasoning of the critics of such plans is along the following lines: The equitable power of federal courts is properly used to devise remedies that do no less and *no more* than eliminate the wrong that violates the Constitution; the wrong in school cases is the segregation imposed by government officials, not the segregation that comes about through the exercise of private choice by citizens, such as through decisions to cluster together in segregated neighborhoods, even when such choice may be motivated by prejudice; systemwide plans such as those adopted in Charlotte-Mecklenburg, North Carolina, and Denver, Colorado, are overreaching in that they cure not only segregative conditions brought about by government action but those caused by private choice.

Perhaps the most explicit expression of this point of view is contained in the opinion of Justice Rehnquist in *Dayton Board of Education* v. *Brinkman* (1977: 420):

> The duty . . . is to first determine whether there was any action in the conduct of the school board which was intended to, and did in fact, discriminate against minority pupils, teachers or staff. . . . If such violations are found, the District Court in the first instance . . . must determine how much *incremental segregative impact* these violations had on the racial distribution of the Dayton school population as presently constituted, when that condition is compared to what it would have been in the absence of such constitutional violations. The remedy must be designed to redress that difference.

Justice Rehnquist conceded that determining "incremental segregative impact" (the difference between the segregation that exists now and that which would exist if the government had done no wrong) is "a difficult task." The question is whether it is possible at all.

Critics of "racial balance" remedies have suggested two approaches — "free choice" and "neighborhood assignment" — that they say would be designed to redress the wrong of government-imposed separation without overreaching. Neither approach withstands scrutiny.

Freedom of choice. If segregation violates the Constitution only when it is imposed by government, why would not a remedy that gives all parents and children a free choice of schools they will attend cure the wrong? The Supreme Court's answer came in *Green* v. *School Board of New Kent County* (1968). Having recently emerged from an era of massive resistance in which even token desegregation was forbidden, a rural school system in Virginia proposed in 1967 to meet its obligations by allowing black children to elect to attend its all-white school and white children to choose the all-black school. Only a handful of black children and no white children made that choice. In rejecting the New Kent School Board's plan as inadequate, the Supreme Court took note of practical conditions existing in many parts of the South that inhibited the exercise of free choice by black people — their status of economic dependency and fears of economic and physical reprisals if they chose desegregation (*Green* v. *School Board of New Kent County*, 1968: 440-441).[1]

The validity of the Court's observations is hardly limited to the conditions that existed in the Deep South in the 1960s. In any place where racial isolation has been the government-sanctioned norm for many years, whites as well as blacks will be constrained by racial fears and misunderstandings from seeking out interracial contact, especially when the onus of choice is placed upon each individual. Even if the situation were not emotionally charged, simple inertia might impel large numbers of people to opt for the status quo over the unknown benefits of a change that cannot be described in advance. In short, it cannot be said that replacing a long-entrenched government racial assignment system with a program of allowing individual choice will recreate the situation that would have existed in the absence of the government wrong. In fact, any "free choice" program is likely to fall far short of abolishing the effects of government-imposed segregation.

Neighborhood assignment. If free choice would not be adequate to eliminate discrimination and restore the rights of black children, some have suggested that replacing the racially dual assignment system with a "neutral" system would accomplish the task. Since school boards ordinarily seek to have students attend the schools closest to their homes, substituting neighborhood assignments for racial assignments would seem logical.

The difficulty with this line of reasoning is that it assumes (1) that the racial composition of neighborhoods has been uninfluenced by the segregated character of the public schools and (2) that government housing policies have not contributed to racially segregated neighborhoods in the same way government school policies established segregated schools. Both of these assumptions are wrong.

The Supreme Court has not yet addressed as a body the latter issue — whether in fashioning a school desegregation remedy, lower courts should take into account the ways in which discriminatory housing policies (such as enforcement of racially restrictive covenants, approval of the discriminatory practices of real estate brokers, segregated placement of public and other subsidized housing) contributed to the growth of segregated neighborhoods.[2] But the role of government at all levels in fostering the growth of segregated housing is hardly in dispute.

The Supreme Court *has* shown a keen awareness of the fact that segregated schools have contributed to the establishment of segregated neighborhoods. In *Swann* v. *Charlotte-Mecklenburg Board of Education* (1971: 20), the Court said: "People gravitate toward school facilities just as schools are located in response to the needs of people."

Thus, when schools were rigidly identified as black or white under the old dual systems, it was not unexpected that black and white families would cluster around the schools that their children were permitted to attend.

Less blatant practices may have the same effect. In *Swann*, the Court discussed such practices as locating new schools in the path of white development or building schools to a size which would accommodate only black children in the area. The opinion concluded:

> Such a policy [segregative site selection] does more than simply influence the short-run composition of the student body of a new school. It may well promote segregated residential patterns which, when combined with "neighborhood zoning" further lock the school system into the mold of separation of the races [*Swann v. Charlotte-Mecklenburg Board of Education,* 1971: 20-21].

In the *Keyes* case, the Court examined the impact of other types of segregative school policies — for instance, the common practice of creating optional zones which permit white students to transfer out of neighborhood schools that have growing black populations. These and other practices

> have the clear effect of earmarking schools according to their racial composition, and this, in turn together with the elements of student assignment and school construction, may have a profound reciprocal effect on the racial composition of residential neighborhoods within a metropolitan area, thereby causing further racial concentration within the schools [*Keyes v. School District No. 1, Denver, Colorado,* 1973: 202].

What the Court has recognized is that, appealing as it may sound, a "neutral" system of neighborhood assignment cannot redress the wrong of deliberate school segregation. It leaves out of account the fact that racially separate neighborhoods themselves are a product of school segregation laws and policies.

In fact, granting that some segregation would likely exist even if government had never decreed it, there may be no way to extract it from the immeasurable consequences of a public order which separated and stigmatized black people for more than two centuries. If that is so, Justice Rehnquist's quest for "incremental segregative impact" is an exercise in fiction.

In the film *It's a Wonderful Life,* the protagonist, played by Jimmy Stewart, is on the verge of suicide because he considers his life a failure when a "guardian angel" intervenes. The angel is able to recreate the distressed circumstances of the hero's town, friends, and family as they would have been if the hero had never lived, and thus to demonstrate to him that he had made a real contribution to the well-being and prosperity of all. The movie ends happily.

Lacking such divine intervention, there is no way in school segregation cases to recreate the situation that would exist if the wrong had never occurred. What, then, is a court conscientiously concerned with "tailoring the scope of the remedy to fit the scope of the wrong" to do? Unfortunately for public understanding, the Court has not addressed the dilemma squarely, but rather has dealt with it in the obscure language of legal presumptions. Justice Rehnquist would place on black parents and children the legal burden of proving that segregation would not exist in any event. Since there is no way to meet this burden, plaintiffs would rarely, if ever, achieve more than a token remedy.

A majority of the Court has rejected the Rehnquist view and has held that if government practices played a substantial role in creating segregation in a public school system, the burden is on the defendants to prove that any segregation they propose to allow to remain was innocently caused. Since public officials can no more easily meet this burden than black parents could meet the Rehnquist burden, most court orders call for eliminating segregation as completely as is feasible, the remedy that critics dub "racial balance."

Underlying the majority's use of legal presumptions and its decision to place the burden of proof on school officials are an awareness that fashioning a remedy is hardly a scientific endeavor and a practical determination that the risks of doing too little far exceed those of doing too much.

If a court does too little, that is, permits the continuation of some segregation that may be attributable to government actions, the legal harm is irreparable. Some minority children will spend their entire school careers in the racially isolated classrooms designed for them by government authorities. If, on the other hand, a court should err by doing too much, ordering more desegregation than is warranted, the harm will be far more limited and temporary. Parents who would choose to send their children to racially homogeneous, isolated schools will find their freedom constrained in that they will no longer be able to assure that choice by locating in a segregated neighborhood. However one may assess the legal harm of such a constraint, it is only of a temporary nature. The Court, in *Swann* (1971: 31-32), made it clear that lower courts could maintain "racial balance" orders for only a limited period of time:

> It does not follow that the communities served by such [court-ordered desegregated] school systems will remain demographically stable, for in a growing mobile society, few will do so. Neither school authorities nor district courts are constitutionally required to make year-by-year adjustments of the racial composition of student bodies once the affirmative duty to desegregate has been accomplished and racial discrimination through official action has been eliminated from the system.

When the duration of a desegregation remedy is thus limited, the dangers of doing "too much" are minimized, if not eliminated. For if segregation is a result of private preferences or other factors not traceable to government discrimination, it will reemerge, creating in practice the condition (what "would have been in the absence of . . . constitutional violations") that Justice Rehnquist would like to attain but about which he can only speculate.

Indeed, there are grounds for suggesting that the Court's current formulation of remedy errs on the side of doing too little rather than too much. It is reasonable to assume that continuing private preferences for racial separation are in part a product of years of conditioning of attitudes under the government-imposed regimen of segregation. If the period allowed for active court supervision of the effort to "accomplish the affirmative duty to desegregate" and to eliminate official discrimination is a short one — and most courts interpret *Swann* to permit them 3 to 5 years for "racial balancing" — it is questionable whether there is sufficient time to counteract the effects on attitudes of years of state-imposed segregation.

Further, hardly anyone doubts that the old order of segregated inferior education visited severe, if immeasurable, penalties on the economic status and earning abilities of black people. Had segregation not limited their opportunities, many blacks would undoubtedly have achieved an economic status that would permit them to live in more affluent neighborhoods and have a freer choice of public schools. If a return to neighborhood schools is permitted after a relatively brief period of "racial balancing," many black families will be forced into segregated situations they would never have occupied if not for the original state policy of segregation.

Finally, the Court thus far has refused to apply the understanding it displayed in *Swann* and *Keyes* of the impact of school segregation practices on demographic patterns to situations where black and white communities are separated by school district boundaries. In the common situation of a central-city district that is 80 percent black in its enrollment surrounded by suburban districts that are 90 percent white the Court has not yet been willing to assume that practices confining black students to particular schools in the central city are necessarily related to the all-white character of suburban schools and neighborhoods. Nor has the Court said explicitly that racial housing and zoning practices that have kept black families out of the suburbs provide a sufficient basis for ordering suburban schools desegregated. Only in cases in which the Court has determined that there was some manipulation of school district lines for purposes of retaining segregation has it approved orders for systemwide desegregation on a metropolitan basis (see *Evans* v. *Buchanan,* 1976, aff'd., 1977); *United States* v. *Board of School Commissioners of Indianapolis,* 1973.

The result is that in Detroit, Atlanta, and other metropolitan areas where it has been established that government authorities segregated black children within the city and kept black families out of the suburbs, remedies have been limited to the token desegregation that could be accomplished within the confines of each jurisdiction.

The quest for causality in school desegregation cases may be viewed as necessary — a product both of the judicial tradition of matching remedies to wrongs and of the distinction between "private" and "state" action that still pervades Fourteenth Amendment jurisprudence. But the effort must be recognized as artificial in many respects. A dominant racial group used government throughout much of the nineteenth and twentieth centuries to enforce its prejudices and fears by segregating minorities. No one can gauge with accuracy the ramifications of this long use of governmental authority as a means for affixing second-class status on black people and rigidly curbing their opportunities. Justice Rehnquist's suggestion that courts must recreate the situation that would have existed without the wrong may be appropriate when the issue is assessing damages for a broken contract, but as applied to the web of history in American race relations it borders on the absurd.

Thus, no court-prescribed remedy, from "freedom of choice" to "racial balance," can be clothed in the mantle of precise compensatory justice. But in seeking to determine whether proposed remedies are too broad or too narrow, certain factors must be taken into account. The impact of segregated, inferior education reaches far beyond the schools to the racial character of neighborhoods and the economic status of black people. The imprimatur of government on practices of racial separation is sure to have conditioned the attitudes of white and black citizens in ways that will take time to erase. And the political power relationships that originally enabled dominant whites to use government as a tool for imposing their will on blacks have changed only to a modest degree — leaving courts in their crucial role of protector of rights that cannot be adequately protected elsewhere in the political process.

Viewed in this context, the limited-duration systemwide remedies approved by the Supreme Court in school desegregation cases can hardly be viewed as too broad. If anything, they may be too limited to right a grievous wrong.

DO SYSTEMWIDE REMEDIES MAKE EDUCATIONAL SENSE?

If the Court's ruminations about causality appear to be appropriate enterprise for philosophers or Talmudic scholars, there is another more practical aspect to the work of the judiciary in shaping remedy. As Justice Warren noted in the second *Brown* decision (1955: 300) concerning implementation:

> Traditionally, equity has been characterized by a practical flexibility in shaping its remedies and by a facility for adjusting and reconciling public and private needs.

Clearly, the more the Court permits remedy to be dictated by mechanistic formulations of cause-effect of the type proposed by Justice Rehnquist, the less ability it will have to take into account practical considerations of what type of desegregation plan is likely to work best for each community. Fortunately, the justices have not donned this straitjacket, though a number of them apparently wish to do so. The question, then, is whether the systemwide remedies frequently mandated by district courts and approved by the Supreme Court have proved to be sound educational policy and meet other community needs. Research and practical experience strongly suggest that the answer is "yes."

First, while the federal courts have refused to revisit the findings made in *Brown* that racial segregation causes harm to black children, all of the major studies since 1954 have confirmed the Court's view (see, for example, Coleman et al., 1966; U.S. Commission on Civil Rights, 1967; Mosteller and Moynihan, 1972). These studies have traced the harm associated with segregation to the importance of peer group influence in determining educational outcomes and to the ways in which schools whose students are mostly black and poor are stigmatized by important groups in the community.

Second, these studies have concluded specifically that children from disadvantaged backgrounds fare better in schools and classrooms where a majority of the students come from advantaged backgrounds than in schools where they are isolated with others of the same background. While race and socioeconomic status obviously are not interchangeable characteristics, in most communities socioeconomic desegregation can be achieved only by providing for significant racial desegregation. The importance of this finding for courts considering desegregation remedies is that only by adopting systemwide plans is it ordinarily possible to establish schools and classrooms consisting predominantly of advantaged students. More limited plans that exempt substantial numbers of schools (to avoid busing or for other reasons) are likely to leave many classrooms with disproportionate numbers of disadvantaged students — the situation that education researchers find least desirable.

Third, the perceptions of parents are in accord with the findings of the researchers. Despite the continuing emotional debate over busing, most parents are less concerned about the means by which their children get to school than about the quality of education offered. And they, too, perceive schools and classrooms that consist largely of advantaged students as providing a better educational environment than those in which most students are disadvantaged (Giles et al., 1975). In Tampa-Hillsborough, Florida, Charlotte-Mecklenburg, North Carolina, and other places where courts have ordered systemwide desegregation, parents have accepted the plans, despite the fact that extensive busing was required, apparently because they regard the classroom situation created as advantageous, or at least reasonable. Based on this experience, a court legitimately concerned about stability, that is, whether parents are likely to accept a reassignment plan or to destabilize it by relocating or enrolling their children in private schools, would almost always prefer a systemwide remedy to more limited proposals.

The major exception to this experience has occurred in central cities where "systemwide remedies" exclude suburban areas that lie in separate school districts, resulting in a situation in which, even when desegregated, every city school contains high proportions of minority and disadvantaged students. Social scientists do not agree completely on whether the instability of city-only systemwide plans is due to the continuing trend toward suburbanization of affluent whites or whether school desegregation itself has an independent role in causing "white flight" (see Rossell, 1978; Coleman, 1975; Farley, 1975). In either event, the problem lies less in the breadth of the plan than in the fact that, in contrast to Charlotte-Mecklenburg and Tampa-Hillsborough, courts have found themselves unable to adopt a systemwide remedy that embraces the entire metropolitan community.

Where school desegregation *is* metropolitan in character, there is growing evidence that it leads not only to stability in the public schools but also to increased housing integration. One recent study of seven communities that had desegregated schools on a metropolitan basis found that residential desegregation occurred far more rapidly than in similar communities where school desegregation was more limited or was not ordered at all (Pearce, 1980). The explanation is that once schools are no longer earmarked as white or black by the racial composition of the public schools, families are freer to exercise residential choice. Some court orders, such as in Louisville, encourage the process by exempting students in integrated neighborhoods from transportation requirements. As implementation of metropolitan desegregation continues, it will lead to a decline in the need for busing.

No one claims that school desegregation orders have proved to be a panacea. Functional illiteracy, unemployment, and asocial behavior still are pervasive facts of life for youth in poor and minority areas, although it is worth noting that they are at their worst in the largest cities, where the barrier of racial isolation has not even been dented. Even in schools that have been physically desegregated many problems may remain. Teachers, counselors, and staff may be ill-prepared to work with minority and poor children. Testing devices may be used to lock students into tracks for low achievers, isolating them as effectively as if the school had never been desegregated. Even when desegregation takes place in the early grades, children may arrive at school with accumulated disadvantages of a life in poverty that are difficult to overcome.

Recent court decisions have taken practical note of some of these problems. In 1977, the Supreme Court sustained orders that, as part of desegregation remedy, state resources be made available for in-service training of teachers and for compensatory programs in reading and mathematics (*Milliken* v. *Bradley,* 1977: 282).[3] Lower court orders have sought to deal with the most arbitrary practices of classifying and stereotyping minority children (see *Larry P.* v. *Riles,* 1972, aff'd 1974). These decisions — which tread a careful line between the judiciary's proper role in removing structural or procedural unfairness form public institutions and inappropriate efforts to dictate substantive educational policy — cannot, of course, assure effective teaching or improvements in student achievement. They can remove impediments to these goals.

What is striking, however, is not the persistence of problems but the progress that has been made. Case studies support the more general social science research about the gains associated with desegregation. In a comprehensive summary of the evidence from about 65 communities, social scientists Crain and Mahard (1978) note that 4 of every 5 studies show gains by minority students, and that no study has suggested that black or white students suffer academically from desegregation. Equally as important, the desegregation breakthroughs that occurred in the late 1960s were followed by substantial increases in the enrollment of minority students at major universities and professional schools and by advances in the job market. In ways that researchers find difficult to quantify, desegregation appears to have given minority children access to the opportunities they need to realize their potential and join the mainstream.

In sum, more than a decade's experience suggests that the system-wide remedies meet the standards of practicality and effectiveness that courts (and citizens) appropriately use as a measuring rod. Once the initial phase of conflict and resistance to change has been surmounted, systemwide desegregation has been marked by community acceptance, stability, and educational gains. The notable exceptions have occurred in cities in which courts have permitted the scope of the remedy to be limited to a district consisting disproportionately of minority and poor students. In fact, if there is a lesson to be learned from the experience of the past ten years, it is that, even at the cost of substantial busing, the more comprehensive the desegregation plan, the more likely it is to be successful.

CONCLUSION

The future course of school desegregation efforts in the courts is by no means certain. If the Supreme Court, as it did in *Milliken I* (1974: 814) persists in regarding school district boundaries as a nearly insuperable barrier to desegregation (a decision that Justice Marshall characterized as "more a reflection of a perceived public mood that we have gone far enough . . . than it is the product of neutral principles of law"), ending racial isolation in many urban areas may become a practical impossibility.[4] If politicians in Congress and elsewhere increase their pressure, the courts ultimately may be impelled to pull back even from the types of systemwide remedies that they are currently mandating.

The nature of the threat to school desegregation efforts should be clear. If these efforts are curtailed, it will not be because of a belated recognition that the *Brown* decision was not solidly grounded in constitutional jurisprudence. Nor will it happen because the courts, in fashioning systemwide remedies, have departed from the principles of *Brown* to impose their own social and educational policies, or because desegregation remedies in practice have proved a failure. On the contrary, the history of *Brown* has been a remarkable demonstration of how the courts, acting within appropriate limits, can set in motion a chain of events that can lead to significant social change.

If regression does come, it will stem from the fact that school desegregation poses the most difficult task that the judiciary has set for itself — protecting the rights of the politically powerless in situations in which they cannot receive adequate protection elsewhere in the political process. The courts have faltered before in dealing with the claims of racial minorities, as when the Supreme Court helped signal the end of Reconstruction with the observation that, when emancipated, slaves should "cease to be the special favorite of the laws" (Civil Rights Cases, 1883). If one thing is certain, however, it is that the nagging question of racial discrimination in public institutions will not disappear.

NOTES

1. In view of the fact that fourteen years had gone by without any desegregation in most of the South, the Court did not propose in *Green* that lower courts engage in a community-by-community inquiry into whether such restraints existed on the exercise of free choice. Such an inquiry would have delayed the desegregation process for several more years. Instead, the Court, exercising its authority to seek practical solutions, decided to make "effectiveness," that is, whether black and white children actually enrolled in desegregated schools, the test of whether free choice would be permitted.

2. In Swan v. Charlotte-Mecklenburg Board of Education (1971), the Court said it would reserve this question for future consideration. In his concurring opinion in the Milliken case (1977), Justice Stewart expressed an individual view that deliberate government housing policies that excluded black people from suburbs could provide a basis for a metropolitan school desegregation remedy. The argument for ameliorating the results of government housing discrimination in a school decree, rather than requiring it to be attacked separately, is one of practicality. Housing discrimination takes many years to correct, and there is no persuasive reason that several generations of children should be compelled to attend the segregated schools created by such practices while housing patterns are being changed.

3. The Court concluded that many of the educational problems of minority children were fairly traceable to state-imposed segregation.

4. For a discussion of Milliken v. Bradley (1974), see Taylor (1975).

CASES

BOLLING v. SHARPE (1954) 347 U.S. 497

BROWN v. BOARD OF EDUCATION [BROWN I] (1954) 347 U.S. 483

BROWN v. BOARD OF EDUCATION [BROWN II] (1955) 349 U.S. 294

CIVIL RIGHTS CASES (1883) 109 U.S. 3

DAYTON BOARD OF EDUCATION v. BRINKMAN (1977) 433 U.S. 406

EVANS v. BUCHANAN (1976) 416 F. Supp. 328 (D. Del.); aff'd. 555 F.2d 373 (3rd Cir., 1977)

GAYLE v. BROWDEN (1956) 352 U.S. 903

GREEN v. SCHOOL BOARD OF NEW KENT COUNTY (1968) 391 U.S. 430

HOLMES v. CITY OF ATLANTA (1955) 350 U.S. 879

KEYES v. SCHOOL DISTRICT NO. 1, DENVER, COLORADO (1973) 413 U.S. 189

LARRY P. v RILES (1972) 343 F. Supp. 1306 (N.D. Cal.); aff'd. 502 F.2d 963 (9th Cir., 1974) (per curiam)

MAYOR OF BALTIMORE v. DAWSON (1955) 350 U.S. 877

MILLIKEN v. BRADLEY [MILLIKEN I] (1974) 418 U.S. 717

MILLIKEN v. BRADLEY [MILLIKEN II] (1977) 433 U.S. 267

STRAUDER v. WEST VIRGINIA (1879) 100 U.S. 303

SWANN v. CHARLOTTE-MECKLENBURG BOARD OF EDUCATION (1971) 402 U.S. 1

UNITED STATES v. BOARD OF SCHOOL COMMISSIONERS OF IN-DIANAPOLIS (1973) 474 F.2d 81 (7th Cir.)

REFERENCES

BLACK, C. L. (1959) "The lawfulness of the segregation decision." Yale Law Journal 69: 421-430.

CAHN, E. (1956) "Jurisprudence." New York University Law Review 31: 182-195.

COLEMAN, J. S. (1975) "Racial segregation in the schools: new research with new policy implications." Phi Delta Kappan 57, 10: 75-78.

———— E. Q. CAMPBELL, C. J. HOBSON, J. McPARTLAND, A. M. MOOD, F. D. WEINFELD, and R. L. YORK (1966) Equality of Educational Opportunity. Washington, DC: Government Printing Office.

CRAIN, R. L. and R. E. MAHARD (1978) "Desegregation and black achievement: a review of the research." Law and Contemporary Problems 42, 3: 17-56.

FARLEY, R. (1975) "Residential segregation and its implications for school integration." Law and Contemporary Problems 39, 1: 164-193.

GILES, M. W., E. F. CATALDO, and D. S. GATLIN (1975) "Desegregation and the private school alternative," in G. Orfield (ed.) Symposium on School Desegregation. Washington, DC: Government Printing Office.

KLUGER, R. (1976) Simple Justice. New York: Knopf.

MOSTELLER, F. and D. P. MOYNIHAN (1972) On Equality of Educational Opportunity. New York: Random House.

PEARCE, D. (1980) Breaking Down Barriers: New Evidence on the Impact of Metropolitan School Desegregation on Housing Patterns. Washington, DC: National Institute of Education.

ROSSELL, C. H. (1978) "School desegregation and community social change." Law and Contemporary Problems 42, 3: 133-183.

TAYLOR, W. L. (1975) "The Supreme Court and urban reality: a tactical analysis of *Milliken v. Bradley.*" Wayne Law Review 21: 751-758.

U.S. Commission on Civil Rights (1967) Racial Isolation in the Public Schools. Washington, DC: Government Printing Office.

PART II

**THE EFFECTS OF DESEGREGATION
ON STUDENTS**

2

REDUCING RACIAL PREJUDICE IN DESEGREGATED SCHOOLS

JOHN B. McCONAHAY

Where there has been empirical research on specific practices and issues, the data point clearly to this conclusion: Racial prejudice can be
reduced in desegregated schools by bringing students together under
conditions of equal status that emphasize common goals and deem-
phasize individual and intergroup competition. There is nothing new in
that statement. It is a paraphrase of Allport's (1954) contact hypothesis
and of the statement by social scientists which was filed as part of the
proceedings culminating in the *Brown* decision (Cook, 1979). However,
those conditions are hard to implement and may never have been implemented in their entirety in any desegregated school to this date
(Cook, 1979).

I begin this chapter with its conclusion because I am attempting to do
two things here. First, I will review the existing literature on the practices that improve race relations in desegregated schools. Second, I will
go beyond this and make recommendations on all of the current issues in
the effects of desegregation practices on race relations and I will even
make recommendations on issues for which we do not yet have any

AUTHOR'S NOTE: This chapter was presented to the National Panel on School
Desegregation at its meeting in Key West, Florida, in October 1979. The author wishes
to express special thanks to Richard Ashmore, Janet Schofield, and Willis Hawley for
their helpful comments and criticisms of an earlier draft of this chapter.

specific research (for example, the best social class composition of the desegregated school). Furthermore, because the existing research gave such strong support to the contact hypothesis, I have used it in deriving recommendations vis-á-vis those issues for which we have no specific data. Hence, I want the reader to be aware at the outset of the strong support the contact hypothesis receives in the existing literature. If later research changes the picture, then the recommendations will be changed in future reviews.

OVERVIEW OF THE LITERATURE

Of the recent reviews of the effects of school desegregation on racial attitudes and behaviors, five (Cohen, 1975; St. John, 1975; Stephan, 1978; McConahay, 1978; Cook, 1979) agree unanimously that the literature is a methodological cesspool. In my own review of over 50 published and unpublished studies conducted between 1960 and 1978, I did not find even one true experiment, and only four of the quasi-experimental studies had enough methodological rigor to make them worth reporting in any detail (Gerard and Miller, 1975; Schofield and Sagar, 1977; Shaw, 1973; Silverman and Shaw, 1973). On the basis of these studies, I concluded that, while desegregation had not produced a situation in which race is irrelevant, there were more amicable interracial contacts and friendships than one could have expected under segregation. In addition, when the data were reported, gender (another way of dividing people into outgroups and ingroups) proved to be a more important factor than race in determining seating and friendship patterns in desegregated schools.

Segregation versus desegregation is not the issue in this chapter, however. Therefore, we are not limited to studies comparing the two types of schools; we can draw upon a number of studies that focus upon practices in already desegregated schools. These studies are more methodologically sophisticated than most of the segregation versus desegregation studies. A few of them are true experiments, but most are based upon some sort of cross-sectional, correlational analysis. Hence, the reader should be warned that these studies have the problems of the direction of cause and effect and controlling for other factors which are associated with correlational studies in general. In addition, it is frequently the case that both the independent variables and the dependent variables are based upon the respondents' perceptions rather than upon direct observation. For example, instead of observing seating patterns (the independent variable) and then relating that to the number of outgroup friends the students have (the dependent variable), the students are asked to recall how often they sit next to or near outgroup persons (the independent variable) and that is related to how many outgroup friends the students report that they have (the dependent variable). Despite these weaknesses, until we have better research these studies are a reasonable first approximation of what practices foster reduced prejudice.

For our purpose, the most important study published since my last review was by Slavin and Madden (1979). As the title of their article indicates they set out to examine with survey data the "School Practices that Improve Race Relations." The study is important not only for its policy intent but because it is based upon a sample of over 2000 students from 71 northern and southern high schools. Hence, it is a good supplement to most of the earlier studies, which were done in only one or a few schools or in one school system.

Slavin and Madden used four measures of racial attitudes and two measures of interracial behavior obtained from a questionnaire administered to students.[1] They had eight school-level independent variables and three individual-level independent variables. The latter were obtained in part from the same student questionnaires as the race relations dependent variables and in part from a questionnaire administered to teachers at the schools from which the student sample was drawn. Two types of analyses were done using multiple regression. In the first, the analyses were at the school level. That is, they tried to determine the policies and characteristics of schools that were, on the average, less prejudiced than other schools in their sample. Separate school-level analyses were run for blacks and whites. The second type of analysis was at the individual level. That is, they attempted to determine the factors associated with more and less prejudiced individual students. Again, these analyses were done separately for blacks and whites. In general, both levels of analysis for both racial groups revealed that working together on class projects or playing together on athletic teams was associated with less behavioral and attitudinal prejudice than either attending schools where the teachers had gone to workshops on race relations or participating in class discussions of race issues. Contact was found to be the key variable in Slavin and Madden's results, as it is in the contact hypothesis.

EVOLUTION OF POLICIES

These general findings are important, but they must be implemented through a set of specific practices and policies. The central focus of this chapter will be upon those specific issues, practices, and policies that arise in the process of attempting to desegregate schools in ways that will maximize good race relations. The various policy issues will be discussed in a somewhat arbitrary progression from those of more concern to policy makers at the macro or school system level through those of more concern to policy makers at the school level to those of concern to policy makers at the micro or individual classroom level.

THE TIME DIMENSION

We start with probably the most important and probably the least researched dimension of desegregation policy: the time dimension. My review of the literature (McConahay, 1978) found that most studies were cross-sectional (that is, contained no time dimension) and very few covered more than a year. These short-term studies, especially those done in the first or second years of desegregation, need to be interpreted in a longer time frame.

First, racial attitudes and behaviors in the first years of desegregation are going to be strongly influenced by community events. If community and school leaders support desegregation and the specific means used in the community to bring it about (pairing, magnet schools, busing, and so on), this will be reflected inside the schools and classrooms. Community controversy and mixed or negative signals from community and school leaders will have some negative impact upon both positive behaviors (friendly contacts, friendships, increased tolerance) and upon negative behaviors (hostile contacts, fights, intolerance) inside the school. But even when the community is quite tranquil during desegregation, the actual process is disruptive for students (Clotfelter et al., 1980). It takes more than a year for these effects of external and internal history to weaken.

Second, the long- and short-run effects of specific programs might be quite different. Teaching minority history might create hostility at first, though the long-range effects might be quite positive. Similarly, some programs might appear to have no impact in the first few weeks or a year, but might have powerful long-term effects.

The only published research covering more than just a year was by Gerard and Miller (1975) and their associates. They studied positive behaviors via sociometric choices (friends, school work partners, and ball teammates) over a period from just before desegregation to at least four and in some cases five or six years after desegregation. Gerard and Miller conclude that very little positive change occurred over this period. However, on the basis of my own examination of their data, I conclude more optimistically that "the data show that the likelihood of an Anglo choosing minority students as friends and schoolwork partners increased somewhat over the years after desegregation, the only exception being the choices of Mexican Americans as schoolwork partners" (McConahay, 1978: 93). Unfortunately, this conclusions applies to the outcome of four years of the entire process of desegregation and does not shed any light upon the long-term effects of specific policies.

It would be useful if we had more research on the time dimension to guide us, but even without such research, policy makers can take time into account by limiting the publicity and emphasis they give to the short-run evaluation of specific desegregation programs. Because of the community conflict and the tensions created by bringing previously separated racial and ethnic groups together in one school, these short-term evaluations will be biased in the direction of finding no effects or negative effects (more hostility, less tolerance). (For a further elaboration of this point, see Clotfelter et al., 1980.)

RACIAL COMPOSITION OF THE SCHOOL

The numbers game is important from the standpoint of community politics, balancing the entire school system, and white flight. However, I will ignore these issues for now and, for analytic purposes, I will pretend that I can concentrate on the racial composition of the school only as it affects racial attitudes and behaviors inside the school.

There are two distinguishable quantitative dimensions of racial composition: (1) the percentages of ethnic groups and (2) the absolute number of each group as well as the total number in the school. There have been five published correlational studies of racial percentages (Gottlieb and Ten Houten, 1965; Justman, 1968; Kurokawa, 1971; St. John, 1964; St. John and Lewis, 1975). In general, these studies suggest that approximately equal proportions are best for maximizing contact and friendship formation between ingroup and outgroup members. If one or the other of the groups in a school has a large percentage (over 70%), it has the power to determine the signs and behaviors by which *in-school* status is ascribed or achieved. For example, as a group becomes proportionally larger, the respect or prestige it accords athletic success relative to academic success will be reflected in the status hierarchy of the school as a whole. If the proportionally larger ethnic group gives greater prestige to athletic achievement than the proportionally smaller group, then athletic achievement will be relatively more important than academic achievement for attaining in-school prestige. Members of the racial or ethnic groups in the numerical minority protect themselves by attempting to isolate themselves from the larger group. Even when the proportions are about equal there is some tendency for the ethnic group members to isolate themselves, but this is less so than when the proportions are decidedly one-sided (Gottlieb and Ten Houten, 1965).

So far as I know, there has been no research on the effects upon race relations of the absolute numbers of blacks, whites, and others or the total numbers of students in a school — there should be, however. Consider two schools that are 30% black, one having 100 students and one having 1000 students. Other things equal, which one will have more racial isolation (fewer outgroup contacts and friendships)? We do not know on the basis of any specific research. However, the work of Milgram (1970) and Tucker and Friedman (1972) suggests that in larger schools (regardless of racial composition), there will be smaller friendship circles. Furthermore, Barker and Gump (1964) and Morgan and Alwin (1980) found less extracurricular participation as school size increased (also see Katz and Kahn, 1978: 108). Hence, we might expect proportionally fewer opportunities for friendly interracial contacts and more racial isolation as the absolute size of the school (and the numbers in each ethnic group) increases.

The proportions and numbers of members of ethnic groups in a school may be determined by other factors, such as costs or (especially) the need for systemwide racial balance. However, on the basis of both the white flight findings (Rossell, 1979) and what was reviewed above, I would recommend schools that are (1) relatively small and (2) approximately equally proportioned. This will maximize the likelihood that the desegregation experience will be as meaningful as possible and will produce the most positive attitude change (for those who are desegregated). This may mean, of course, that in systems in which the proportions of ethnic group members are grossly unequal, some schools will have to be left segregated in order to achieve nearly equal proportions in others.

SOCIAL CLASS COMPOSITION OF THE SCHOOL

Though there is a large body of research on the effects of the social class (SES) composition of schools upon cognitive and certain noncognitive outcomes for students (see Alexander et al., 1979), researchers in the field of race relations have regarded SES as something to "control" (Slavin and Madden, 1979; Gerard and Miller, 1975; St. John and Lewis,

1975) and not a factor to analyze. Hence, we have no specific research to guide us on this issue.

Some students of the contact hypothesis have interpreted its equal status clause to mean equal SES in the larger community (Armor, 1972). According to this view, desegregated schools that are all one social class should produce less prejudiced students than schools that are heterogeneous with respect to SES. That might be the case. In a socially heterogeneous desegregated school, students of one race and one social class might observe students from both a different race and social class and attribute social class differences between the two groups to racial differences. Furthermore, a strong determinant of interpersonal attraction is similarity of attitudes and behaviors (Bleda, 1974; McConahay, 1978). Adding social class differences in attitudes and behaviors to racial differences may decrease the likelihood of friendships in socially heterogeneous schools. Finally, there is evidence that among whites the different social classes exhibit different varieties of prejudice. Among working- and lower-class whites, racism is influenced heavily by a perceived threat from blacks (Ashmore and McConahay, 1975). Among middle- and upper-class whites, racism is influenced more by values and symbols (McConahay and Hough, 1976). Therefore, it would be easier to tailor programs to combat racism within desegregated schools that were socially homogeneous.

Despite these possible benefits from having desegregated schools that are homogeneous with respect to SES, I would not recommend them. First, at this time, the black population of the United States is disproportionately working and lower class. Consequently, there are very few middle- and upper-class blacks to desegregate with their social class peers in the white community. Middle- and upper-middle-class schools would remain virtually segregated or desegregated in only token fashion. Desegregation, then, would be a matter of mixing working- and lower-class whites and blacks. As a deliberate policy, this sort of school desegregation would exacerbate the already existing anger of working-class whites (Day, 1974; Kopkind, 1974). In addition, since working- and lower-class whites are more likely than higher-status whites to be personally threatened by the idea of desegregation (Ashmore and McConahay, 1975), desegregated schools composed entirely of working- and lower-class students can be volatile.

Second, though America's schools are in a state of de facto segregation by social class, it would be politically dangerous as well as personally distasteful to many policy makers to establish a deliberate policy of creating socially homogeneous desegregated schools.

Third, even in schools where the external SES of the black and white students is the same, both blacks and whites attribute higher competence and status to the whites in most interaction situations (Cohen, 1975). This means that, even in socially homogeneous schools, special policies and programs must be instituted to create the situation of equal status specified in the contact hypothesis as a precondition for positive changes in racial attitudes and behaviors (see the discussion of interracial work groups below).

Until future research shows that it is not desirable, I think that socially heterogeneous desegregated schools are preferable to socially homogeneous schools. The exact mix of social classes is hard to specify; however, each social class should be represented by more than a token number or percentage.

TEACHER ATTITUDES

There has been some evidence reported in the literature that teacher prejudice and student prejudice are positively correlated, that is, the more prejudiced the teacher, the more prejudiced the student (Gerard and Miller, 1975). However, other studies have found that this relationship is highly dependent upon the combination of the race of the teacher and the grade and race of the students (Forehand et al., 1976). Despite the complexity of this relationship in the studies to date, it is likely on theoretical grounds that prejudiced teachers will not accord equal status to students of both races in a biracial classroom and may lead discussions of race relations in a biased or perfunctory manner.

While it may be that less prejudiced teachers generally produce less prejudiced students, how do we get less prejudiced teachers? It cannot be done by a policy directive. It might be done by testing for racial attitudes when teachers are hired, given tenure, or promoted. However, testing for political and social beliefs in this one context might open a Pandora's Box that many of us will regret in other contexts.

Teacher attitudes might be changed by programs and special workshops designed to expose and change their prejudices. These will be discussed below. Furthermore, though they might not change attitudes, workshops and other programs designed to combat racism and prejudice, along with other clear signals from the highest-level school officials regarding how to behave, will inhibit the direct expression of racism on the part of prejudiced teachers. Perhaps that is all we can hope for at this time; behaving in a nonracist manner might lead prejudiced teachers and administrators to change their attitudes as well (McConahay, 1978).

GENDER OF STUDENTS

It appears that the popularity of black girls declines as the proportion of whites in a school increases. On the other hand, the popularity of black and white boys and white girls is either unaffected or increased as the proportion of the outgroup in a school increases (St. John and Lewis, 1975). Consistent with this finding was the finding of Schofield and McGivern (1978) that during the first year of desegregation in a "magnet" school, sixth-grade black males and white females were significantly more positive about their experiences than were black females and white males in the same grade. Except for these studies, we do not have any general knowledge of how the gender composition of a school or class affects racial attitudes and behaviors.

AGE OF DESEGREGATION

The results of prior (hence younger) desegregation upon racial attitudes and behaviors in desegregated schools are mixed (McConahay, 1978). What we know about racial socialization in general (Katz, 1976; McConahay and Hough, 1976; Sears and McConahay, 1973) suggests that the earlier a child is brought into contact with children of other races the better. Racial attitudes are acquired early and become harder to change, other things being equal, as the child matures. In addition, in the early grades it is easier to create opportunities for contact within classrooms than it is in the later grades, where specialized academic interests may make this more difficult.

Therefore, from the standpoint of race relations, the younger that students are desegregated, the better. Unfortunately, white resistance and white flight is increased when younger students are desegregated (Rossell, 1979). This may cause short-run problems, but, in the long-run desegregating from kindergarten through high school is best.

MULTIETHNIC TEXTBOOKS

One approach to changing student attitudes and behaviors without direct contact between the races is the use of multiethnic textbooks. The general purpose of these texts is to show that America was not built and is not now exclusively peopled by white Anglo-Saxon Protestants. Regardless of their direct effect on racial attitudes and behavior, these texts should be used in all schools because they give a more accurate picture of America yesterday and today than do texts written from one

racial perspective. Nevertheless, the use of these texts was not significantly related to a single measure of racial attitude and behavior in Slavin
and Madden's (1979) sample of schools of either whites or blacks. For
tenth graders, at least, multiethnic texts do not appear to be a very
effective way to combat prejudice.

MINORITY HISTORY

Along with multiethnic texts, specific courses in minority history and
culture have been added to the curriculum of the higher grades. These
courses were found by Slavin and Madden (1979) to have a weak effect
for whites (only one of six measures significantly related), and they had
no effect on blacks. Whatever their merits on other grounds, these
courses have little effect on racial attitudes and behavior in desegregated
schools.

TEACHERS' WORKSHOPS

One of the major proposals to produce less bias in teachers' behavior
(if not their attitudes) has been that of workshops for teachers designed
to reduce their prejudice (Forehand and Ragosta, 1976). I do not know of
any rigorous evaluation of these workshops, but to the student of racial
prejudice it appears chimerical to think that one or two workshops could
undo 20 to 65 years of prejudice. However, if the workshops communicate the concern and commitment of the top school system administrators, the teachers might learn how to modify their behavior (regardless of their attitudes) in a less biased direction. (See the discussion of
teacher attitudes, above.)

Whatever effects these workshops might have on teachers, they are
not particularly effective in reducing average prejudice scores for those
schools that have them. Slavin and Madden (1979) found significant (but
weak) effects for the presence of workshops on only one of six measures
of prejudice for both whites and blacks. It should be noted, however,
that though the measure of prejudice affected for whites was different
from the one for blacks, both measures were scales of behavior rather
than of attitudes.

MULTIRACIAL COMMITTEES

In many schools the principals, faculty, staff, and students have put together committees representing the various racial groups in the school to hear grievances and promote racial harmony. So far as I know, this is the only governance or management practice that has been studied, and, again, it was Slavin and Madden who studied it. They found no relationships between the presence or absence of multiracial committees and the average school-level prejudice score for either whites or blacks on all six measures of prejudice. Once again, whatever the merits of these committees on other grounds, the best current research suggests that they are irrelevant to racial attitudes and behaviors.

INTERRACIAL ATHLETIC TEAMS

The only extracurricular activity that has been studied so far is athletics. Both earlier research (McConahay, 1978) and the most recent research (Slavin and Madden, 1979) have reported that playing on an interracial team was significantly associated with less prejudice for both whites and blacks. In the Slavin and Madden study, this was true even with gender, racial composition of school, SES composition of school, and individual SES controlled. This particular finding is important from the standpoint of the contact hypothesis because, when the teams are interracial, the contact — while individually competitive — is also in pursuit of a superordinate goal.

RACIAL COMPOSITION OF CLASSROOMS IN SCHOOLS

The debate on classroom composition has centered on whether and to what extent each classroom must be a numerical microcosm of the entire school or grade in the school. When students are grouped (or tracked) into classrooms having fairly homogeneous levels of ability or achievement, the problems of boredom due to material that is too easy for some students and anxiety and loss of self-esteem due to material that is too hard for other students are minimized. Thus, students work at their own levels and are alleged to learn more (Hawley, forthcoming).

Unfortunately, homogeneous ability or performance classes also tend to be racially homogeneous (that is, segregated) as well. In the upper grades, racial segregation is also fostered by the differences among ethnic groups in their career interests and aspirations. Hence, intended or not, academic tracking can produce segregated classrooms within desegregated schools.

The research results suggest that racially balanced classes are more likely than unbalanced classes to produce less prejudiced attitudes and behaviors. Though Slavin and Madden (1979) found that tracking was not related to interracial attitudes and behaviors in their macro-level study of tenth-grade students, another macro-level study by Koslin et al. (1972) found that on all three of their measures the interracial attitudes and behaviors of third graders were more favorable in racially balanced than in unbalanced classes. In a micro study, Schofield and Sagar (1977) compared seventh- and eighth-grade students in the same school. They found that the eighth graders, who were rigidly tracked on the basis of academic interests which produced predominantly black or white classes, were more likely to eat lunch in same-race clusters than were the seventh graders, who were in untracked, racially heterogeneous classes. This tendency to cluster by race increased for the eighth graders as the year progressed, but it did not for the seventh graders.

Schofield (1979) did a follow-up study of the seventh graders in the first study during the next year, when they had entered the rigidly tracked eighth grade. She found that they too tended to cluster increasingly in same-race groups as the year progressed. Hence, being desegregated in balanced classrooms in the seventh grade did not offset the effects of being resegregated in the eighth grade. In both years, the segregated eighth graders became increasingly racially segregated in their social contacts. This finding is especially important because these seventh-eighth graders were students in a magnet school in which the administration and faculty stressed good race relations and provided many opportunities for students to have desegregated experiences outside of class.

Everyone would like for a practice that improves race relations to also enhance academic performance. Unfortunately, it appears that the decision on tracking hinges upon trading off race relations against academic achievement. Tracking may improve academic performance, but it also leads to segregation in the classroom and inhibits good race relations. I therefore recommend against tracking, because I think there are other ways to enhance academic performance that also improve race relations (see below). These practices cannot be applied in segregated classrooms.

ABILITY GROUPING WITHIN THE CLASSROOM

Most of what was said above about tracking or ability grouping by classes applies to ability grouping in the classroom. Whatever its merit for enhancing academic performance, the practice resegregates pupils within the classroom along race and social class lines (Ashmore and McConahay, 1975). The only direct research on the practice found that it did not have an effect on racial prejudice. Slavin and Madden (1979) reported no relationship across all six of their measures for both blacks and whites. In short, it did not increase prejudice among the tenth graders studied, but it did not decrease it either.

CLASS DISCUSSIONS OF RACIAL ISSUES

Another technique for possibly changing racial attitudes and behaviors which does not require interracial contact is to hold discussions of race-related issues. Any college professor who has taught a seminar in race relations and then read the final exams and term papers of his or her students should not have much faith in the ability of discussions to change attitudes among college students. It does not appear to be very effective for changing the attitudes of tenth graders either. For blacks, Slavin and Madden (1979) found no relationship between class discussions and any of their six measures of prejudice at either the school or individual level of analysis. For whites the picture is more complicated. At the school level of analysis, the presence of class discussions in a school was weakly but significantly related to their two measures of unprejudiced behavior. Class discussions were not related to any of their four school-level measures of white attitude. At the individual level, having discussions was related to one of their two behavioral measures and two of their four attitudinal measures. However, the significant relationships were quite weak in all cases.

It appears, then, that discussions of racial issues have no effect upon blacks, have some effect upon white racial behaviors, and have little effect upon white attitudes. They do not hurt, but, relative to other practices, they are not as effective.

INTERRACIAL WORK GROUPS

According to Slavin and Madden (1979), the strongest effects in their data were associated with assigning students to work on class projects in interracial teams. This was especially true for whites, where work group assignment was significant for five of six school-level analyses and six of six individual-level analyses. Furthermore, their measures of the strength of these effects (the betas or standardized regression coefficients) were stronger for these relationships than for any other policy or practice they studied. Patchen et al. (1977) reported similar findings.

Buttressing these correlational data are the results of a series of field experiments conducted in the last decade by different research teams in a wide range of school settings, grades, and regions of the country. These teams used different techniques, but they all had in common an attempt to create interracial work groups in which status and participation inside the groups were equal and intragroup and interethnic competition were minimized or eliminated. Furthermore, because most of these studies were true experiments, with appropriate, randomly assigned control groups, we can have a great deal of confidence in their results.

One of the pioneers in this area of research is Cook. After developing his approach in a series of laboratory studies using college students (Cook, 1969), he and his colleagues set up a field experiment in the seventh and tenth grades of the newly desegregated Denver public schools. (Weigel et al., 1975). Each of ten English teachers (who did not know the hypotheses) taught one class using an approach in which the class was divided into interracial groups. The modal group was composed of three Anglos, one black, and one Mexican-American. As a control, the same teacher taught another class using a lecture-oriented "whole-class" method. For each teacher, the experimental and control classes were decided by chance, making this a true experiment. The experiment lasted four and one-half months in the tenth grade and seven months in the seventh grade. At the end of this study, it was found that the interracial group classes had substantially more cross-ethnic helping behavior for all ethnic groups and greater respect, liking, and friendship choices for Mexican-Americans on the part of whites relative to the control group classes. However, racial attitudes (as measured by at-home interviews three months after the experiment) did not differ between the experimental and control condidtions.

DeVries et al. (1978) reported stronger results on the basis of four field experiments using a technique they developed known as the "Teams-Games-Tournament" or TGT. In the TGT approach, the class is divided into interracial groups of four or five members from all achievement levels and both sexes. The teammates sit together at all times and engage in peer tutoring of one another in academic disciplines such as English, mathematics, and social studies. Then, at the end of a week, a class tournament is held in which students from the teams compete individually in skill contests with students of comparable ability from other teams in the class. The team scores are then the sum of the scores achieved by individuals in the skill contests. Hence, the TGT technique has cooperation within work groups and competition across work groups, but all groups are interracial or interethnic. In studies using seventh- to twelfth-grade classes in Maryland and Florida, the TGT was compared to randomly assigned control classes using traditional teaching methods. Relative to the control group, the TGT technique produced more cross-racial sociometric friendship choices in each of the four experiments.

Perhaps the most impressive results for interracial work groups have been reported by Aronson and his associates (Aronson and Bridgeman, 1979; Aronson et al., 1978). In a series of field experiments in southwestern Texas and northern California, they used a method known as the jigsaw technique to improve not only racial attitudes but also academic performance. In the jigsaw technique, the students in a classroom are divided into six-person interracial and interethnic learning groups. The material to be learned is divided into six parts or paragraphs and each group member is given only one part of the material. Then each student must master his or her part of the material and teach it to the other students in his or her group. Thus, the jigsaw technique incorporates Cohen's (1975) finding that blacks must be "expert" in a central aspect of the group task in order to overcome the "interracial interaction disability" which makes true equal status so hard to achieve in interracial contacts. Furthermore, the learning task is interdependent. A student will not pass if he or she only learns his or her own part of the material, and unless he or she teaches it to the other group members, they will do poorly on the exam. Finally, there is no competition among learning groups in the classroom, so that competition is less than in the TGT technique. Of course, these were American classrooms in the various experiments and, therefore, the competition inherent in individuals needing to pass or get good grades on the exam was still present. The results of the experiments with the jigsaw technique showed that, relative to the control group classrooms, this technique produced more cross-racial and cross-ethnic sociometric choices, fewer ethnic stereotypes, higher self-esteem, and better academic performance.

The concept of interracial work groups as a means of reducing prejudice and improving race relations has a great deal of empirical support. It is rare in social science to find such robust results across such a wide range of techniques, empirical evaluation methodologies, grade levels, regions of the country, and curricula. It is premature to recommend the jigsaw technique or TGT or any other specific operationalization of the concept, but it is clear that this is the most effective practice for improving race relations in desegregated schools that we know of to date.

It is equally clear that the general theory of prejudice reduction which shaped most of the interracial work groups research — the contact hypothesis — has received a great deal of support as well. The techniques that were experimentally studied consciously attempted to create equal status and common goals without interracial or interethnic competition. When we consider the racial context in which these studies were conducted, the overall level of competition built into American education, and the short duration of the studies, these results can only increase our confidence in the general thrust of the contact hypothesis.

CONCLUSION

In the above discussion of policies and issues, the various practices were treated mostly in isolation from one another and as if the choice were a simple binary one of "to do it or not to do it." But many policy choices involve more complicated weighing of how to allocate limited resources of time, money, and personnel among policies. Hence, I conclude this chapter with some more general comparative recommendations.

First, where we had empirical data to guide us, the importance of contact under the conditions specified in the contact hypothesis was truly impressive. Those practices that brought students of different races together were most effective in reducing isolation and prejudice (for example, interracial work groups) while those that separated the races (such as multiracial texts) were least effective. Hence, more resources ought to be put into practices and structures that emphasize projects done in interracial groups and into varsity and intramural sports than into curricula that rely upon textbooks and special classes to change attitudes and improve relations.

Second, when desegregation plans are drawn up, consideration should be given to the need to have a large enough percentage of each race present in each desegregated school so that contact can be made in a situation of equal power and status inside the school. Unfortunately, in many central cities there are not enough whites to do this in every school and in many suburbs and small towns there are not enough blacks to create equal numbers or proportions in each school unless some schools are left composed of all one race (segregated). This must be balanced against other political and legal considerations, but the attempt to create desegregated schools with about equal proportions of the races should be considered, nevertheless.

Third, in the upper grades, where different career and academic goals might separate the races, extracurricular activities could provide many important opportunities for direct contact. The extracurricular budget for each school should be flexible enough that more funds could be made available to those activities (different activities at different schools) that are working to bring the races together, while funds should be reduced for activities that have been "captured" by one race or another.

Finally, tracking and ability grouping appear to be particularly retrogressive policies from the standpoint of race relations. Whatever their value for the cognitive aspects of education, they completely defeat the purposes of desegregation whenever they result in segregated classes or segregated work groups within nominally desegregated schools. There is evidence that interracial work groups not only improve race relations but also improve academic achievement (Aronson and Bridgeman, 1979). However, with segregation created by tracking or grouping there is no opportunity for us to give these contact groups a chance.

NOTE

1. Slavin and Madden (1979) say that they have three measures of attitudes and three measures of behavior, but the item, "Would you like to have more friends of a different race?" which they classify as a measure of behavior, is clearly a measure of attitudes.

REFERENCES

ALEXANDER, K. L., J. FENNESSEY, E. L. McDILL, and R. J. D'AMICO (1979) "School SES influences — composition or context?" Sociology of Education 52: 222-237.
ALLPORT, G. W. (1954) The Nature of Prejudice. Reading, MA: Addison-Wesley.
ARMOR, D. J. (1972) "The evidence on busing." Public Interest 28: 90-126.
ARONSON, E. and D. BRIDGEMAN "Jigsaw groups and the desegregated classroom: in pursuit of common goals." Personality and Social Psychology Bulletin 5: 438-446.
———, N. BLANEY, C. STEPHAN, J. SIKES, and M. SNAPP (1978) The Jigsaw Classroom. Beverly Hills, CA: Sage.
ASHMORE, R. D. and J. B. McCONAHAY (1975) Psychology and America's Urban Dilemmas. New York: McGraw-Hill.
BARKER, P. R. and P. V. GUMP (1964) Big School, Small School: High School Size and Student Behavior. Stanford, CA: Stanford University Press.
BLEDA, P. R. (1974) "Toward a clarification of the role of cognitive and affective processes in the similarity-attraction relationship." Journal of Personality and Social Psychology 29: 368-373.

CLOTFELTER, C., J. B. McCONAHAY, C. H. ROSSELL, and W. D. HAWLEY (1980) "Quantitative measures of school desegregation." (unpublished)

COHEN, E. G. (1975) "The effects of desegregation on race relations." Law and Contemporary Problems 39: 271-299.

COOK, S. W. (1979) "Social science and school desegregation: did we mislead the Supreme Court?" Personality and Social Psychology Bulletin 5: 420-437.

———— (1969) "Motives in conceptual analysis of attitude-related behavior," in W. J. Arnold and D. Levine (eds.) Nebraska Symposium on Motivation. Lincoln: University of Nebraska Press.

DAY, N. (1974) "Busing: a symposium." Ramparts (December): 40-42.

DeVRIES, D. L., K. J. EDWARDS, and R. E. SLAVIN (1978) "Biracial learning teams and race relations in the classroom: four field experiments using Teams-Game-Tournament." Journal of Educational Psychology 70: 356-362.

FOREHAND, G. and M. RAGOSTA (1976) A Handbook for Integrated Schooling. Washingtin, DC: U.S. Office of Education.

———— and D. ROCK (1976) Conditions and Processes of Effective School Desegregation. Princeton, NJ: Educational Testing Service.

GERARD, H. B. and N. MILLER (1975) School Desegregation. New York: Plenum.

GOTTLIEB, D. and W. D. TEN HOUTEN (1965) "Racial composition and the social systems of three high schools." Journal of Marriage and the Family 27: 204-212.

HAWLEY, W. D. (forthcoming) Increasing the Effectiveness of School Desegregation: Lessons from the Research. Washington, DC: National Institute of Education.

JUSTMAN, J. (1968) "Children's reactions to open enrollment." Urban Review, 3, 11: 32-34.

KATZ, D. and R. KAHN (1978) The Social Psychology of Organizations. New York: John Wiley.

KATZ, P. A. (1976) "The acquisition of racial attitudes in children," pp. 125-156 in P. A. Katz (ed.) Towards the Elimination of Racism. New York: Pergamon.

KOPKIND, A. (1974) "Busing into Southie." Ramparts (December): 34-38.

KOSLIN, S., B. KOSLIN, R. PARGAMENT, and H. WAXMAN (1972) "Classroom racial balance and students' interracial attitudes." Sociology of Education 45: 386-407.

KUROKAWA, M. (1971) "Mutual perceptions of racial images: white, black and Japanese Americans." Journal of Social Science 27: 213-235.

McCONAHAY, J. B. (1978) "The effects of school desegregation upon students' racial attitudes and behavior: a critical review of the literature and a prolegomenon to future research." Law and Contemporary Problems, 42, 3: 77-107.

———— and J. C. HOUGH Jr. (1976) "Symbolic racism." Journal of Social Issues 32, 2: 23-45.

MILGRAM, S. (1970) "The experience of living in cities." Science 167: 1461-1468.

MORGAN, D. L. and D. F. ALWIN (1980) "When less is more: school size and social participation." Social Psychology Quarterly 43: 241-252.

PATCHEN, M. D., J. D. HOFMANN, and W. R. BROWN (1977) "Determinants of students' interracial behavior and opinion change." Sociology of Education 50: 55-75.

ROSSELL, C. H. (1979) "The causes of white flight from school desegregation and some policy options." (unpublished)

ST. JOHN, N. H. (1975) School Desegregation: Outcomes for Children. New York: John Wiley.

—— (1964) " De facto segregation and interracial association in high school." Sociology of Education 37: 326-344

—— and R. G. LEWIS (1975) "Race and the social structure of the elementary classroom." Sociology of Education 48: 346-368.

SCHOFIELD, J. W. (1979) "The impact of positively structured contact on intergroup behavior: does it last under adverse conditions?" Social Psychology Quarterly 42: 280-284.

—— and E. McGIVERN (1978) "Who likes desegregated schools? The effect of sex and race on students' attitudes." Presented at the meeting of the American Educational Research Association, Toronto, March.

—— and H. A. SAGAR (1977) "Peer interaction patterns in an integrated middle school." Sociometry 40: 130-138.

SEARS, D. O. and J. B. McCONAHAY (1973) The Politics of Violence: The New Urban Blacks and the Watts Riots. Boston: Houghton Mifflin.

SHAW, M. E. (1973) "Changes in sociometric choices following forced integration of an elementary school." Journal of Social Issues 29: 143-157.

SILVERMAN, I. and M. E. SHAW (1973) "Effects of sudden mass school desegregation on interracial interactions and attitudes in one southern city." Journal of Social Issues 29: 133-142.

SLAVIN, R. E. and N. A. MADDEN (1979) "School practices that improve race relations." American Educational Research Journal 16: 169-180.

STEPHAN, W. G. (1978) "School desegregation: an evaluation of predictions made in *Brown* v. *Board of Education*." Psychological Bulletin 85: 217-238.

TUCKER, J. and T. S. FRIEDMAN (1972) "Population density and group size." American Journal of Sociology 77: 742-746.

WEIGEL, R. H., P. L. WISER, and S. W. COOK (1975) "The impact of cooperative learning experiences on cross-ethnic relations and attitudes." Journal of Social Issues 31: 219-244.

3

MINORITY ACHIEVEMENT:
POLICY IMPLICATIONS OF RESEARCH

ROBERT L. CRAIN
RITA E. MAHARD

This chapter reviews a particular portion of the school desegregation literature — the studies of the effect of school desegregation on minority achievement. These studies look at the achievement test performance of minority students after a school system has been desegregated. The studies are usually small, unpublished studies dealing with single cities. These are, of course, not the only kinds of studies that can contribute to our knowledge of how desegregation works and how it can work better. Indeed, almost any laboratory or classroom study of student learning contributes valuable information about how to make desegregated schools more effective. However, these studies are unique in their ability to test hypotheses about the relative effectiveness of different kinds of desegregation plans. A study in a single city cannot do this, since normally there is only one kind of desegregation plan present; but if we bring together a large number of these studies, using each one as an evaluation of a certain kind of desegregation, we can draw some overall conclusions.

There is another literature which can also be useful, that from large-scale national studies based on simultaneous achievement testing in a large number of schools. The Coleman report (Coleman et al., 1965) is the best known of these, but there are several others, and one book has attempted to pool the conclusions from all of these studies (Bridge et al., 1979). These large-scale studies can be used to compare the performance of minority students in various kinds of segregated and racially mixed schools. However, they have an important drawback: They pool together racially mixed schools that are newly desegregated with those that are "naturally" integrated — meaning that they have served an integrated or two adjoining segregated neighborhoods for a long time, and the students have not gone through the experience of a formal desegregation plan. Does this make a difference? We do not know, but until we do we must be cautious about assuming that the large-scale studies will tell us useful things about how to operate a desegregation plan.

With that caveat, let us consider the two main findings that have appeared consistently in these studies. First, minority students in predominantly Anglo schools score higher on achievement tests. Second, this does not seem to be because of the "whiteness" of the school but because predominantly white schools have student bodies with higher socioeconomic status. These two findings suggest that the best desegregation plan is one that creates predominantly white schools using white students from relatively affluent families. However, studies found a slightly different pattern, and their findings are worth consideration. The first, by Winkler (1975), found that black students who came from segregated elementary schools into predominantly white junior high schools did not experience a gain in achievement; there were gains only for those desegregated in elementary school. A second study (National Opinion Research Center, 1973) found that in newly desegregated southern high schools achievement tended to be lower in schools where blacks made up less than 20 percent of the student body. Black male students had especially low scores in these schools. We shall see that both of these findings are consistent with the literature we review here.

Finally, we can draw upon studies made of individual students in desegregated situations. In a recent study, Patchen et al. (1980) make important negative contributions by failing to support one popular theory of desegregation's effects: the theory that black students benefit from the "lateral transmission" of values or behavioral norms from white students. Both studies show that actual personal contact with white students in desegregated schools is irrelevant to achievement performance. If black students were somehow learning better study habits or developing more achievement-oriented values from associating with whites, then we would expect achievement gains to be greater for those with white friends. This is not what these two studies found. By seeming to refute this line of argument, these papers bring an alternative hypothesis to the forefront: the teacher expectation theory of desegregation. This theory, derived from the work of Rosenthal and Jacobson (1968), argues that students perform better when teachers have higher expectations about their ability to learn. This suggests that the predominantly middle-class desegregated school benefits black students because the teachers pace their teaching to what they see as the average level in the class — which will be higher than the level they would expect if they were teaching in an all-black school.

Another line of research has implications for desegregation policy. Several studies (Forehand et al., 1976; Coulson et al., 1977; Crain et al., 1981) show that black achievement is higher in schools where staff racial attitudes and the overall racial climate of the classroom is more positive. This implies that certain kinds of desegregation plans produce enhanced achievement by creating more favorable racial situations. Thus it seems that existing theory suggests that there should be differences in the effectiveness of different kinds of desegregation plans. It is the purpose of this chapter to begin searching for evidence that this is the case.

SAMPLE OF STUDIES

The small-scale studies of minority achievement after desegregation constitute a fugitive literature. Very few of the studies are published in journals or books. Many are unpublished doctoral dissertations, obtained through University Microfilms; others are reports of school system evaluations or papers read at the American Educational Research Association meetings, and were identified using the ERIC retrieval system. After a lengthy search, we located 93 studies which measured the impact of desegregation on minority achievement.[1] Nearly all of these studies deal only with black students, so that we had to make a special effort to look at the effects of desegregation on Hispanic students. We excluded a large number of papers. Many of these were studies that compared students in racially segregated and racially mixed schools, but with no indication that a formal desegregation plan had been put in place. We judged that these studies would tell us little that the more sophisticated large-scale studies such as the Coleman Report had not already shown. We also dropped a number of studies in which the research design does not meet a minimum standard of quality. For example, we discarded studies which simply compared the achievement of black students in desegregated schools with black students in segregated schools with no reasonable effort to verify that the two sets of students were of similar background or had similar test scores prior to desegregation.

The 93 studies were a very mixed bag, and their results were equally mixed. Following a procedure suggested by Glass and Smith (1979) for meta-analyses, we divided the 93 studies into 323 samples of students. If a research project studied several samples of students — who differed in age or in the research method used to measure the effect of desegregation on them — these were treated as separate samples. Slightly over half of the samples showed an increase in achievement after desegregation, while the remainder were divided between samples that showed no change and samples that lost ground. It is important to keep in mind that the point of all these studies is to measure the effect of desegregation, meaning the difference between the achievement of desegregated minority students and the achievement that those same students would have had if they had attended segregated schools. This must necessarily be a hypothetical question, which can be answered only by inference, since no student can possibly be desegregated and segregated simultaneously. The question of how to draw this inference most accurately has plagued desegregation research for the past decade.

The first review of this literature, and the impetus for all the work since then, was provided by St. John (1975). While she found that more studies showed desegregation improving achievement than not, she nevertheless concluded that the quality of the studies was too uncertain, and the results too mixed, to make a definitive conclusion. Weinberg (1977), reviewing nearly the same set of studies, was less cautious and concluded that desegregation did raise achievement. Bradley and Bradley (1977) reviewed a small number of these same studies and concluded that there were so many methodological problems that it was impossible to draw any conclusion about the effects of desegregation. More recently, Krol (1978) conducted a meta-analysis patterned after the work of Glass and Smith, and found a general positive effect of desegregation. In an earlier paper, we reviewed 41 studies and came to the same general conclusion — that desegregation tended to raise achievement test scores. However, all of these papers have been forced to dwell at length on various problems created by the different kinds of methodologies used.

In assessing the methodology of a study we must ask two general questions: First, are the desegregated students typical of students experiencing desegregation? Second, how can one best estimate what their achievement performance would have been in the absence of desegregation? Many of the studies we reviewed had problems with both of these issues. Most studies of desegregation were conducted almost immediately after the desegregation plan studied was put into effect. This meant that the students were not representative of graduates of desegregated schools — they were still in school in nearly every case and, in a number of cases, they began desegregation not at kindergarten or first grade but after they had already attended segregated schools. Thus their experience is not representative of a future cohort of students who would experience 12 or 13 years of desegregation by the end of high school. Many critics have commented about the unfairness of evaluating desegregation prematurely, when the students have only experienced 1 or 2 years in desegregated schools. However, critics have not paid attention to the other side of that issue — the fact that many of these students began desegregated schooling after first attending segregated schools.

The problem of choosing a comparison group is sometimes very difficult. In many communities every school is desegregated, so that no minority students remain in segregated schools to serve as a comparison group for the desegregated students. In this circumstance there are a variety of makeshift solutions, none of them completely satisfactory. Even when some segregated schools remain, the problem of deciding whether the segregated and desegregated minority students are truly similar is a difficult one. If one of the two groups comes form a more affluent background, the test scores of that group's members will normally be higher. Statistical procedures to correct for this bias are inadequate.

Our first task was to attempt to separate the genuine effects of desegregation from the false effects created by the methodological decisions made in an effort to deal with these two general issues.[2] To determine the bias introduced by incomplete treatments, we recorded a variety of dates — when the students were desegregated, when they were posttested, and, if the design was longitudinal, when they were pretested. From this we could determine the number of years in segregated schools before beginning desegregation and the duration of desegregation at the time achievement effects were estimated. We found that we could separate the studies into seven general categories according to the type of methodology used to create a comparison between desegregated and segregated black students. We then ranked the seven strategies according to our best judgment about their relative effectiveness.

Group 1. The best design is a randomized experiment — when desegregated and segregated students are selected by a flip of the coin, guaranteeing that there could be no differences between the two groups (other than that which might occur by a statistical fluke analogous to having a coin come up heads many times in a row).

Groups 2 and 3. The next best designs use a group of segregated black students as a control group, but without randomly assigning some students to desegregated and others to segregated schools. All of these studies pretested the desegregated and segregated students before or simultaneously with desegregation in order to show that they began with roughly equal achievement levels (or to statistically correct for differences if they were present). We divided control group studies into two categories, because some of them went one step further, and described the desegregation plan in such a way that the reader could conclude that the desegregated students were not chosen because they wanted to be reassigned, or because they appeared to be better candidates for desegregation, but because of an arbitrary geographic pattern which seemed to preclude much chance of a strong difference between these students and those left out of the plan. (Another example: Some volunteers for desegregation were compared with students who volunteered for desegregation too late to be accepted, on the assumption that these students were similar in their motivation.) The studies which did not explain why some students were desegregated rather than others were placed in a third category.

Group 4. These included cross-sectional studies with segregated black student control groups. In a very small number of studies a black control group was used without a pretest to demonstrate that their scores were similar to those of desegregated students before the plan took effect. Most of these studies were dropped from our analysis, but a few were kept when there was some evidence of similarity between the two groups.

If a randomized experiment provides the best estimate of the effects of desegregation, these inferior designs provide estimates that have more error, either overestimating or underestimating the effects of desegregation. This is a serious problem, but the problems that arise if there are no segregated black students to use as a control are even more serious. The next three designs not only introduce error into our estimate of the effects of desegregation, but they introduce a systematic negative bias — all three designs tend to underestimate the effects of desegregation.

Group 5. This group is made up of studies using cohort designs. In cases where all black students are desegregated, the best option is to simply compare the performance of desegregated black students to the performance of black students in the same grade a few years earlier. Unless there has been a drastic population shift in the community, these students should come from the same sort of family backgrounds. However, there has been a steady decline in achievement test scores in the

United States until recently. This decline, if it occurred in a desegregated community, would make desegregation appear to have a negative effect.

Group 6. When all black students are desegregated, one option is to compare the performance of black students to the performance of white students in the same community. The achievement of white students is, of course, an inadequate proxy for the performance of blacks. Worse yet, during the later elementary school years, when many of these studies were done, there normally is an increase in the "gap" between white and black scores. Thus a study of desegregated black students might find that in the third grade, before desegregation, they were a certain distance behind white students, and that this distance had increased after desegregation when the students were in the sixth grade. This normal increase in the gap would thus be misread as evidence that desegregation had lowered achievement.

Group 7. Finally, the researcher may choose to simply compare the performance of black students to the national norms on the achievement test being used. But, again, black students in later elementary school years can be expected to fall further behind the test norms, making it appear that desegregation had lowered achievement.

For each of the 323 samples under study, we recorded the age of the students at desegregation and the dates of pretesting and posttesting, as well as the type of control group design used. Multiple regression equations were then constructed in order to estimate the effects of these factors. We found that the duration of desegregation made no difference. Students who had experienced 4 years of desegregation did not show a stronger effect of desegregation than those desegregated only 1 or 2 years. This was a very surprising conclusion. We also discovered that the age at which desegregation began made a very important difference. We found 11 samples of students who were desegregated at kindergarten and found the effects of desegregation to be positive in every case. At the other extreme, when students were desegregated for the first time in secondary school, less than half of the samples showed positive effects of desegregation.

It appears that the beneficial effects of desegregation take place during the very earliest primary school grades, and students who are desegregated after that time inadequately represent the true effects of desegregation. Thus, when grade of desegregation was entered into a regression equation in an effort to predict the effect of desegregation on achievement, we found that the lower the grade of first desegregation, the higher the achievement effect. We also found, as expected, that the type of study design was significantly related to outcome. Those studies which used white students or test norms as a proxy for segregated black

TABLE 3.1   Percentage of Studies Showing Positive Desegregation
            Outcomes, by Grade at which Students Were Desegregated and
            Type of Research Design

Type of Design	Grade of Desegregation					Raw Average
	K	1	2-3	4-6	7+	
Random experimental	100 (1)	100 (8)	71 (7)	60 (5)	—	81 (21)
Longitudinal	100 (2)	73 (11)	46 (46)	62 (39)	69 (29)	59 (127)
Cohort comparison	100 (5)	78 (23)	56 (25)	40 (37)	45 (11)	56 (101)
Norm-referenced	100 (3)	0 (2)	43 (14)	37 (19)	0 (8)	35 (46)
Column average	100 (11)	77 (44)	50 (92)	49 (100)	52 (48)	56 (295)

student achievement found much weaker effects of desegregation. At
the other extreme, desegregation plans that were studied using a randomized experiment showed stronger effects of desegregation. Both
grade at initial desegregation and type of design were significantly related to the outcome.

Table 3.1 shows the percentage of studies that yielded positive results
at each grade of initial desegregation and with each type of design. To
simplify the table we have collapsed the two nonrandom longitudinal
designs with black control groups, combined the small number of cross-
sectional studies with the cohort designs, and collapsed studies that used
white student achievement as a control group with those that used test
norms. All 11 studies of students desegregated at kindergarten show
positive effects of desegregation. Similarly, a high percentage of the
studies of students desegregated in first grade show favorable results. In
general, the studies that used randomized experiments were somewhat
more likely to find positive results in the upper elementary school
grades, and the norm-referenced studies were least likely to find positive
results. At the extreme, none of the eight studies using white or test
norm controls of students desegregated in secondary school show positive desegregation effects.

Having established that the methodology used affected the chances
of obtaining a positive effect of desegregation, our next task was to
attempt to estimate what the magnitude of the effect of desegregation on
black achievement would be if the strongest methodological design was
used. In order to do this, we had to create a common unit of measurement to describe the effects of desegregation. Some studies reported
results in grade equivalents, others in raw test score points, some in
changes in IQ, and others with more elaborate statistics. Following
Glass, we converted these all into standard deviation units. (In the upper

elementary school grades a standard deviation unit is equal to about three grade levels; in the lower primary grades a standard deviation is a smaller number of grades. A typical student of below-average perform-ance who moved up one standard deviaiton would move from the 17th percentile to the fiftieth, and his or her IQ would change from 90 to 105.) We used the reference tables for the Comprehensive Test of Basic Skills (CTBS) to convert scores given in grade equivalents to standard devia-tion units — a somewhat dangerous practice, since a variety of different tests were used and each had its own statistical characteristics. The CTBS is the most commonly used test, however, and if tests are properly normed, the grade equivalent/standard deviation conversion should be the same for all tests. After these conversions were made, our statistical estimates of the effect of desegregation research designs and of using different grades at initial desegregation were used to estimate how much each study's result would be raised or lowered if that study had been, in fact, a study of students desegregated at first grade, using a randomized experimental design. We found that our best estimate of the achieve-ment gain was about one-third standard deviation. This would raise a student's achievement in the first grade by a fraction of a year; but, if that student held on to this advantage throughout school, he or she would be approximately one grade level higher than if he or she had been in a segregated school.

In the course of doing this analysis we were able to identify those studies which were methodologically strongest. We found 23 studies which were made of students desegregated at either kindergarten or first grade, and which used black students in a segregated school as a control group or compared scores to those of previous cohorts. As Table 3.2 shows, the authors of these studies analyzed 45 samples of students involved in 19 desegregation plans in 18 cities (2 desegregation plans, a decade apart, were studied in Nashville). Of the 45 studies, 40 show positive effects and, of those for which a size of effect could be esti-mated, desegregation raised achievement by a quarter of a standard deviation, or .3 of a grade year or more.

Apparently St. John (1975) and Bradley and Bradley (1977) were correct in arguing methodological factors made an important difference in the study of desegregation. This analysis satisfies us that desegrega-tion has consistently positive effects for black students. There has been very little work on the achievement effects of desegregation for Hispanic students, but what research there is shows a similar pattern. The Cole-man report (Coleman et al., 1966: 310) found that Hispanics showed higher achievement test scores in schools with more white students. Mahard and Crain (1980) made a second study using data from the National Longitudinal Study (NLS) of the high school graduating class

TABLE 3.2 Results of Studies of Students Desegregated at Kindergarten or First Grade, Where Adequate Research Design Was Used

State, City[a]		Grade at Desegregation	Design	Effect(s)[b]	Source
Northeast					
Connecticut:	Hartford (met)	K	Random	.37s	Mahan and Mahan (1971)
		1	Random	.12s .32s	Mahan and Mahan (1971)
	New Haven (met)	1	Random	.35s	Wood (1968)
		1	Random	.24s	Samuels (1977)
New Jersey:	Newark (met)	1	Random	1.60s	Zdep (1971)
New York:	New Rochelle	K	Longitudinal	(+)	Wolman (1964)
		1	Longitudinal	.70s .75s	Bowman (1973)
	Rochester (met)	1	Random	.2y .7y .1y	Rock et al. (1968)
		K	Longitudinal	.93s	Rentsch (1967)
		1	Longitudinal	.03s	Rentsch (1967)
Midwest					
Illinois:	Evanston	1	Cohort	−.01s −.05s	Hsia (1971)
	Peoria	1	Longitudinal	.07s −.06s	Lemke (1979)
Michigan:	Ann Arbor	1	Cohort	.05s	Carrigan (1969)
	Grand Rapids	K	Longitudinal	.1y	Scott (1970)
		1	Longitudinal	.1y .3y	Scott (1970)
Minnesota:	Minneapolis	1	Longitudinal	(+) (+)	Danahy (1971)

South

Georgia:	Dekalb County	1	Longitudinal	– .2y	Moore (1971)
Mississippi:	anon. (northeast)			.26s .53s	Moorehead (1972)
	Gulfport	1	Longitudinal	.7y	Frary and Goolsby (1970)
South Carolina	Beaufort County	K	Cohort	.3y	Chenault (1976)
Tennessee:	Nashville	1	Longitudinal	.05s .43s	Anderson (1966)
	Nashville[c] (met)	1	Cohort	.28s .19s .36s	Nashville-Davidson
				.24s .19s .41s	County Public Schools (1979)

West

California:	Berkeley	1	Cohort	(0)	Dambacher (1971)
	Pasadena	1	Cohort	.18s	Luneman (1973)
		K	Cohort	.49s .49s .60s	Kurtz (1975)
		1	Cohort	.20s .02s	Kurtz (1975)
Nevada:	Las Vegas	1	Cohort	.1y	Clark County School District (1975)

a. "met" indicates metropolitan plan.

b. "s" indicates effect in standard deviation units; "y" indicates effect in grade level years.

c. Two separate desegregation plans were studied in Nashville.

of 1972, and found a positive correlative between attending predominantly white schools and achievement for Mexican-Americans, Puerto Ricans, and Cubans. We also found one technically adequate study of a specific desegregation plan (Morrison, 1972) of Anglo-American, Mexican-American, and black achievement in a large urban school system (probably Houston). Morrison found Mexican-American achievement to be higher in desegregated schools. When Hispanics were first desegregated in grade three, the desegregated group had lower test scores than those in segregated schools; by the eighth grade they were slightly over one year ahead. The effects of desegregation were stronger for Hispanics than for blacks (see Morrison, 1972: viii, 120).

Our efforts to arrive at an accurate estimate of the overall effect of desegregation on achievement has implications for policy as well as research methodology. The finding that strong effects of desegregation occur in the earliest primary grades are a strong argument against delaying desegregation past grade one. Only a few school systems leave the early primary grades segregated; the most significant is Dallas. Our analysis indicates that this is a very unfortunate policy. Many school systems leave kindergarten students segregated. This analysis suggests that it would be academically very beneficial to include minority kindergarten students in a desegregation plan. All 11 studies recorded in Table 3.1 show positive effects — even those with severly biased methodologies. In Table 3.2, the 5 studies which measure the effect of desegregation at kindergarten in standard deviation units show a mean gain of .57 standard diviations. If such gains persist into upper elementary school, this would represent a gain of nearly two grade levels in achievement.

This analysis also has implications for an understanding of how desegregation works. Our analysis found no effect of duration of desegregation on achievement. One study in particular makes this point very well. Iwanicki and Gable (1978) evaluated the Hartford desegregation project in middle elementary school. These students had been desegregated at early grades. They found over one-year periods in mid-elementary grades no greater rate of growth for desegregated students than for those who remained in the segregated schools. When we contrast this to the highly favorable findings in this same district for desegregation at kindergarten and first grade (see Table 3.2), we are led to conclude that desegregation creates a sudden burst of achievement growth lasting through the early grades of elementary school, but that the desegregated students merely maintain this higher level of achievement, and do not increase it through the later years of elementary school. None of our present theories of the way desegregation works would explain this pattern. More research needs to be done following students over a long period of time in several districts in order to determine if this is indeed the typical pattern. If it is, we will have to rethink the impact of desegregation, viewing it as a kind of early childhood intervention. Research on desegregated Head Start programs would also be helpful in this regard.

READING AND LANGUAGE ARTS SKILLS

In order to further understand the effect of desegregation, we looked at achievement test performance on each subtest of the achievement batteries administered in the 93 studies. In many cases separate subtest gains were reported, and, where they were, we found an interesting pattern. Averaging all the samples of desegregated students together, we find that desegregation increases each subtest about equally. (There is a slight tendency for mathematics gains to be greater than reading gains but the difference is small and not significant.) However, when we looked separately at those samples of students who showed the smallest gains in achievement after desegregation, we found that their scores in the reading comprehension subtest lagged behind their scores in mathematics, spelling, or vocabulary. In school districts where students experienced greater gains than normal, reading subtest scores outpaced the other subtests.

There are two interpretations to this finding. One is that it is a statistical artifact — since reading comprehension is a critical element in achievement test performance, it may be simply that a good score in achievement requires a high level of reading performance. The second interpretation is a substantive one: Minority students come into desegregated schools with difficulties in reading comprehension. Schools that are unable to provide help to these students will not find their performance helped by desegregation; those that are able to make a special effort to deal with reading problems will find students benefiting from the entire curriculum and scoring well on all parts of the test. The language arts subtest shows the same pattern — very low scores in schools where students do not benefit from desegregation very much, very high scores where they do. This suggests that a desegregated school must make special efforts to work with language problems, which are perhaps related to the need to learn standard English grammar. This would seem to imply that teachers in desegregated schools should make special efforts to assist their black students in reading comprehension. We are reluctant to make such a policy recommendation on the basis of a single piece of research, but we do believe that additional research on the relationship of desegregation to various areas of achievement is likely to be quite valuable.

There are very few studies of desegregation in secondary school. Those that were done and which reported performance on tests in subject matter areas showed an interesting pattern, however. In secondary schools where minority students benefited little from desegregation, their performance in subject matter tests — science, history, and so on — lagged well behind their performance in reading and mathematics. In schools where achievement gains were large, it was greatest in these subject matter tests. This result seems consistent with the findings of the National Opinion Research Center (1973) study, which argued that the overall social climate of the secondary school was critical for minority student performance. If a bad racial climate inhibits the academic motivation of black students, this effect should appear most strongly in those tests which measure material specifically taught in secondary school classes. Overall reading and math performance, much of which is carried forward from earlier grades, would not be hindered as much by the negative social climate that inhibits learning. Put more simply, a negative secondary school racial climate does not make black students stupid, but it does prevent them from learning in the courses they take. This result must be considered tentative because of the very small number of studies involved.

There is one exception to the general pattern that tests in all areas of achievement show approximately equal gains as a result of desegregation when all studies, of both successful and unsuccessful desegregation plans, are considered. The largest gains appear consistently on tests of general intelligence. Increases in IQ scores after desegregation generally outrun performance on all subareas of standard achievement tests. In 29 cases where a comparison was possible, IQ scores were greater than the average of the other subtests in 16 cases and less than the average in only 5.

Table 3.3 reports the IQ gains following desegregation for 38 samples of students studied by 12 authors. We have divided the studies into 3 categories based on overall quality of the methodology used. Standing alone is the Wood (1968) study, a randomized experiment conducted in Hartford, Connecticut. It shows gains of 4 or more IQ points during the first year of desegregation and is a technically excellent study. In the second group we list 6 studies in which the IQ growth of desegregated students is compared to that of segregated students — our next best design to randomization. Of the 18 studies in this category, 13 show IQ gains resulting from desegregation, with half the studies showing gains of 3 IQ points or more. In the last grouping we include 5 studies that we think should not be taken as seriously as the others because of technical problems, even though these studies also show IQ gains resulting from desegregation. The last 4 of these studies are technically weaker designs, having no segregated black control group for comparison. The first study is a technically excellent design done in Hartford, but the students used in this study are, to a large degree, the same students studied by Wood; we have discounted this study in order to avoid being overly influenced by a single desegregation plan.

From these studies we estimate that desegregation tends to raise black achievement by approximately 4 IQ points on average. If this is correct, it represents a significant increase in performance on these tests. The average pretest scores in this collection of studies is around 91 — a 4-point increase would erase nearly half of the "gap" between that and the norm of 100.

At one time it was believed that IQ tests measured an ability to learn which was physiological, unaffected by school environment. This view is no longer held, and some research has shown that certain kinds of school curricula have greater impact on IQ than others. For example, the Stanford Research Institute study of the Follow-Through experiment (Stallings, 1978) found that students in "traditional" Follow-Through compensatory programs showed gains in basic skill scores but little gain on a nonverbal IQ test (the Ravens test). Conversely, students in more self-directed learning environments showed less increase in basic skills but more gain in IQ. It seems reasonable to argue that the desegregated classroom is a cognitively more stimulating environment, if for no other reason than that the student is confronted with a variety of stimuli and behaviors which he or she would not experience in the more homogeneous environment of his or her neighborhood school.

FINDINGS RELEVANT TO
DESEGREGATION POLICY

We now come to the heart of this exercise — having removed the extraneous effects of differences in methodology from the results of these 93 studies, we are in a position to inquire whether certain kinds of desegregation plans seem to have stronger effects on desegregation than others. One important conclusion is a negative one — issues related to voluntary versus mandatory desegregation and one-way versus two-way busing seem irrelevant. Mandatory plans and voluntary plans show approximately equal achievement gains.[3] We also can find no evidence that formerly black schools differ from formerly white schools in their achievement impact.

TABLE 3.3 Results of 13 Studies of Desegration and Black IQ Gains

State, City	Grade	Method	Effect (IQ)	Source
Connecticut: Hartford	K-1	Randomized	4.5[a]	Wood (1968)
	2-3		5.5[a]	
	4-5		4.0[a]	
Florida: Brevard County	10	Longitudinal	10.7[a]	Williams (1968)
Kentucky: (anon)	5-6	Longitudinal	-4.5	Meketon (1966)
	5-6		7.3	
Michigan: Flint	5	Longitudinal	2.0	Van Every (1969)
New York: Rochester	1	Longitudinal	1.2	Rentsch (1967)
	2		0	
	3		6.6	
	4		.4	
	5		-2.5	
New York: Syracuse	1	Longitudinal	-1.1	Beker (1967)
	2		-.6	
	3		3.7	
	1		1.6	
	2		5.9	
	3		5.0	
Oklahoma: Tulsa	3	Longitudinal	7.2[a]	Griffin (1969)
			7.2[a]	
			6.2[a]	

State	Place	Grade	Design	Value	Study
Connecticut:	Hartford	K	Randomized	6.0[a]	Mahan (1968)
		1		1.3	
		2		4.7	
		3		7.6[a]	
		4		−1.2	
		5		.4	
Florida:	Hillsborough County	4	Norms	6.5[a]	Taylor (1974)
Michigan:	Ann Arbor	K	Cohort	5.2	Carrigan (1969)
		1		3.4	
		2		2.4	
		3		−3.9	
		4		−4.2	
		5		−1.6	
Mississippi:	anon. (northeast)	1	Cohort	5	Moorehead (1972)
				7[a]	
New York:	White Plains	2	Cohort	−1	Bondarin (1970)
		5		1	

a. $p < .05$.

One important finding is that the metropolitan desegregation plans analyzed show stronger achievement effects than other studies. Recall that in Table 3.2 there were several northeastern studies of metropolitan plans. These plans, in Hartford and New Haven, Connecticut, Newark, New Jersey, and Rochester, New York, all involved the voluntary transfer of black students from inner-city schools to suburban schools and were all evaluated with experimental designs. In these cases, the number of students who would be willing to attend suburban schools far exceeded the number of spaces available to them, so that students were chosen by lottery. When those students selected for the plan were compared to those who were not, in every case sizable achievement gains were reported.

The other type of metropolitan plan is the result of the merger of suburban and central city school districts. In this data set we have only one example — the Nashville-Davidson County public schools were merged and desegregated shortly thereafter. This, the second Nashville study recorded in Table 3.2, shows sizable achievement gains for black students. Another study, which we located too late to be entered into our computer file of studies, comes from Louisville, Kentucky, where consolidation of the city and suburban districts took place in 1975. The newly formed Jefferson County school system compared the performance of fifth-grade black students in 1978 to those in the fifth-grade in 1975, when desegregation began, and found black students' overall performance rising from the twenty-fifth percentile nationally to the thirty-third percentile. At the same time, white students rose from the fiftieth percentile to the fifty-fourth (Raymond, 1980). These striking gains do not appear for older students, who were desegregated after starting school in segregated classes. The other major metropolitan desegregation plan is Newcastle County, Delaware, the result of the merger of several suburban systems with the Wilmington public schools. We have not received any achievement data for minority students there.

Table 3.4 shows the expected achievement gain for students in metropolitan desegregation plans and in other types of communities. These expected scores are statistically adjusted to eliminate differences in methodological quality and the effects of desegregation at later grades. The estimates of effect are computed by assuming that the studies in all four kinds of situations were randomized experimental evaluations of students desegregated at first grade in all four types of communities. Since we estimate that the average gain is .3 of a standard deviation, we show in Table 3.4 effects of desegregation varying on both sides of this .3 value. The important point in Table 3.4 is not the magnitude of the four values, but their relative relationship. What we

TABLE 3.4   Effect of Desegregation, by Type of School District Setting

	Mean Effect (standard deviation)	Number of Samples
Central city	.285	(97)
Suburb	.241	(76)
Countywide	.339	(31)
Metropolitan	.364	(30)

find there is that metropolitan studies show the strongest effect of desegregation, while studies in suburbs and in central cities show weaker effects. Lying between the two are the results of studies made in countywide school systems, which are common in the South. A countywide system is a kind of metropolitan desegregation plan, but different in the sense that desegregation does not involve the reassignment of black students into schools that were traditionally administered by a school district serving only suburban students. Thus it is a different form of metropolitan desegregation but shows results similar to the plans that are normally referred to as metropolitan in nature.

Why should metropolitan desegregation plans show stronger desegregation effects? There are two plausible explanations, although neither of them can be tested with these data. The first is that metropolitan desegregation represents the most complete form of socioeconomic desegregation. Minority students from low-income central-city neighborhoods are reassigned to suburban schools in affluent areas. If the plan were limited only to the central city, the number of middle-class white students available would be sharply reduced. By the same argument, desegregation within suburban schools might be relatively ineffective because the minority children living in suburban ghettos would not be as poor as those living in central cities — thus improvement to the same level of achievement in desegregated schools would not be as marked a gain for them, since their performance in segregated schools would already be fairly high. This hypothesis would explain why countywide plans would be as effective as other kinds of metropolitan plans, since both would involve the full range of socioeconomic differences in the area.

There is a second explanation as well, having to do with the administration of school districts. This hypothesis argues that suburban school districts, spared the conflict and tension that surround the operation of many central-city school districts, have been able to recruit stronger teaching staffs and better principals and provide a more effective administrative environment for their schools. Once a metropolitan school district is created or minority students are reassigned to suburban schools, these schools are able to maintain their stronger academic traditions. However, this hypothesis does not agree with one study; Natkin (1980) found that black students bused to suburban schools did no better on achievement tests than those who remained in the newly desegregated inner-city schools. Had there been a strong difference in the quality of teaching or administration in the two kinds of schools, one would have expected the bused students to do better. The suburban Louisville schools were affected by staff desegregation as well as student desegregation. Intuitively, we would expect this to have both negative and positive effects on black students in suburban schools. They would be harmed by the dislocation of teaching staff and the high turnover of staff in these schools. At the same time, they would probably benefit from the presence of more black teachers in the suburban schools. In this sense we would expect formal metropolitan desegregation plans involving the merger of suburban and central-city districts to be more effective in the long run than voluntary plans, which sometimes leave virtually all-white teaching staffs in the suburban schools serving the inner-city minority transfer students.

THE RACIAL COMPOSITION OF DESEGREGATED SCHOOLS

We also looked at the effectiveness of desegregation in schools of different racial compositions. We were guided by two findings from the literature. The first is that the various large-scale studies of schools have found black achievement directly related to percentage white in the school — the whiter the school, the higher the minority achievement. The second, from the National Opinion Research Center, was that there was an optimal point in percentage white — that when percentage white exceeded 80 percent, achievement began falling. In Table 3.5 we have plotted the expected achievement gain once the effects of differences in methodology and grade of desegregation have been removed, and find similar patterns in both the North and the South. In the South the pattern is quite clear and is statistically significant.[4] Achievement reaches a peak for schools between 19 percent and 29 percent black and drops off on either side in a reasonably steady manner. In the North the pattern is more complex. There is, again, a high point in the 9 percent to 18 percent range, with a decline in both directions, although the decline is not completely even and the overall pattern is not statistically significant. The differences are not small. In the North, a school with a relatively small black population has achievement scores which are a tenth of a

TABLE 3.5　Desegregation Effect, by Percentage Black of Desegregated School (size of effect [std. dev.] and number of samples)

	Region			
	North		South	
Percentage Black	SD	N	SD	N
1-8	.304	(19)	.319	(12)
9-18	.430	(29)	.398	(8)
19-29	.243	(29)	.494	(7)
30-37	.274	(27)	.364	(20)
38-44	.188	(26)	.274	(10)
44-100	.303	(20)	.278	(33)
Total	.270	(143)	.331	(89)

standard deviation higher than schools with larger black populations. In the South, the difference may be as much as .2 of a standard deviation.

The finding that schools with smaller black populations have higher achievement can be explained in two ways. First, if the main effect of desegregation is to place students from low-income families into schools with affluent students, the more white students, the greater the average income level in the school. (We cannot test this directly, since none of the 93 studies reported the actual social class of either the black or white students.) Secondly, a smaller black population makes it more difficult to resegregate the school by creating an all-minority class of supposedly low-ability students. Presumably, such a segregated classroom would be detrimental to achievement.

The finding that achievement is lower in the schools with the smallest percentage black population is also consistent with theory as well as with the National Opinion Research Center study (1973). The argument is simply that the overwhelmingly white school is a hostile environment for black students: There are not enough black students and not enough black teachers to provide minority students with the sense of being integrated into the school. The argument would be that they would continue to feel like outsiders, not really a part of the school situation and inhibited in their learning because of this. (See Crain et al., 1981, for an elaboration of this argument.)

Civil rights advocates have frequently argued for the establishment of a "critical mass" of black students, insisting that desegregation plans now spread black students so thinly that they make up less than 15 percent or 20 percent of the school. These achievement results seem consistent with that request. At the same time, these data provide additional support for the metropolitan desegregation argument. For it is only with metropolitan desegregation that one can be guaranteed a large enough population of white students to provide for predominantly (but not overwhelmingly) white student bodies.

CONCLUSION

It is often said that science is a cumulative process — that each research paper makes a small contribution as it is built upon by others. Certainly, the many students who wrote doctoral dissertations about school desegregation over the past 20 years were not able to anticipate that the advent of high-speed computers and the development of meta-analysis would enable their work to make a contribution of this kind. But this is exactly what has happened. The overall pattern of results of these studies has been obscured by methodological errors which are nearly unavoidable in many cases. Because of this, it was impossible from a quick reading of them to even say whether or not desegregation was beneficial for minority achievement. But once reasonable estimates have been derived for the correction factors due to inadequate methodology, a clear pattern emerges.

We can see from this analysis that desegregation is indeed beneficial, although it must begin in the earliest grades. We have also seen what research has led us to suspect for some time — that desegregation in a predominantly white society requires predominantly white schools, and desegregation in a society where whites have run to the suburbs to establish a "white noose" around declining minority central cities requires metropolitan desegregation. We have also learned some things that were not expected. The discovery that a school can have too many white students and thus harm black achievement confirms what up to now had been a largely speculative argument for a "critical mass" of black students in desegregated schools.

There is a great deal more work to be done. Our finding that desegregation enhances IQ test scores as much or more than it does achievement test scores calls into question a lot of our assumptions about the meaning of intelligence, and invites us to think more about why desegregation is beneficial. Similarly, the finding that desegregation's success seems peculiarly dependent on scores in reading comprehension and language arts invites researchers to think further about this issue. Finally, and most important, the discovery that effects of desegregation are almost completely restricted to the early primary grades — that desegregation is successful as an early childhood intervention — means that we must begin rethinking what desegregation is doing for black students.

Some policy implications are clear — early desegregation, metropolitan desegregation, desegregation in predominantly white schools but with a critical mass of black students. In terms of the policy options available to officials in federal and local administrations, the success of voluntary one-way transfer programs to suburbs is particularly relevant. Some states have enabling legislation to permit this to occur. While there is a great deal of opposition from central-city administrations, central-city teachers' unions, and some central-city black political leaders, there is also a good deal of support — from suburban school administrators with declining enrollments, from integrationist groups in the suburbs, and from black parents themselves. While this is hardly a substitute for court-ordered metropolitan desegregation, it is a reasonable first step that can be taken without waiting for the courts. Since it is a policy that has little opposition from the traditional antibusing groups that have frightened so many school boards, this is a policy some school systems may wish to follow in order to demonstrate their willingness to at least take partial steps toward desegregation.

NOTES

1. The 93 studies are, alphabetically: Aberdeen (1969); Anderson (1966); Baltzell (1974); Banks and Di Pasquale (1969); Barnett (1972); Bartz (1978); Beers and Reardon (1974); Beker (1967); Benjamin (1975); Bennett (1974); Bondarin (1970); Bowman (1973); Bryant (1968); Calhoun (1978); Carrigan (1969); Chenault (1976); Clark (1971); Clark County School District (1975); Clinton (1969); Dambacher (1971); Danahy (1971); Denmark (1970); Dressler (1967); Evans (1973a, 1973b); Felice (1974); Fortenberry (1959); Fox et al. (1968); Frary and Goolsby (1970); Gardner et al. (1970); Gerard and Miller (1975); Graves and Bedell (1967); Griffin (1969); Hsia (1971); Iwanicki and Gable (1978, 1979); Jonsson (1967); Justin (1973); Justin and Thabit (1975); Klein (1967); Kurtz (1975); Laird and Weeks (1966); Lemke (1979); Levy (1970); Linney (1978); Los Angeles Desegregation Monitoring Committee (1980); Luneman (1973); Mahan and Mahan (1970, 1971); Marcum (1968); Marcus and Sheehan (1978); Mayer et al. (1974); Maynor and Katzenmeyer (1974); Meier (1975); Meketon (1966); Moore (1971); Moorefield (1968); Moorehead (1972); Moreno (1971); Morrison (1972); Nashville-Davidson County Public Schools (1979); Natkin (1980); Papay (1976); Pascarelli et al. (1979); Perry and Kopperman (1973); Prewitt (1971); Prichard (1969); Purl and Dawson (1973); Rentsch (1967); Rock et al. (1968); Sacramento City Unified School District (1971); Samuels (1958); Samuels (1971); Savage (1971); Schellenberg and Halteman (1976); Scott (1970); Shaker Heights School Board (1972); Sheehan and Marcus (1978); Shutman (1974); Slone (1968); Smith (1978); Smith (1976); Smith (1971); Stallings (1959); Starnes (1968); Stephenson and Spieth (1972); Syracuse City School District (1967a, 1967b); Taylor (1974); Teele (1973); Thomas (1977); Thompson and Dyke (1972); Van Every (1969); Walberg (1971); Williams (1968); Wolman (1964); Wood (1968); Zdep (1971).

2. The analysis of the effect of methodology on the estimate of the effect of desegregation is described in much more detail in Crain and Mahard (1981).

3. In an earlier paper (Crain and Mahard, 1978), we noted that mandatory plans seemed to show higher achievement gains. We were reluctant at that time to accept this as a firm finding and were apparently wise to do so, since with the larger sample we cannot find any difference between the two types of plans.

4. The significance tests reported here are based on the number of authors, rather than the total number of samples, since multiple samples from the same author do not constitute independent populations.

REFERENCES

ABERDEEN, F. D. (1969) "Adjustment to desegregation: a description of some differences among Negro elementary school pupils." Ph.D. dissertation, University of Michigan (University Microfilms No. 70-4025).

ANDERSON, L. V. (1966) "The effect of desegregation on the achievement and personality patterns of Negro children." Ph.D. dissertation, George Peabody College for Teachers (University Microfilms No. 66-11237).

BALTZELL, D. C. (1974) "Rapid desegregation and academic achievement in a large urban school district." Presented at the annual meeting of the American Educational Research Association, Chicago, April.

BANKS, R. and M. E. DI PASQUALE (1969) A Study of the Educational Effectiveness of Integration. Buffalo, NY: Buffalo Public Schools.

BARNETT, S. (1972) Evaluation of San Francisco Unified School District Desegregation/Integration 1971-1972. San Francisco: San Francisco Unified School District.

BARTZ, D. E. (1978) Desegregation in Kalamazoo, Michigan. Charleston: Eastern Illinois University, Department of School Services Personnel.

BEERS, J. S. and F. REARDON (1974) "Racial balancing in Harrisburg: achievement and attitudinal changes." Integrated Education 12, 5: 35-38.

BEKER, J. (1967) "A study of integration in racially imbalanced urban public schools." Syracuse University Youth Development Center. (unpublished)

BENJAMIN, R. C. (1975) An Evaluation of the Cluster Program in Lansing. Lansing, MI: Lansing School District, Office of Evaluation Services.

BENNETT, J. E. (1974) "The effects of integration on achievement in a large elementary school." Florida Journal of Educational Research 16: 12-15.

BONDARIN, A. (1970) The Racial Balance Plan of White Plains, New York. New York: Center for Urban Education, Program References Service.

BOWMAN, O. H. (1973) "Scholastic development of disadvantaged Negro pupils: a study of pupils in selected segregated and desegregated elementary classrooms." Ph.D. dissertation, State University of New York at Buffalo (University Microfilms No. 73-19176).

BRADLEY, L. and G. BRADLEY (1977) "The academic achievement of black students in desegregated schools." Review of Educational Research 47: 399-449.

BRIDGE, G., C. JUDD, and P. MOOCK (1979) The Determinants of Educational Outcomes: The Effects of Families, Peers, Teachers and Schools. New York: Teachers College Press.

BRYANT, J. C. (1968) "Some effects of racial integration of high school students on standardized achievement test scores: teacher grades and drop-out rates in Angleton, Texas." Ph.D. dissertation, University of Houston.

CALHOUN, P. C. (1978) "A study of the effects of forced desegregation pairing of a low socioeconomic status black elementary school with a middle socioeconomic status white elementary school on achievement, social interaction, and enrollment." Ph. D. dissertation, Georgia State University.

CARRIGAN, P. M. (1969) School Desegregation via Compulsory Pupil Transfer: Early Effects on Elementary School Children. Ann Arbor, MI: Ann Arbor Public Schools.

CHENAULT, G. S. (1976) "The impact of court-ordered desegregation on student achievement." Ph. D. dissertation, University of Iowa (University Microfilms No. 77-13068).

Clark County School District (1975) Desegregation Report. Las Vegas, NV: Author.

CLARK, E. N. (1971) "Analysis of the differences between pre- and post-test scores (change scores) on measures of self-concept, academic aptitude and reading achievement earned by sixth grade students attending segregated and desegregated schools." Ph. D. dissertation, Duke University (University Microfilms No. 72-307).

CLINTON, R. R. (1969) "A study of the improvement in achievement of basic skills of children bused from urban to suburban school environments." Master's thesis, Southern Connecticut State College.

COLEMAN, J. S., E. Q. CAMPBELL, C. J. HOBSON, J. McPARTLAND, A. M. MOOD, F. D. WEINFELD, and R. L. YORK (1966) Equality of Educational Opportunity. Washington, DC: Government Printing Office.

COULSON, J. E., S. D. HANES, D. G. OZENE, C. BRADFORD, W. J. DOH-ERTY, G. A. DUCK, and J. A. HEMENWAY (1977) The Third Year of Emergency School Aid Act (ESAA) Implementation. Santa Monica, CA: System Development Corporation.

CRAIN, R. L. and R. E. MAHARD (1981) Desegregation Plans that Raise Black Achievement: A Review of the Research. N-1210-NIE. Santa Monica, CA: Rand Corporation.

—————— (1978) "Desegregation and black achievement: a review of the research." Law and Contemporary Problems 42: 17-56.

—————— and R. E. NAROT (1981) Making Desegregation Work: How Schools Create Social Climates. Cambridge, MA: Ballinger.

DAMBACHER, A. D. (1971) A Comparison of Achievement Test Scores Made by Berkeley Elementary Students Pre and Post Integration Eras, 1967-1970. Berkeley, CA: Berkeley Unified School District.

DANAHY, A. H. (1971) "A study of the effects of busing on the achievement, attendance, attitudes, and social choices of Negro inner city children." Ph. D. dissertation, University of Minnesota (University Microfilms No. 72-14285).

DENMARK, F. L. (1970) "The effect of integration on academic achievement and self-concept." Integrated Education 8, 3: 34-43.

DRESSLER, F. J. (1967) Study of Achievement in Reading of Pupils Transferred from Schools 15 and 37 to Peripheral Schools to Eliminate Overcrowding, to Abandon an Obsolete School, and to Achieve a More Desirable Racial Balance in City Schools. Buffalo, NY: Buffalo Public Schools, Division of Curriculum Evaluation and Development.

EVANS, C. L. (1973a) Desegregation Study II: Academic Effects on Bused Black and Receiving White Students, 1972-73. Fort Worth, TX: Fort Worth Independent School District.

—————— (1973b) Short-Term Desegregation Effects: The Academic Achievement of Bused Students, 1971-72. Fort Worth, TX: Fort Worth Independent School District.

FELICE, L. G. (1974) The Effect of School Desegregation on Minority Group Student Achievement and Self-Concept: An Evaluation of Court-Ordered Busing in Waco, Texas. Waco, TX: Research Development Foundation.

FOREHAND, G. A., M. RAGOSTA, and D. A. ROCK (1976) Conditions and Processes of Effective School Desegregation. Princeton, NJ: Educational Testing Service.

FORTENBERRY, J. H. (1959) "The achievement of Negro pupils in mixed and nonmixed schools." Ph.D. dissertation, University of Oklahoma (University Microfilms No. 59-5492).

FOX, D. J., C. STEWARD, and V. PITTS (1968) Services to Children in Open Enrollment Receiving Schools: Evaluation of ESEA Title I Projects in New York City, 1967-1968. New York: Center for Urban Education.

FRARY, R. B., and T. M. GOOLSBY, Jr. (1970) "Achievement of integrated and segregated Negro and white first graders in a southern city." Integrated Education 8, 4: 48-52.

GARDNER, B. B., B. D. WRIGHT, and R. DEE (1970) The Effect of Busing Black Ghetto Children into White Suburban Schools. Chicago: Social Research, Inc.

GERARD, H. B. and N. MILLER [eds.] (1975) School Desegregation: A Long-Range Study. New York: Plenum.

GLASS, G. V and M. L. SMITH (1979) "Meta-analysis of research on class size and achievement." Educational Evaluation and Policy Analysis 1, 1: 2-16.

GRAVES, M. F. and F. D. BEDELL (1967) A Three-Year Evaluation of the White Plains Racial Balance Plan. White Plains, NY: Board of Education.

GRIFFIN, J. L. (1969)"The effects of integration on academic aptitude, classroom achievement, self-concept and attitudes toward the school environment of a selected group of Negro students in Tulsa, Oklahoma." Ph.D. dissertation, University of Tulsa (University Microfilms No. 69-17923).

HSIA, J. J. (1971) Integration in Evanston, 1967-1971: A Longitudinal Evaluation. Evanston, IL: Educational Testing Service, Midwestern Office.

IWANICKI, E. F. and R. GABLE (1979) Final Evaluation Report 1978-79, Hartford Project Concern Program. Hartford, CT: Hartford Public Schools.

——— (1978) "A quasi-experimental evaluation of the effects of a voluntary urban/suburban busing program on student achievement." Presented at the annual meeting of the American Educational Research Association, Toronto, March.

——— (1977) An Evaluation of the 1976-77 Hartford Project Concern Program. Hartford, CT: Hartford Public Schools.

——— (1976) An Evaluation of the 1975-76 Project Concern Program. Hartford, CT: Hartford Public Schools.

JONSSON, H. A. (1967) Report of Evaluation of ESEA Title I Compensatory Activities for 1966-1967. Berkeley, CA: Berkeley Unified School District.

JUSTIN, N. E. (1973) "Integration, not just black and white: insights from seven Florida studies," in N. E. Justin and H. A. Kersey (eds.) Florida Education in the 1970s. Dubuque, IA: Kendall/Hunt.

——— and J. THABIT (1975) "Black and white achievement before and after integration." Intellect 102: 458-459.

KLEIN, R. S. (1967) "A comparative study of the academic achievement of Negro tenth grade high school students attending segregated and recently integrated schools in a metropolitan area of the South." Ph.D. dissertation, University of South Carolina.

KROL, R. (1978) "A meta analysis of comparative research on the effects of desegregation on academic achievement." Ph.D. dissertation, Western Michigan University (University Microfilms No. 79-07962).

KURTZ, H. (1975) The Educational and Demographic Consequences of Four Years of School Desegregation in the Pasadena Unified School District. Pasadena, CA: Pasadena Unified School District.

LAIRD, M. A. and G. WEEKS (1966) The effect of busing on achievement in reading and arithmetic in three Philadelphia schools. Philadelphia: Philadelphia School District.

LEMKE, E. A. (1979) "The effects of busing on the achievement of white and black students." Educational Studies 9: 401-406.

LEVY, M. (1970) A Study of Project Concern in Cheshire, Connecticut: September 1968-June 1970. Cheshire, CT: Department of Education.

LINNEY, A. (1978) "A multivariate, multilevel analysis of a midwestern city's court ordered desegregation." Ph.D. dissertation, University of Illinois — Urbana-Champaign.

Los Angeles Desegregation Monitoring Committee (1980) Permits with Transportation: Additional Analysis and a Follow-Up Report. Los Angeles: Los Angeles Unified School District.

LUNEMAN, A. (1973) "Desegregation and student achievement: a cross-sectional and semi-longitudinal look at Berkeley, California." Journal of Negro Education 42: 439-446.

MAHAN, T. W. (1971) "The impact of schools on learning: inner city children in suburban schools." Journal of School Psychology 9, 1: 1-11.

———— and A. M. MAHAN (1970) "Changes in cognitive style: an analysis of the impact of white suburban schools in inner city children." Integrated Education 8, 1: 58-61.

MAHARD, R. E. and R. L. CRAIN (1980) "Effects of desegregation on academic achievement," in W. D. Hawley (ed.) An Assessment of Effective Desegregation Strategies: Preliminary Report. Durham, NC: Duke University, Center for Educational Policy.

MARCUM, R. B. (1968) "An exploration of the first year effects of racial integration of the elementary schools in a unit school district." Ph.D. dissertation, Stanford University (University Microfilms No. 69-10784).

MARCUS, M. M. and D. S. SHEEHAN (1978) "The relationship between desegregation, student attitude and student background and achievement characteristics." Presented at the annual meeting of the American Educational Research Association, Toronto, March.

MAYER, R. R., C. S. KING, A. BORDERS-PATTERSON, and J. W. McCULLOUGH (1974) The Impact of School Desegregation in a Southern City. Lexington, MA: D.C. Heath.

MAYNOR, W. and W. G. KATZENMEYER (1974) "Academic performance and school integration: a multi-ethnic analysis." Journal of Negro Education 43: 30-38.

MEIER, J. A. (1975) Longitudinal Effects of Desegregation, 1972-1975. Dallas: Dallas Independent School District.

MEKETON, B. (1966) "The effects of integration upon the Negro child's responses to various tasks and upon his level of self-esteem." Ph.D. dissertation, University of Kentucky.

MIDDLETON, E. J. (1974) "The effects of desegregation on the academic achievement of black and white high school seniors in St. Mary Parish, Louisiana." Ph.D. dissertation, University of Colorado (University Microfilms No. 74-22372).

MOORE, L. (1971) "The relationship of selected pupil and school variables and the reading achievement of third-year primary pupils in a desegregated school setting." Ph.D. dissertation, University of Georgia (University Microfilms No. 72-11018).

MOOREFIELD, T. E. (1968) "The busing of minority group children in a big city school system." Ph.D. dissertation, University of Chicago.

MOOREHEAD, N. F. (1972) "The effects of school integration on intelligence test scores of Negro children." Ph.D. dissertation, Mississippi State University (University Microfilms No. 72-20270).

MORENO, M. C. (1971) "The effect of integration on the aptitude, achievement, attitude to school and class and social acceptance of Negro and white pupils in a small urban school system." Ph.D. dissertation, Fordham University (University Microfilms No. 71-27014).

MORRISON, G. A., Jr. (1972) "An analysis of academic achievement trends for Anglo-American, Mexican-American, and Negro-American students in a desegregated school environment." Ph.D. dissertation, University of Houston (University Microfilms No. 73-08927).

Nashville-Davidson County Public Schools (1979) Achievement Performance over Seven Years. Nashville, TN: Author.

National Opinion Research Center (1973) Southern Schools: An Evaluation of the Emergency School Assistance Program and of School Desegregation. Chicago: Author.

NATKIN, G. L. (1980) "The effects of busing on second grade students achievement test scores (Jefferson County, Kentucky)." Presented at the annual meeting of the American Educational Research Association, Boston, April.

PAPAY, J. P. (1976) Effects of Induced Desegregation. Dallas: Dallas Independent School District, Department of Research, Evaluation, and Information Systems.

PASCARELLI, E. T., H. TALMADGE, and S. R. PINZUR (1979) "Summative evaluation of longitudinal student achievement data in a desegregated school district." Presented at the annual meeting of the American Educational Research Association, San Francisco, April.

PATCHEN, M., G. HOFMANN, and W. BROWN (1980) "Academic performance of black high school students under different conditions of contact with white peers." Sociology of Education 53: 33-51.

PERRY, G. A. and N. KOPPERMAN (1973) A Better Chance: Evaluation of Student Attitudes and Academic Performance 1964-1972. Boston: A Better Chance.

PREWITT, H. D. (1971) "The influence of racial integration on scholastic achievement in the elementary schools of Lufkin, Texas." Ph.D. dissertation, Texas A&M University (University Microfilms No. 72-05705).

PRICHARD, P. N. (1969) "The effects of desegregation on selected variables in the Chapel Hill City school system." Ph.D. dissertation, University of North Carolina (University Microfilms No. 70-03301).

PURL, M. C. and J. A. DAWSON (1973) The Achievement of Students in Primary Grades After Seven Years of Desegregation. Riverside, CA: Riverside Unified School District.

RAYMOND, L. (1980) "Busing: five years later — test score trends: blacks gain, whites hold." Louisville Times (May 13).

RENTSCH, G. J. (1967) "Open-enrollment: an appraisal." Ph.D. dissertation, State University of New York at Buffalo (University Microfilms No. 67-11516).

ROCK, W. C., J. E. LANG, H. R. GOLDBERG and L. W. HEINRICH (1968) A Report on a Cooperative Program Between a City School District and a Suburban School District. Rochester, NY: City School District.

ROSENTHAL, R. and L. JACOBSON (1968) Pygmalion in the Classroom: Teacher Expectations and Pupils' Intellectual Development. New York: Holt, Rinehart and Winston.

Sacramento City Unified School District (1971) Focus on Reading and Math, 1970-71: An Evaluation Report on a Program of Compensatory Education, ESEA Title I. Sacramento, CA: Author.

ST. JOHN, N. H. (1975) School Desegregation: Outcomes for Children. New York: John Wiley.

SAMUELS, I. G. (1958) "Desegregated education and differences in academic achievement." Ph.D. dissertation, Indiana University (University Microfilms No. 58-2934).

SAMUELS, J. M. (1971) "A comparison of projects representative of compensatory, busing, and non-compensatory programs for inner-city students." Ph.D. dissertation, University of Connecticut (University Microfilms No. 72-14252).

SAVAGE, L. W. (1971) "Academic achievement of black students transferring from a segregated junior high school to an integrated high school." Master's thesis, Virginia State College.

SCHELLENBERG, J. and J. HALTEMAN (1976) "Busing and academic achievement: a two-year follow up." Urban Education 10: 357-365.

SCOTT, W. (1970) A study of bused and non-bused children. Grand Rapids, MI: Grand Rapids Public Schools.

Shaker Heights School Board (1972) An Interim Evaluation of the Shaker School Plan. Shaker Heights, OH: Shaker Heights Public Schools.

SHEEAN, D. S. and M. M. MARCUS (1978) The Effects of Desegregation on Student Attitudes and Achievement. Dallas, TX: Dallas Independent School District, Department of Research, Evaluation, and Information Systems.

SHUTMAN, E. (1974) "The relationship of desegregation and of consistent attendance to reading achievement of primary-grade Negro pupils." Ph.D. dissertation, University of Southern California (University Microfilms No. 74-21508).

SLONE, I. W. (1968) "The effects of one school pairing on pupil achievement, anxieties and attitudes." Ph.D. dissertation, New York University (University Microfilms No. 68-11808).

SMITH, A. B. (1978) "A study of the educational effectiveness of desegregation." Ph.D. dissertation, University of Oklahoma.

SMITH, A. D. (1976) "The impact of desegregation on the Florida statewide twelfth-grade achievement test scores of black and white students in a rural and an urban Florida county." Ph.D. dissertation, University of Florida (University Microfilms No. 76-12133).

SMITH, A. D., A. DOWNS, and M. LACHMAN (1979) Achieving Effective Desegregation. Lexington, MA: D. C. Heath.

SMITH, L. R. (1971) "A comparative study of the achievement of Negro students attending segregated junior high schools and Negro students attending desegregated junior high schools in the city of Tulsa." Ph.D. dissertation, University of Tulsa (University Microfilms No. 71-22730).

STALLINGS, F. H. (1959) "A study of the effects of integration on scholastic achievement in the Louisville public schools." Ph.D. dissertation, University of Kentucky.

STALLINGS, J. (1978) Study of the Follow-Through Experiment. Palo Alto, CA: Stanford Research Institute.

STARNES, T. A. (1968) "An analysis of the academic achievement of Negro students in the predominantly white schools of a selected Florida county." Ph.D. dissertation, University of Southern Mississippi (University Microfilms No. 68-14712).

STEPHENSON, R. and P. SPIETH (1972) Evaluation of Desegregation 1970-1971. Miami: Dade County Public Schools, Department of Program Evaluation.

Syracuse City School District (1967a) Study of the Effect of Integration — Croton and
    Edward Smith Elementary School Pupils. Washington, DC: Government Printing
    Office.
———— (1967b) Study of the Effect of integration — Washington Irving and Host Pupils.
    Washington, DC: Government Printing Office.
TAYLOR, D. R. (1974) "A longitudinal comparison of intellectual development of
    black and white students from segregated to desegregated settings." Ph.D. disserta-
    tion, University of South Florida.
TEELE, J. E. (1973) Evaluating School Busing: A Case Study of Boston's Operation
    Exodus. New York: Praeger.
THOMAS, K. D. (1977) "The effect of busing on school success of minority students in
    urban elementary schools." Ph.D. dissertation, North Texas State University.
THOMPSON, C. E. and F. L. DYKE (1972) First Interim Evaluation Report: Urban-
    Suburban Pupil Transfer Program, 1971-1972. Rochester, NY: Rochester City
    School District.
VAN EVERY, D. F. (1969) "Effect of desegregation on public school groups of sixth
    graders in terms of achievement levels and attitudes toward school." Ph.D. disser-
    tation, Wayne State University (University Microfilms No. 70-19074).
WALBERG, H. J. (1971) "An evaluation of an urban-suburban school busing program:
    student achievement and perceptions of class learning environment." Presented at
    the annual meeting of the American Educational Research Association, New York,
    February.
WEINBERG, M. (1977) Minority Students: A Research Appraisal. Washington, DC:
    National Institute of Education.
WILLIAMS, F. E. (1968) "An analysis of some differences between Negro high school
    seniors from a segregated high school and a non-segregated high school in Brevard
    County, Florida." Ph.D. dissertation, University of Florida (University Microfilms
    No. 69-17050).
WOLMAN, T. G. (1964) "Learning effects of integration in New Rochelle." Integrated
    Education 2, 6: 30-31.
WOOD, B. H. (1968) "The effects of busing vs. non-busing on the intellectual function-
    ing of inner city, disadvantaged elementary school children." Ph.D. dissertation,
    University of Massachusetts (University Microfilms No. 69-5186).
WINKLER, D. R. (1975) "Unequal achievement and the schools." Integrated Educa-
    tion 14, 1: 24-26.
ZDEP, S. M. (1971) "Educating disadvantaged urban children in suburban schools: an
    evaluation." Journal of Applied Social Psychology 1, 2: 173-186.

4

MINORITY CHILDREN:
DESEGREGATION, SELF-EVALUATION,
AND ACHIEVEMENT ORIENTATION

EDGAR G. EPPS

In "The Nature and Meaning of Negro Self-Identity," Proshansky and Newton (1968: 209) point out that "most theorists and reasearchers have assumed that [for black children] segregation in the schools, whether de facto or legal, has devastating consequences for the development of a positive self-image." Chief Justice Warren, speaking for the United States Supreme Court in *Brown* v. *Board of Education* (1954: 494), wrote that "the policy of separating the races is usually interpreted as denoting the inferiority of the Negro group. A sense of inferiority affects the motivation of a child to learn. Segregation with the sanction of law, therefore, has a tendency to retard the educational and mental development of Negro children." In the 27 years since the *Brown* decision, black children have experienced both segregated and desegregated educational environments. During that period, many researchers have attempted to determine the impact of school desegregation on the self-image and motivation of black children. This chapter reviews some of that research and discusses the implications of the research findings for educational policy makers.

SELF-IMAGE

CONCEPTUAL ISSUES

There is little agreement among researchers on the meaning of the terms "self-image," "self-esteem," and "self-concept." Some researchers use the terms interchangeably; others draw distinctions. Coopersmith (1975: 148) views the self-concept as "the symbol or image which the person has formed out of his personal experiences" and self-esteem as "the person's evaluation of that image." Strike (1981: 235) treats self-concept and self-image as synonymous terms, but states that it is important to distinguish between self-respect and self-image. Porter and Washington (1979: 54) "divide self-esteem into two components: racial and personal. Racial self-esteem refers to how the individual feels about the self as black, i.e., about his group identity. . . . Personal self-esteem [refers to] esteem for one's individuality regardless of racial group — how one feels about the self in a comprehensive sense." Coopersmith (1975: 148) also notes that "in addition to a global self-concept that summarizes the broad range and variety of personal experiences persons form more specific self-concepts that are more limited and particularistic." He goes on to state that "the question of whether certain features of experience such as race, sex, or size are so salient that they pervade virtually all aspects of the self-concept has not been established." Hare (1980b) writes that it is important to look at dimensions of self-esteem, such as how the person evaluates himself in the home setting, the school setting, and while interacting with peers. It has also been pointed out that individuals do not give equal weight to all aspects of their experience (Rosenberg, 1968).

Some selectivity is clearly involved in the development of self-esteem. An individual will choose among various types of qualities and characteristics — valuing those characteristics at which he believes he is good and disregarding or undervaluing those characteristics or qualities at which he views himself as being poor. One's self-esteem may be based upon such varied characteristics as athletic prowess, dress and physical appearance, attractiveness to the opposite sex, skill at verbal repartee, and skill at fighting, as well as academic achievement. The particular combination of attributes that constitute the basis of high self-esteem varies from individual to individual, but is systematically related to the social and cultural background of the individual and to the values held by persons who are close to him, such as parents and friends. Finally, it is important to note that some researchers distinguish between general self-esteem and academic-specific self-esteem or self-concept of academic ability (Brookover and Erickson, 1975). In this review, the following distinctions will be made: for global self-image, the term general self-esteem will be used; for academic self-image, the term self-concept of academic ability will be used; and for racial self-image, the term racial self-identity will be used.

RESEARCH ON RACIAL SELF-IDENTITY

Research in this general area attempts to determine the extent to which black children or other minority children develop racial self-hatred, a low sense of self-worth, dominant group preference, or rejection of their own group as a result of growing up in a racist society. The research usually involves asking children to choose pictures or dolls that are "like me" or "unlike me"; to select the "good child" or the "pretty child," or the child he or she would like to work or play with. Inferences are then made from these choices about the children's self-images and racial self-identity *without making direct assessments* of the children's self-esteem or racial self-evaluation.

Recent reviews of research in this area (Banks and Rompf, 1973; Weinberg, 1977; Spencer, 1976; Stephan, 1978) indicate that there are numerous methodological and conceptual problems which make it difficult to draw firm conclusions. Porter and Washington (1979) point out that responses among preschool children vary by age, sex, and social class. A major problem is inadequate controls. This is very important in making comparisons over time and across settings. Specific inadequacies cited by reviewers in addition to lack of controls include questionable research designs, poor sampling, the use of a wide variety of instruments and proceduces, the use of samples of different age, sex, and status composition, and the study of children in different social contexts (laboratories, playgrounds, schools, different geographic regions, different desegregation status, and so on). Generalizing from this complexity is difficult.

Spencer (1976) argues that few researchers give adequate consideration to the developmental issues regarding concept acquisition (self, other, race, ethnicity). In her research, Spencer found a significant nonlinear relationship between racial attitudes and self-concept. Specifically, 80% of the 4 and 5 year olds were found to have both "majority culture preference racial attitudes. and positive self-esteem. She states:

> Previous to this research, virtually all research on the personality disposition of Black Americans has accepted the assumption that given

the racial preferential behavior of black children (i.e., doll choice, racial statements, etc.), blacks must necessarily suffer from low self-esteem or negative self-concepts. Generally, this inference has been made without assessing self-concept and racial attitudes in the same population [Spencer, 1976: 200].

The research demonstrates clearly that young black children do not internalize the negative societal evaluation of blacks, even as they learn that blacks are devalued in society.

Other research suggests that black children's preference behavior has changed since the earlier work of Clark and Clark (1947). Winnick and Taylor (1977) found that almost double the number of black children in their study (64 percent) showed preference for their own race, as was found in the study published by Clark and Clark. In addition, Banks (1976) points out that the appropriate research question is not whether black children make more cross-race choices than whites; it is the extent to which choices made by black children differ due to chance. Using this criterion, his analysis of the results of the most prominent studies of preference behavior in blacks indicated that in only 6 percent of the experiments did black children demonstrate preference.

Banks and Rompf (1973: 782) demonstrated that black children do not exhibit global self-hatred as earlier studies had suggested (for example, Clark and Clark, 1947). They conclude:

Within an experimental design where social and task structure were manipulated, preference behavior on the part of black children was found to be highly variable. If a generalized internal process like self-concept were motivating preference behavior, such variance would not be anticipated or explained. To the extent that such behavior covaries with experimentally controllable factors, it is extremely difficult to attribute it to internal traits.

DESEGREGATION EFFECTS ON RACIAL IDENTITY

The most extensive study of racial identity in the context of desegregation was conducted in Riverside, California (Gerard and Miller, 1975). The results of this study indicated that a child's ethnic identity and self-attitude are not closely linked: When data measuring these two factors were analyzed together, they showed no significant relationship. Photographic assessment of ethnic identity, a technique that uses photographs of male and female black, Mexican-American, and Anglo children, was used in this study. The clearest result, as one would expect, is that children of all ethnic groups were most likely to choose a same-race same-sex picture as "most like me." This pattern was more pronounced after two years of desegregation, fewer minority group children choosing a picture of an Anglo child in the third year. McAdoo (1977) studied the development of racial attitudes in Mississippi, Michigan, and Washington, D.C., over a period of five years. She found that a child's preference for his or her own race increased after he or she attended an interracial school. Weinberg (1977: 169) has observed: "Racial self-awareness has apparently increased sharply, both in the North and in the South. Racial self-acceptance has also undoubtedly risen. But the degree of such a rise has been overstated."

DESEGREGATION EFFECTS ON SELF-ESTEEM

Several comprehensive reviews of both published and unpublished studies on the impact of desegregation on children's self-esteem available prior to 1977 have been published (Epps, 1975, 1978; St. John, 1975; Stephan, 1978; Weinberg, 1977). These reviews have all found a mixed pattern of results, some finding that black students have higher self-esteem in segregated schools and others finding black students with higher self-esteem in nonsegregated schools. Still other studies have found no significant differences between students in segregated and nonsegregated schools. A few of the more recent studies will be reviewed here.

Hare (1977) studied 210 fifth graders in an attempt to assess how children of varying backgrounds differ in their levels of general and area-specific (school, peer, and home) self-esteem. The children attended desegregated schools in Evanston, Illinois. Although the sample contained limited numbers of black middle-class and white lower-class children, socioeconomic status was also examined as an influence on these dimensions of self-esteem. The findings indicate that there are variations in general and area-specific self-esteem across both race and status lines, but no differences by sex. There was no racial difference in general self-esteem. However, whites scored higher than blacks in school self-esteem. There were significant socioeconomic status differences among measures of general, school, and peer self-esteem, with the higher-status students having the higher scores.

Hare (1977) reports that home self-esteem is the best predictor of general self-esteem for black children and for blue-collar white children. School self-esteem, the best predictor of general self-esteem for white-collar whites, is not significantly related to general self-esteem for the other groups. In other words, school self-evaluation seems to have little bearing on the total self-esteem of black children or lower-class children.

Caution is advised in generalizing from this study because of the small samples used in some comparisons and because Evanston may be a unique environment in some respects.[1]

Cicirelli (1977) used the Purdue Self-Concept Scale (PSCS) to study 345 primary grade children attending inner-city schools in a metropolitan area. There was a decline in self-concept with grade level, and blacks scored higher than whites. An analysis of black second-grade children's scores indicated that the race differences were due to the high level of the scores of children whose families were on welfare; these children score significantly higher than other blacks. The results were explained as possibly being due to low evaluative expectations in the welfare environment, increasingly salient black pride, or defensiveness. The black and white children in this study live in the same neighborhood and attend the same schools, therefore the differences displayed seem to indicate home influences or ethnic influences rather than neighborhood or community influences. Although it is still possible for the school to have differential impacts on children of different racial groups even when they are in the same classrooms, this study provides no evidence on this source. Cicirelli (1977: 215) states that "it is conceivable that parents and teachers have lower expectations for these [welfare] children than would be the case for their slightly more advantaged peers; however, this should be submitted to empirical test."

Hunt and Hunt (1977), in a reanalysis of Rosenberg and Simmons's (1971) Baltimore data, explored the mediating processes that sustain self-image in black males. The analysis sample consisted of 690 male students in the fifth through twelfth grades. A recent version of the Rosenberg self-esteem scale was used, along with items indicating specific terms of self-description (such as well-behaved, good at sports, hard worker in school). There was also a school attachment scale, a sense of control/personal efficacy measure, and a measure of sex-role identification (conceptions of maleness). Students in segregated and desegregated schools were compared. The results indicate that black males' self-esteem is higher in segregated schools and their sense of control/efficacy higher in desegregated schools. These authors present evidence to support the hypothesis that sense of control in these black youth is associated with low school attachment and is, thus, based on nonschool factors. According to the authors, "the findings . . . suggest a pattern of self-image maintenance among black boys not so much through *rejection* of conventional values and institutions and clear *substitution* of compensatory terms of self-respect, as through *distance* and *diffusion* — identification of the dimensions of self with a wide range of both conventional and unconventional terms of identity" (Hunt and Hunt, 1977: 552).

Using a different assessment scale, Hughes and Works (1974) undertook a study that reached the opposite conclusion from that of the study by Hunt and Hunt. They compared the self-concepts of black teenagers in a predominantly black high school and in a predominantly white high school. The self-concepts of the black males in the predominantly black school were more positive than those of their counterparts in the predominantly white school, but the racial composition of the school was not associated with the self-esteem of the females. The authors conclude that attendance at a desegregated predominantly white high school may have harmful consequences for the black male.

Hare (1980a) also reported sex differences among black males and females attending desegregated elementary schools. However, students differed more in achievement than in self-esteem. There were no significant differences in general self-esteem, home self-esteem, or self-concept of academic ability. However, boys were significantly higher than girls on a self-rating of the importance of sociabilities, and tended to be higher in peer self-esteem. Black females tended to be higher than black males on school self-esteem, and were significantly higher than black males in anxiety and achievement orientation (achievement values). Black girls also were significantly higher than black boys in both reading and math achievement as measured by standardized test scores. It is of interest to note that white boys had significantly higher self-esteem than white girls, and that whites did not differ in achievement. Black and white males did not differ in self-esteem or self-concept of ability; however, black girls had significantly higher self-concept of ability than white girls, in spite of the fact that white girls had significantly higher achievement scores.

Gerard and Miller (1975) found that on all measures of self-attitudes administered prior to desegregation, except the need for school achievement, Anglo children scored significantly more favorably than black and Mexican-American students. The authors state that response bias may have influenced outcomes on some of the scales utilized, thus possibly confounding the results. Since these results are consistent with others reported elsewhere in the book, the authors are inclined to view these as genuine racial/ethnic differences. Controls for socioeconomic status also failed to account for the ethnic differences. The only significant change after desegregation involved younger black children. These children displayed much greater increases in general anxiety than either Anglo or Mexican-American children three years after desegregation. It should be noted that factor analyses yielded different factor structures for each of the ethnic groups, which suggests that the scales may be measuring different underlying constructs for each ethnic group. Drawing conclusions about ethnic differences is thus a bit hazardous.

It seems clear that generalizing about the impact of desegregation of the racial aspect of self-concept is unwarranted. As Christmas (1973) and Weinberg (1977) concluded after reviewing the literature, the findings are generally inconclusive. However, Weinberg feels that on balance the research is more favorable than unfavorable. The research certainly does not support the contention that desegregaton is harmful to black self-identity.

MOTIVATION TO ACHIEVE

Gerard and Miller (1975) drew heavily on achievement motivation theory in their research design. The indices of achievement-relevant motivation used in their study included: (1) a ring-toss game which yielded measures of goal discrepancy — the difference between expected performance and actual preformance, and number of unusual shifts, such as raising goals after poor performance; (2) an eight-item sense of control over the environment scale; (3) a six-item scale to assess intellectual achievement responsibilities (IAR), which yielded two scores — a "lack of effort" score and a "lack of ability" attribution score; and (4) a measure of tendency to delay degratification. The authors hypothesized that minority scores should improve on these measures after exposure to white classmates in desegregated schools. The analysis attempted to answer three questions: (1) Do the measures show the expected differences for age and ethnic group? (2) Do the measures predict school achievement? (3) Is there any indication that desegregation has an impact on achievement-related behavior?

On the ring-toss goal setting measures and the fate control measures, the age and ethnic group responses were about as predicted, with older children and Anglo children having more favorable scores. On the IAR measures, an age effect was found for "effort" attribution, but not for "ability" attribution. There were no ethnic differences on the "effort" attribution measure, but Mexican-American children were more likely than either Anglos or blacks to attribute failure to their own ability. Blacks and Anglos did not differ on the IAR. The results for delay of gratification were as predicted: older children and Anglos were more likely than younger children or minority children to delay gratification.

To answer the second question, regarding the relation of motivation to achievement, a standardized achievement test score (three levels within each ethnic group) was included in an analysis along with school grade, sex, and ethnic group. The goal setting (ring-toss) measure was not related to achievement for any group; fate control was significantly related to achievement for Anglos and Mexican-Americans, but not for blacks. The "effort" subscale of the IAR was not related to achievement. However, attributing one's failures to lack of "ability" was associated with low achievement, but only for girls. The results for delay of gratification were inconclusive. Gerard and Miller (1975: 139) conclude: "In summary, our analysis demonstrates that only a miniscule proportion of the variance in achievement can be accounted for by achievement motivation or at least our measures of it. We obtained a moderate relationship for fate control and for self-attributions of ability, but the other four variables appeared to be virtually unrelated to achievement scores."

The impact of desegregation analysis indicated that there was no effect of desegregation on goal-setting scores for third and fifth graders, but first-grade minority children performed better after one year of desegregation than the comparison (predesegregation) group. The authors recommend caution in interpreting this result, because there were only ten black children in the group that showed improvement. However, comparing children who had one year of desegregation experience with those who had three years of desegregation experience suggests that goal setting of minority children improves as desegregation experience increases. Amount of desegregation experience did not appear to affect fate control. However, after three years of desegregation, "all children were much less likely to delay gratification than were their age mates two years earlier" (Gerard and Miller, 1975: 144).

Perhaps the most important analysis in Gerard and Miller's study looked at the effect of teachers' attitudes on children's achievement orientations. On the goal setting measure, it was found that desegregation experience was mediated by teachers' attitudes. While Anglo children were not affected, third- and fourth-grade black and Mexican-American children in classrooms with teachers who were moderate or high in discrimination improved their goal setting less than did minority children in classrooms of teachers who were low in discrimination. The measure of teacher discrimination was derived from teachers' tendencies to overestimate the achievement inferiority of minority children.

The ESAA In-Depth Study of 1974-75 (Wellisch, 1976) attempted to relate school effort to provide minority-oriented cultural enrichment materials and activities to school success in raising student achievement. The rationale is based on the assumption that such cultural enrichment programs lead to improved self-image among minority children, and that improved self-image is related to improved academic achievement. A positive relationship between cultural enrichment activities and minority achievement scores was found, but there was no direct measure of self-image. Other research (for example, Carey and Allen, 1977) found no such relationship. However, the ESAA impact studies did find support for the positive relationship between sense of control and achievement (Coulson, 1975; Coulson et al., 1976, 1977).

While these data do not provide direct evidence that desegregation enhances minority children's sense of control, or that a strong sense of control causes high achievement, they do suggest that there is a correlation between a child's sense of control and his or her level of achievement. Evidence gathered by other researchers indicates that the sense of control among minority students is greater in desegregated schools than in segregated schools (Hunt and Hunt, 1977).

In a study of 513 fifth graders attending desegregated schools in a moderate-sized midwestern city, Hare (1980b) looked at ethnic differences in children's sense of control and achievement orientation. Whites scored significantly higher than blacks on both measures. Also, with race controlled, high socioeconomic status children scored higher than low socioeconomic status children on these same measures. It is quite probable that these differences can be attributed to cultural variation in perception of the opportunity structure as well as actual differences in the way youngsters in the different race and class groups experience day-to-day life.

Ramirez and Price-Williams (1976) ask if it is valid to apply an Anglo-American definition of achievement motivation based on individualistic achievement striving to groups that place greater emphasis on group or family expressions of achievement and approval. The tradition of group-related achievement may have relevance for organization of classroom instruction in desegregated schools as a means of increasing motivation and achievement among minority children.

Ruhland and Feld (1977) studied the development of achievement motivation in black and white children in two working-class elementary schools, one 33 percent black, and the other 85 percent black. The results indicated that the black and white children did not differ in "autonomous" achievement motivation, which is learned at home prior to school age. However, white students scored significantly higher on social comparison motivation, which is acquired during the elementary school years. Autonomous standards define excellence in relation to one's own past performance. Social comparison standards are based on comparisons between one's own performance and that of others. These findings on autonomous motivation provide clear support for Banks and McQuarter's (1978) contention that the roots of low achievement in blacks are not located in family and early socialization experiences. As Ruhland and Feld (1977) assert, the classroom is a major source of information about how one's ability compares with the abilities of one's peers. If teachers have low expectations for minority students, or if they provide other inaccurate feedback, they may subvert the process of developing effective social comparison motivation and self-evaluation skills. Evidence from several studies suggests that black students are less accurate than whites, in segregated or desegregated settings, in estimating their own achievement levels (Busk et al., 1973: Hare, 1980a; Massey et al., 1975). Teachers may be providing inappropriate feedback to minority students (for example, saying work is satisfactory when a student is performing below standards). It is also possible that the social comparison process represents a cultural conflict for some minority students whose backgrounds are not supportive of individualistic competition; some groups stress family- or group-oriented achievement and discourage competition with peers.

In summary, this review, like others (Epps, 1975, 1978; Porter and Washington, 1979; St. John, 1975; Weinberg, 1977), concludes that the results of research on racial self-identity, self-concept and self-esteem, and achievement orientation of black students yield mixed or conflicting results. Some studies find higher self-esteem for black students in segregated schools; others report higher scores for integrated schools; still others report no difference. These differences in results can be attributed to methodological weaknesses in some studies, the use of many different instruments to assess personality characteristics, comparisons of different age, sex, and geographic location groups, and comparisons of results from different time periods. However, in spite of these shortcomings, some conclusions seem warranted.

First, it is virtually impossible to determine with certainty whether or not desegregation has short-term or long-term beneficial or harmful effects on minority students' self-esteem, aspirations, or motivation. There is fairly consistent evidence that desegregation has a facilitating effect on students' sense of control. Black students' aspirations for future education are usually high in both segregated and desegregated schools. Self-concept of academic ability is also surprisingly high in view of the relatively low academic achievement of black students (Brookover et al., 1979).

Second, whatever the impact of desegregation, minority students, especially blacks, typically have acceptable levels of general self-esteem. That is, most studies find minority students scoring equal to or higher than whites in general self-esteem.[2] The work of Hare (1980a, 1980b) provides important insights that can help to guide policy makers. This research strongly suggests that it is the area of school-related self-esteem that may need enhancing in minority students. Hare's results, along with those of Brookover and his associates (1979) and that of Busk and associates (1973), also provide a basis for inferring that minority students use different reference groups than whites in forming their evaluations of their academic performance.

Third, minority students' achievement values or orientations are usually lower than those of white students. However, much of this difference is associated with social class. There is also a strong probability that the instruments used to assess achievement values are based upon Anglo-American middle-class norms and may not accurately assess minority achievement motivation, which may be more strongly oriented to family and group achievement than to individualistic competition.

Fourth, results vary so much across settings that it makes little sense to talk of gross comparisons such as desegregation versus segregation. Experiences vary within classrooms and schools to such an extent that site-specific assessment is necessary for an understanding of desegregation's impact on students. For example, Felice and Richardson (1977) report that dropout rates for bused minority students are similar to but slightly higher than those for nonbused minority students. This general finding is less interesting than the fact that dropout rates for bused students are strongly affected by the socioeconomic status composition of the school and by teacher expectations at the receiving school. The authors explain: "Desegregation produces a positive benefit for this most crucial dimension of minority student educational accomplishment, when the school to which the minority student is bused is one where teachers' expectations are positive and supportive" (Felice and Richardson, 1977: 242).

Fifth, Scheirer and Kraut (1979) have examined the assumption that raising students' self-concepts will result in improved academic achievement. Their review of published studies and doctoral dissertations found little evidence that self-concept enhancement causes improved achievement. In fact, there is a strong suggestion that improvements in achievement lead to improved self-concept. Scheirer and Kraut (1979: 144) argue:

> In this view, self-concept change is likely to be an outcome of increased achievement with accompanying social approval, rather than an intervening variable necessary for achievement to occur. This view also provides an alternative explanation for the relative success of the Brookover [et al., 1967] and the Gray and Klaus [1970] programs, for both interventions focused on parents' creating more positive, and thus more rewarding, interactions with their children.

Finally, it seems clear that if the goals of desegregation include both the enhancement of self-concept and achievement, there is a need to consider how the school environment can be reorganized so as to enhance achievement, and, in the process, enhance self-concept as well. The following section addresses this issue.

SCHOOL CLIMATE:
ENHANCING SELF-ESTEEM AND MOTIVATION

School learning climate is defined as "the norms, beliefs and attitudes reflected in institutional patterns and behavioral practices that enhance or impede student achievement" (Lezotte et al., 1980: 4). This definition of school learning climate implies a concern for the educational environment of the whole school. While it is also possible to think of the learning climate of a classroom, an effective classroom isolated in a low-achieving school can have little impact on the total school environment. Therefore, it seems more efficient to concentrate on school learning climate rather than classroom learning climate.

This focus on school learning climate is based on recent research which demonstrates that some schools attended by lower-class minority children are much more successful than others in terms of students' scores on achievement tests (Brookover and Schneider, 1975; Brookover and Lezotte, 1979; Edmonds, 1979). The school climate concept is important for desegregation planners for two reasons. First, the learning environment in desegregated schools can have either an enhancing or impeding effect on student learning, self-esteem, and racial attitudes. Second, in urban districts with large minority populations some schools remain minority-isolated even with the best of planning. It is necessary to implement programs in these schools to make sure that isolation does not result in inferior education. Knowledge of the characteristics of achieving schools can assist planners in developing programs for effective education in minority-isolated schools as well as in biracial or multiethnic schools.

Lezotte and associates (1980) point out that achievement is apparently unrelated to the climate when composite level of SES and race of the student body are used as a proxy for climate. They assert, however, that school learning climate correlates positively with achievement when climate is viewed as

the dynamic patterns of classroom interactions and teaching process (with the classroom as a unit of analysis); organizational structures based on differences in philosophy and practices (tracking); differences in the school setting due to time spent on lessons, attendance rates, and perceptions of levels of discipline; the overall atmosphere or ethos of a building; the intellectual and academic emphasis and norms in a building; and the normative patterns of teacher and student expectations, evaluations, beliefs and group practices (Lezotte et al., 1980: 55).

According to Brookover and associates (1979: 147), the following characteristics of the school social system relate to high achievement and other desired outcomes:

> First of all, believe that all children can and will learn whatever the school defines as desirable and appropriate. Expect all children to learn these patterns of behavior rather than differentiate among those who are expected and those who are not expected to learn. Have common norms that apply to all children so that all members of the school social system expect a high level of performance by all students. With these evaluations, expectations, and norms characterizing the school social system, the patterns of interaction between teacher and pupil should be characterized by consistently appropriate and clearly recognized reinforcement of learning behavior. Failure should be followed by immediate feedback and reinforcement should be given only when correct responses are made. This type of school environment is best characterized by what has come to be known as the Mastery Model (Bloom, 1976).

Perhaps the most important theme of this school climate research is that the schools can be held responsible for levels of pupil achievement regardless of students' racial or socioeconomic status. As Edmonds (1979) points out, the factors that appear to contribute to high achievement are under the control of the school system. Instructional leadership, high expectations, positive learning atmosphere, and specific emphasis on instruction in basic skills are consistently essential institutional determinants of pupil performance. Edmonds contends that strong administrative leadership is indispensable. This leadership is necessary to bring together the various elements of good school learning environments. He states that "effective schools get that way partly by making it clear that basic school skills take precedence over all other school activities." It is also necessary for pupil progress to be monitored systematically so that the principal and the teachers can remain constantly aware of pupil progress in relationship to objectives.

Brookover et al. (1979) also stress that high achieving schools are characterized by the students' feeling that they have control of their academic work and that their own efforts make a difference in their academic success. Tracking appears harmful to the development of this sense of control. Teachers and principals in high achieving schools are able to convince students that they are committed to seeing that their students learn their academic work. High expectations are communicated to students so that they know they are expected to learn and that they are expected to conform to the school norms of high achievement standards. In lower achieving schools, students feel a sense of futility. They believe that the system is organized in such a way that they cannot achieve, that teachers are not committed to their achievement, and that teachers have little faith in their ability to learn. Low expectations are characteristic of teacher attitudes, student attitudes, and the attitudes of the administrators. Therefore, little time or effort is devoted to instruction, and much effort is devoted to control. Since teachers and administrators believe that only a few of their students can learn, tracking or ability grouping is likely to characterize lower achieving schools. Students are also likely to be praised for substandard performance. One result of this inappropriate feedback is that students in low achieving schools may have high self-concept of academic ability and at the same time low sense of control (high sense of futility). This is especially true of predominantly black schools.

In the next section of this chapter, descriptions of some cooperative learning strategies and some team learning strategies are presented. The research suggests that such strategies may be used to improve minority students' achievement in desegregated schools, to increase interracial cooperation, and to enhance self-esteem and motivation.

COOPERATIVE VERSUS INDIVIDUALISTIC INSTRUCTION

Johnson and Johnson (1979: 105-106, 108), in a comprehensive review of cooperative and competitive educational processes, state:

There is evidence that there is a greater perceived likelihood of success and that success is more important in cooperative than in competitive and individualistic learning situations. . . . Experimental evidence also indicates that cooperative learning experiences, compared with individualistic ones, result in more intrinsic motivation, less extrinsic motivation, and less need for teachers to set clear goals for students. . . . One of the most important social problems facing our country is prejudice toward groups and individuals that are in some way different from the middle-class white majority. There is a need for instructional strategies that will reduce prejudice among students at the same time that they maximize achievement. There is evidence that cooperative learning experiences, compared with individualistic ones, encourage the liking of peers who are both smarter and less smart than oneself.

. . . In studies involving students — from different ethnic groups, handicapped and non-handicapped, male and female — at the junior high school level, the evidence indicates that cooperative learning experiences, compared to competitive and individualistic ones, promote more positive attitudes toward members of different ethnic groups and sexes and toward handicapped peers. . . . There is also evidence that cooperative learning experiences, compared with individualistic ones, result in higher self-esteem. . . . Cooperative attitudes are related to basic self-acceptance and positive self-evaluation compared to peers; competitive attitudes, to conditional self-acceptance; individualistic attitudes to basic self-rejection.

Slavin and DeVries (1979: 136-137) present considerable evidence that learning in teams can produce the type of cooperative learning environments described by Johnson and Johnson:

If a school wants to promote positive race relations, to increase students' academic performance, to encourage mutual concern, and to develop self-esteem, team techniques may be a means to accomplishing those goals. They are practical and inexpensive, require no special training, and generate enthusiasm. Further, they have been extensively researched and field-tested in hundreds of classrooms.

However, Slavin and DeVries (1979: 123) make a distinction between the games approach and the cooperative techniques used with experimental groups at the University of Minnesota (Johnson and Johnson, 1979). The cooperative experimental groups have not demonstrated greater effects on achievement than standard techniques used with control groups. If one is concerned about raising achievement of minority children, it is not enough to set up a cooperative reward and task structure and wait for achievement to increase. The team techniques that have been most successful in increasing academic performance require individual accountability on the part of students (for example, Teams-Games-Tournaments; Jigsaw).

Additional support for the effectiveness of the games approach has been reported by Lucker et al. (1976). These researchers found that, while whites performed equally well in interdependent (using games) or traditional classes, blacks and Mexican-Americans performed significantly better in the interdependent classes. In interdependent classes, the achievement level for minorities and whites did not differ; in traditional classes, the white children performed significantly better than minority children. Compared to students in traditional classrooms, students in interdependent learning groups increased in self-esteem, decreased in preference for competitive behavior, and viewed their classmates as learning resources.

Cohen (1980) cautions against uncritical adoption of the cooperative approach of the Johnsons or the team learning strategies of Slavin and DeVries and Lucker. Schofield and Sagar (1979) also express reservations about the long-term effectiveness of group learning strategies. In both cases the reservations are based on observed patterns of interracial interaction in classrooms that suggest that status differences in socioeconomic background and reading ability affect patterns of interaction in groups. Since these status differences usually favor whites, patterns of dominance and friendship selection usually favor whites as well. These patterns are difficult, though not impossible, to change. Careful attention has to be paid to organizing the group process so that it does not reinforce already existing patterns of status association and competence expectations. Cohen (1980: 273) states that "combining racial groups with similar levels of academic achievement makes it much easier to produce equal status relationships." Cohen also recommends reorganizing classrooms so as to minimize the continued use of reading competence as the major source of students' expectations about competence in general. This involves the use of multiple abilities in the curriculum and the use of small groups in instruction.

There is ample evidence that school environments are often less congenial to minority children than to middle-class white children. Teachers tend to rate white children higher in competence and sociability. Black children are usually rated lower on both competence and ability. While these kinds of teacher attitudes exist, we are a long way from achieving the goal of equally effective integrated education. Restructuring schools so that they utilize cooperative learning structures and team techniques should help to overcome some of these problems. However, it will also be necessary to change teacher and administrator attitudes about instructional processes as well as about the learning potential of minority students.

Esposito (1973) reviewed the research literature on the impact of ability grouping on three aspects of children's schooling: academic achievement, affective development, and ethnic and socioeconomic isolation. From this review one can draw the following conclusions: (1) the evidence on academic achievement is inconsistent with respect to high ability students, sometimes showing advantages for homogeneous grouping and sometimes showing advantages for heterogeneous grouping; (2) homogeneous grouping almost always produces lower academic achievement than heterogeneous grouping in average and below-average groups; (3) homogeneous grouping almost always results in segregating students ostensibly according to ability, but practically according to socioeconomic and ethnic status; (4) homogeneous ability grouping tends to inflate the self-esteem of students in high ability groups, but has negative effects on self-esteem of students in average and below-average groups and tends to stigmatize students in below-average groups as inferior and incapable of learning; (5) homogeneous ability grouping rarely results in the development of instructional practices or techniques that are uniquely adapted to the needs of the different ability groups; and (6) teachers and administrators have low expectations for achievement of students in low ability groups, thereby setting in motion a self-fulfilling prophesy.

There seems to be little educational justification for homogeneous ability grouping. The practice persists in spite of this lack of educational justification, perhaps because of educational inertia or the belief that grouping makes the work of the teacher easier. If the practice cannot be justified on the grounds of enhancing the achievement of average and low ability children, and if the practice results, as it usually does, in segregating children on the basis of class and ethnicity, it should be abolished in all cases in which a case of educational benefit cannot be clearly established. Perhaps the policies of PL 94-142 can be adopted for desegregation planning. The law requires that an individualized education plan be written for each student before he or she can be placed in any special education program, and that the plan be reviewed annually. Individualized education plans are signed by parents, thereby giving parents some control over their children's placement. The most important aspect of any such plan is the provision of effective monitoring to assure that the goals of the plan are being met, and that children are enabled to make upward movement as their achievement improves. One of the most harmful aspects of ability grouping, tracking, and special education placement is the tendency for initial placement to become permanent. There must be assurance of systematic procedures for upward mobility from low ability groups to higher ability groups, from special education to mainstream classrooms, and from lower tracks to higher tracks if the harmful aspects of placement are to be minimized.

Bloom (1976) has developed an instructional approach, based on research and theory, that has demonstrated that effective instruction improves achievement and enhances self-concept without ability grouping. A version of this instructional strategy has been implemented in the Chicago public schools. Evaluation of the 1976-1977 program in 10 schools indicates that pupils taught with mastery learning techniques gained 7.5 months during 7 months of instruction, while the control group of pupils gained only 4.5 months on the Iowa Tests of Basic Skills. There were no measures of self-esteem reported in this study, but if we are correct in inferring from other research that improving achievement enhances self-esteem and motivation, this type of program could help educators achieve the goal of effective desegregation — high quality education for all pupils.

CONCLUSION

In conclusion, recent research indicates that the self-esteem of black children in interracial schools is usually comparable to the self-esteem of white children in the same schools, yet the black children usually get lower grades than the white children and have lower achievement test scores. Their self-esteem is only weakly related to their achievement. How are students able to have such a high concept of their achievement when they are not meeting the school's achievement standards? One plausible explanation is that they are comparing themselves only to their black classmates. We need to develop policies for desegregation that will raise achievement and, through raising achievement, build a stronger relationship between self-esteem and achievement among black pupils.

How can this be done? To begin with, desegregation must be complete. It must be carried out at the classroom level. Students must not be resegregated through tracking. Even ability grouping within classrooms must be eliminated if the goal of desegregation, equality of educational opportunity for all pupils, is to be realized. This will require reorganizing the instructional process through such instructional strategies as mastery learning, multiple-ability group teaching, and teaching-learning games. It is not easy to change schools, but without change there is little hope for making the most of the dream of the *Brown* decision.

NOTES

1. There is also the possibility of an instrument effect. Hare (1977) devised his own instrument for this study. The Hare scale correlates highly with other recognized instruments, such as those developed by Coopersmith (1967) and Rosenberg (1965). Hare's instrument correlates .83 with both the Coopersmith and Rosenberg scales, which correlate about .74 with each other. Thus, it is measuring a dimension that is widely considered to be self-esteem. The question of a self-favorability response set remains to be considered, as it is not mentioned in this chapter. However, construct validity has been established (Shoemaker, 1980).

2. For example, Drury (1980), in a secondary analysis of 194 high schools selected from 11 southern states in 1973 for ESAA, found that when school mean SES and

achievement are controlled school mean self-esteem is significantly higher for blacks than for whites.

REFERENCES

BANKS, W. (1976) "White preference in Blacks: a paradigm in search of a phenomenon." Psychological Bulletin 83: 1179-1186,

—— and G. McQUARTER (1978) "Achievement motivation and black children." IRCD Bulletin 11, 4.

—— and W. ROMPF (1973) "Evaluation bias and preference in black and white children." Child Psychology, 44: 776-783.

BLOOM, B. (1976) Human Characteristics and School Learning. New York: McGraw-Hill.

BROOKOVER, W. and E. ERICKSON (1975) Sociology of Education. Homewood, IL: Dorsey.

—— and L. LEZOTTE (1979) "Changes in school characteristics coincident with changes in student achievement." Occasional Paper No. 17, Institute for Research on Teaching, College of Education, Michigan State University, May.

—— and J. SCHNEIDER (1975) "Academic environments and elementary school achievement." Journal of Research and Development in Education 9: 83-91.

——, E. ERICKSON, and L. JOINER (1967) Self-Concept of Ability and School Achievement: Relationship of Self-Concept to Achievement in High School (Vol. III). East Lansing: Michigan State University, Office of Research and Publications.

——, C. BEADY, P. FLOOD, J. SCHWEITZER, and J. WISENBAKER (1979) School Social Systems and Student Achievement: Schools Can Make a Difference. New York: Praeger.

BROWN v. BOARD OF EDUCATION (1954) 347 U.S. 483.

BUSK, P., R. FORD, and J. SCHULMAN (1973) "Effects of schools' racial composition on the self-concept of black and white students." Journal of Educational Research 67: 57-63.

CAREY, P. and D. ALLEN (1977) "Black studies: expectation and impact on self-esteem and academic performance." Social Science Quarterly 57: 811-820.

CHRISTMAS, J. (1973) "Self-concept and attitudes," in K. Miller and R. Dreger (eds.) Comparative Studies of Blacks and Whites in the United States. New York: Seminar.

CICIRELLI, V. (1977) "Relationship of socioeconomic status and ethnicity to primary grade children's self-concept." Psychology in the Schools 14: 213-215.

CLARK, K. B. and M. P. CLARK (1947) "Racial identification and preference in young children," in T. M. Newcomb and E. L. Hartley (eds.) Readings in Social Psychology. New York: Holt, Rinehart & Winston.

COHEN, E. (1980) "Design and redesign of the desegregated school," in W. Stephan and J. Feagin (eds.) School Desegregation: Past, Present, and Future. New York: Plenum.

COOPERSMITH, S. (1975) "Self-concept, race and education," in G. Verma and C. Bagley (eds.) Race and Education Across Cultures. London: Heineman.

—— (1967) The Antecedents of Self-Esteem. San Francisco: Freeman.

COULSON, J. (1975) The First Year of Emergency School Aid Act (ESAA) Implementation. Santa Monica, CA: System Development Corporation.

————, D. S. HANES, D. G. OZENE, C. BRADFORD, W. J. DOHERTY, G. A. DUCK, and J. A. HEMENWAY (1977) The Third Year of Emergency School Aid Act (ESAA) Implementation. Santa Monica, CA: System Development Corporation.

————, D. G. OZENE, C. BRADFORD, W. J. DOHERTY, G. A. DUCK, J. A. HEMENWAY, and N. C. VAN GELDER (1976) The Second Year of Emergency School Aid Act (ESAA) Implementation. Santa Monica, CA: System Development Corporation.

DRURY, D. (1980) "Black self-esteem and desegregated schools." Sociology of Education 53: 51-59.

EDMONDS, R. (1979) "Some schools work and more can." Social Policy 9, 5: 28-32.

EPPS, E. (1978) "The impact of school desegregation on the self-evaluation and achievement orientation of minority children." Law and Contemporary Problems 42, 3: 57-76.

———— (1975) "Impact of school desegregation on aspirations, self-concept, and other aspects of personality." Law and Contemporary Problems 39: 300-313.

ESPOSITO, D. (1973) "Homogeneous and heterogeneous ability grouping: principal findings and implications for evaluating and designing more effective educational environments." Review of Educational Research 43: 163-179.

FELICE, R. and R. RICHARDSON (1977) "The effects of busing and school desegregation on minority student dropout rates." Journal of Educational Research 70: 242-246.

GERARD, H. and N. MILLER [eds.] (1975) School Desegregation: A Long-Term Study. New York: Plenum.

GRAY, S. and R. KLAUS (1970) "The early training project: a seventh year report." Child Development 41: 909-924.

HARE, B. (1980a) "Looking underneath the central tendency: sex differences within race and race differences within sex." State University of New York at Stony Brook. (unpublished)

———— (1980b) "Self-perception and academic achievement: variations in a desegregated setting." American Journal of Psychiatry 137: 683-689.

———— (1977) "Racial and socioeconomic variation in preadolescent area-specific and general self-esteem." International Journal of Intercultural Relations 1: 31-51.

HOBSON v. HANSEN (1967) 296 F. Supp. 401 (D. D.C.).

HUGHES, R. and E. WORKS (1974) "The self-concepts of black students in a predominantly white and in a predominantly black high school." Sociology and Social Research 59: 50-54.

HUNT, J. and L. HUNT (1977) "Racial inequality and self-image: identity maintenance as identity diffusion." Sociology and Social Research 61: 539-559.

JOHNSON, D. and R. JOHNSON (1979) "Cooperation, competition, and individualization," in H. Walberg (ed.) Educational Environments and Effects. Berkeley, CA: McCutchan.

KATIMS, M., J. SMITH, C. STEELE, and W. WICK (1977) "The Chicago Mastery Learning Reading Program: an interim evaluation." Presented at the annual meeting of the American Educational Research Association, New York.

LEZOTTE, W., S. MILLER, D. HATHAWAY, J. PASSALACQUA, and W. BROOKOVER (1980) School Learning Climate and Student Achievement: A Social Systems Approach to Increased Student Learning. East Lansing: Michigan State University, Center for Urban Affairs, College of Urban Development, and Institute for Research on Teaching.

LUCKER, G., D. ROSENFELD, J. SIKES, and E. AARONSON (1976) "Performance in the interdependent classroom: a field study." American Educational Research Journal 68: 588-596.
McADOO, H. P. (1977) "The development of self-concept and race attitudes in black
children: a longitudinal study," in Report of the Third Conference on Empirical
Research in Black Psychology. Washington, DC: National Institute of Education.
MASSEY, G., M. SCOTT, and S. DORNBUSCH (1975) "Racism without racists:
institutional racism in urban schools." Black Scholar 7: 2-11
PORTER, J. and R. WASHINGTON (1979) "Black identity and self-esteem: a review
of studies of black self-concept." Annual Review of Sociology 5: 33-74.
PROSHANSKY, H. and P. NEWTON (1968) "The nature and meaning of Negro
self-identity," in M. Deutsch et al. (eds.) Social Class, Race, and Psychological
Development. New York: Holt, Rinehart & Winston.
RAMIREZ, M. and D. PRICE-WILLIAMS (1976) "Achievement motivation in chil-
dren of three ethnic groups in the United States." Journal of Cross-Cultural
Psychology 7: 49-60.
ROSENBERG, M. (1968) "Psychological selectivity in self-esteem formation," in C.
Gordon and K. Gergen (eds.) The Self and Social Interaction. New York: John
Wiley.
——— (1965) Society and the Adolescent Self-Image. Princeton, NJ: Princeton Univer-
sity Press.
——— and R. SIMMONS (1971) Black and White Self-Esteem: The Urban School
Child. Washington, DC: American Sociological Association.
RUHLAND, D. and S. FELD (1977) "The development of achievement motivation in
black and white children." Child Development 48: 1362-1368.
ST. JOHN, N. H. (1975) School Desegregation: Outcomes for Children. New York:
John Wiley.
SCHEIRER, M. and R. KRAUT (1979) "Increasing educational achievement via
self-concept change." Review of Educational Research 49: 131-150.
SCHOFIELD, J. W., and A. SAGAR (1979) "The social context of learning in an
integrated school," in R. Rist (ed.) Desegregated Schools: Appraisals of an Ameri-
can Experiment. New York: Academic.
SHOEMAKER, A. (1980) "Construct validity of area specific self-esteem: the Hare
self-esteem scale." Educational and Psychological Measurement 40: 495-501.
SLAVIN, R. E. and D. DeVRIES (1979) "Learning in teams," in H. Walberg (ed.)
Educational Environments and Effects. Berkeley, CA: McCutchan.
SPENCER, M. (1976) "The social-cognitive and personality development of the black
pre-school child: an exploratory study of development process." Ph.D. disserta-
tion, University of Chicago.
STEPHAN, W. (1978) "School desegregation: an evaluation of predictions made in
Brown v. Board of Education." Psychological Bulletin 85: 217-238.
STRIKE, K. (1981) "Toward a moral theory of desegregation," in J.S. Soltis (ed.)
Philosophy and Education: Eightieth Yearbook of the National Society for the
Study of Education (Part 1). Chicago: National Society for the Study of Education.
WEINBERG, M. (1977) Minority Students: A Research Appraisal. Washington, DC:
National Institute of Education.
WELLISCH, J. B., A. MARCUS, A. H. MacQUEEN, and G. A. DUCK (1976) An
In-Depth Study of Emergency School Aid Act (ESAA) Schools: 1974-75. Santa
Monica, CA: System Development Corporation.
WINNICK, R. and J. TAYLOR (1977) "Racial preference — 36 years later." Journal of
Social Psychology 102: 157-158.

5

HISPANIC STUDENTS
AND SCHOOL DESEGREGATION

RICARDO R. FERNANDEZ
JUDITH T. GUSKIN

The past decade has witnessed the rapid growth of bilingual education programs throughout the United States. Beginning with the passage in 1968 of federal legislation and modest appropriations (Title VII of the Elementary and Secondary Education Act), and supported by enforced federal regulations and a number of significant court decisions which culminated in *Lau* v. *Nichols* (1974), bilingual education has come to the forefront of American education practice in urban settings. Fostered by the involvement of community groups from different language and cultural backgrounds, numerous states enacted legislation during the 1970s requiring the use of the home language of students as a vehicle of instruction in content areas while English language skills are being acquired simultaneously. Total yearly federal expenditures for bilingual education, which currently exceed $200 million, are used to serve children of limited proficiency in English from over 70 language groups, although the vast majority of children in need of bilingual programs are still not being served. Bilingual education represents a major thrust in U.S. public education policy. Premised on civil rights law prohibiting discrimination based on national origin (language), the influence of bilingual education on the nation's educational system is evident, in spite of the uncertain prospects it faces in the 1980s.

Parallel to this phenomenon, over the same time period, another thrust in public educational policy became intensified — school desegregation in major urban areas. Supported by a series of court decisions following *Brown* v. *Board of Education* (1954), the movement to end racial segregation of the nation's schools, which had begun to gather momentum in the late fifties and early sixties in the South, began to expand to the North and to the West in the early seventies. While desegregation litigation was still concentrated in the South, there was no public consciousness regarding its potential impact on cultural and linguistic minorities who also face discrimination. Once lawsuits were filed and remedies imposed in cities with significant language minority populations in addition to blacks, another element entered into the picture and it became apparent that factors other than race might be involved. However, consideration of these other racial and ethnic groups in planning and implementing desegregation did not happen to any significant extent until recently (for example, in Los Angeles, Austin, Detroit, Chicago). The dramatic growth of the Hispanic population in the United States, together with its increased visibility, has placed greater emphasis on the need to plan for desegregation along triethnic or multiracial lines.

While blacks and Hispanics publicly espouse similar goals in terms of equality of educational opportunities and quality educational programs, the means to promote these goals often appear to be in conflict. Desegregation and bilingual education emerge as the respective symbols by which these two communities will judge the progress made toward improving their educational condition. Although the compatibility of both programs has been stated (Cárdenas, 1975; González, 1979), there are conflicting, or, at least, varying legal precedents, federal and state legislation as well as regulations, and differing perceptions in each group on the immediate and long-range goals of both desegregation and bilingual education.

There is little information available on Hispanic students, and even less on how they have been affected by school desegregation. The dearth of research evidence on how Hispanics fare in desegregated schools is a major limiting factor to scholars and practitioners interested in this group.

This chapter represents an attempt to provide some basic information about Hispanics and how their needs can be taken into account in the desegregation process. It contains a review of demographic data on this group, the second largest minority group in the United States, a brief overview of how the courts have defined and resolved the issues related to Hispanics and segregation, and a brief summary of selected research studies. In addition, issues and problem areas in desegregation implementation in cities where Hispanics are involved in the process are discussed not only at the macro or district level but also at the school and classroom level.

Most of the recommendations in this chapter are based on the personal experiences of the authors as practitioners in the field of school desegregation planning for many years. Given the paucity of research, many important questions remain unanswered; it is hoped that there will be a growing number of scholars interested in this area in the future.

HISPANICS IN THE UNITED STATES:
AN OVERVIEW

As the second largest minority group in America, Hispanics are faced with problems similar to those that confront members of other minority groups: low educational attainment, segregation, poverty, reduced levels of services in government-funded programs, and discrimination on the basis of national origin or language. Demographic projections vary but invariably confirm sustained growth rates for Hispanics well into the next century.

More than 12 million persons in the United States identify themselves as being Mexican, Puerto Rican, Cuban, or "other Spanish" origin (U.S. Department of Commerce, 1979).[1] In viewing the Hispanic population by national origin, Mexican-Americans, the biggest subgroup, account for 7 million (59 percent of all Hispanic Americans). Puerto Ricans account for 1.8 million (15.1 percent); Cubans, .7 million (5.7 percent); Central and South Americans, .6 million (7.2 percent); and "other Hispanic," 1.5 million (12.6 percent). Given this data, it is clear that Hispanics are becoming a significant sector of the nation's educational system, and this trend will continue through the 1980s and 1990s. Therefore, it is imperative that schools become sensitive to the special educational needs of this minority group.

Geographically, close to 75 percent of all Hispanics reside in 5 states: California, New York, Texas, Florida, and New Mexico. Numerically, California has the largest Hispanic population (3.3 million), but it is also important to note that Hispanics account for over one-third (36 percent) of New Mexico's total population and for one-fifth (21 percent) of the population of Texas[2] (National Center for Education Statistics, 1976).

Hispanics are the youngest ethnic minority in the nation. The youthfulness of the Hispanic population is seen in two types of data: (1) median age — 22.1 years for Hispanics compared to 29.5 years for non-Hispanics and (2) the percentage of the population below age 18 —

42 percent for Hispanics compared to 29 percent for non-Hispanics (U.S. Department of Commerce, 1979). Puerto Ricans have the lowest median age (20.3 years), while the median age of Cubans (36.5 years) is higher than the national average. In considering the school-age Hispanic cohort, 43.1 percent are between ages 5 and 25; for whites the figure is 34.2 percent.

Contrary to popular belief, most Hispanics reside in metropolitan regions. According to census statistics for 1978, 85 percent of all Hispanic families in the United States lived in metropolitan areas, compared to 65.2 percent for non-Hispanics. Further, twice as many Hispanics (51.1 percent) reside in central cities than non-Hispanics (25.6 percent).

The geographic distribution of Hispanics has a direct impact on the nation's educational system. At the state level, certain states with large portions of Hispanics must be aware, both at the policy and programmatic levels, of the special educational needs of Hispanic students. In addition, given the fact that most Hispanics live in metropolitan and/or central-city regions, urban school districts need to become directly involved with the academic advancement of this population. At present, the problems of urban school districts, including white flight, an older white population with fewer (or no) children, and an eroding tax base, are disproportionately falling on Hispanics, blacks, and other minorities, and this situation will probably worsen.

Many Hispanic families speak Spanish at home. According to the figures from the 1976 Survey of Income and Education, 80 percent of all Hispanic Americans live in Spanish-speaking households. Moreover, of the members this group approximately one-third usually speak Spanish (National Center for Educational Statistics, 1976). Of the Hispanics reporting English-language backgrounds, the figure is 14 percent. Further, language spoken is related to place of birth. For example, among foreign-born Mexicans and Cubans, as well as Puerto Ricans born in Puerto Rico, two-thirds report that they usually speak Spanish (National Center for Educational Statistics, 1980).

In considering school-aged Hispanic population cohorts, 96 percent between the ages of 6 and 13 live in a household where some Spanish is spoken (National Center for Educational Statistics, 1975). Among Hispanic students ages 14 to 18 the figure is 78 percent, declining to 15 percent for those ages 19 to 25. In that a large portion of Hispanic students are Spanish-speaking, particularly at the elementary level, schools must implement language service programs to help students with limited English-speaking skills. There is a negative impact on the academic achievement of limited-English-speaking students unless schools provide language programs. This is evidenced by the fact that among Hispanics ages 14 to 25 the school dropout rate is 25 percent annually and, of this group, approximately 45 percent come from Spanish-speaking households (National Center for Educational Statistics, 1980).

Hispanics have lower incomes than non-Hispanics. In 1977, the median incomes for Hispanics and non-Hispanics were $5564 and $6484, respectively. To further highlight the income gap between Hispanics and non-Hispanics, in 1977 21.4 percent Hispanic families had incomes below the poverty level, in contrast to 8.7 percent of non-Hispanics. Without adequate educational services, the income gap between Hispanics and non-Hispanics will remain large. The interrelationship between education and income for Hispanics is circular. First, as the result of their limited education, Hispanics are at a disadvantage in the labor market; secondly, many Hispanic students must drop out of school in order to help their families financially.

A review of Hispanic demographics brings forth some of this population's educational needs. Compared to the general population, Hispanics are a young and fast-growing group, with high concentrations in urban areas. During the next decade Hispanic school enrollments, particularly in central cities, will substantially increase.[3] It is therefore necessary that the nation's educational system address the academic as well as the sociocultural needs of Hispanic youngsters.

LANGUAGE ISSUES AND
THE EDUCATION OF HISPANIC STUDENTS

As stated earlier, a significant number of Hispanic school-age youngsters come from households where Spanish is spoken. Moreover, it is evident that students with limited English-language skills are at a severe educational disadvantage in an all-English curriculum. This is corroborated by the fact that hispanics have high dropout (or "push out") rates, lower achievement scores, and are more likely to be behind their expected grade levels. School authorities often cite English-language "deficiencies" as the foremost reason that Hispanic students do poorly in school. While the acquisition of language skills and proficiency in English are critical to a successful educational experience, many Hispanic students do not understand the instructional language used in the classes in which they are enrolled (Gonzalez, 1979b). A significant portion of Hispanic schoolchildren who need special language services are not enrolled in programs. Indeed, among the 12 states where the need for bilingual programs are greatest, only one-third to two-thirds of the Hispanic children are being served (U.S. Office for Civil Rights, 1978).

Data released by the National Center for Educational Statistics (1978) reveal that there are approximately 3.6 million children in the United States with limited proficiency in English, 70 percent of whom are of Hispanic origin. This may help explain why the Hispanic community's response to their children's educational crisis has centered on the issue of bilingual and bicultural education.

HISPANICS AND DESEGREGATION: LEGAL PRECEDENTS AND STRATEGIES

Since the mid-nineteenth century, Hispanics have struggled for equal educational opportunities in the nation's public schools. In many respects, although they were never subjected to slavery, the history of discrimination against Hispanics has been as debasing as that against blacks, yet this issue has received little public attention. The major drawback in understanding the history of discrimination against and segregation of Hispanic school children is that it has not been well documented.

The earliest litigation by Mexican-Americans against school authorities dates back to 1930. A number of court cases in California and Texas followed during the 1940s and early 1950s (for example, *Méndez* v. *Westminister,* 1946; *Delgado* v. *Bastrop Independent School District,* 1948; *Gonzalez* v. *Sheely,* 1951). Following *Brown* (1954), the question of how Mexican-Americans would be classified in planning for school desegregation was still unresolved. Although in the Southwest and California there were no statutes requiring the segregation of Mexican-American students, it is a fact that separation had existed for decades, at times justified on the grounds that students' limited English-language skills necessitated separate schools or programs, ostensibly to provide special remedial help, which usually never materialized. Many school systems in the Southwest virtually ignored all this litigation and provided separate schools for Mexicans.

There were three noteworthy decisions that took place immediately following *Brown.* In *Romero* v. *Weakley* (1955), though the case was settled out of court, blacks and Chicanos challenged the practice of classifying Chicanos as "whites" and mixing them into black schools for desegregation purposes. The other case, *Hernández* v. *Driscoll Consolidated School District* (1957) dealt with segregated classes on the basis of language. The court ultimately ruled that it was unconstitutional for the Driscoll district to assign Hispanic students to language classes on the basis of "race," rather than lack of English-language skills. The *Hernández* case took on a new significance in that the court identified

Chicanos as being subjected to "unreasonable *race* discrimination." It was not until 1970 that a federal district judge in Texas held that, for the purpose of school desegregation, Mexican-Americans should be treated as an "identifiable ethnic minority group." The body of precedents grew quickly but not until *Keyes* v. *School District No. 1* (1973) did the U.S. Supreme Court recognize Chicanos in the Southwest as being discriminated against and segregated in a manner similar to blacks.

The importance of *Keyes* also lies in the subsequent rejection by the Tenth Circuit Appeals Court of a comprehensive educational plan (which included bilingual education) for Mexican-American students which would have required the maintenance of predominantly Hispanic schools in opposition to the districtwide mandate to desegregate all schools (*Keyes,* 1975). *Keyes* posed the question of what takes precedence when desegregation and bilingual education compete with one another. The legal precedent established there is clear: "Bilingual education, moreover, is not a *substitute* for desegregation. Although bilingual instruction may be required to prevent the isolation of minority students in a predominantly Anglo school system, . . . such instruction must be subordinate to a plan of school desegregation." An obvious comment to be made here is that legally there is no difficulty with bilingual education as *part* of the remedy, but clearly it cannot be *the* remedy for segregated school systems or even portions thereof.

In *Bradley* v. *Milliken* (1975), the court ordered bilingual instruction as part of a series of components in the desegregation remedy, on the basis of a state law requiring such programs. Subsequent legal decisions in *Ross* v. *Eckels* (1972) and *Tasby* v. *Estes* (1976) held that desegregation plans must consider the needs of other groups besides blacks and whites. The terminology of school desegregation planning was expanded by the use of the term "triethnic" to refer to those districts where a third group was "numerically significant" to be considered separately in devising court-ordered remedies.

In recent years the stategy of Hispanic participation in desegregation cases has been limited to intervening at the remedy stage to protect the integrity of existing bilingual programs. In school districts with concentrations of Hispanics and other minorities, planning is usually done in the absence of any input from the Hispanic community, although it is clear that Hispanic pupils are affected by their transfer out of neighborhood schools and by other programmatic changes, especially with regard to staff. In order to protect the interests of Hispanic students, which are often tied to the viability of existing bilingual/bicultural programs or programs to be created at schools where Hispanic children are to be transferred, Hispanic groups have intervened in a number of cases and have succeeded in obtaining recognition by courts, school districts, and black plaintiffs of the unique educational needs of Hispanics.

The fact that blacks have led the legal struggle for desegregation, and that only after a case is won do Hispanics take a manifest interest in it, has caused some advocates of desegregation, both black and white, to conclude rather hastily that Hispanics are opposed to school desegregation and integration. Viewed against the background of the struggle of blacks for equality in American society, and the lack of documentation on how Hispanics have fought against segregation, it is understandable that Hispanics are looked upon as relative newcomers to this struggle.

REVIEW OF SELECTED RESEARCH
AND RELATED LITERATURE

In 1977, the National Institute of Education (NIE) published data collected by the U.S. Office for Civil Rights (OCR) during 1970-1974 and analyzed by the Center for National Policy Review, Catholic University, Washington, D.C. The data clearly point out the broad trends of segregation of Hispanic children in urban public schools throughout the country. They indicated a significant and rapid growth in the number of Hispanic children in these systems, and an increase in the level of their segregation during this period of time.

In one of the earliest articles on desegregation of Hispanic students, Cárdenas (1975) argued against the implicit dichotomy between bilingual education and desegregation and made practical suggestions for implementation of both mandates at the school and classroom levels. González (1979) points out how bilingual education has been left unattended while society has tried to weather black/white polarization during the last 25 years. He emphasizes the need to differentiate among corrective measures for different racial/national origin groups, while recognizing that these remedies are *minimal* responses and that much more is needed to achieve quality education and ultimate societal integration. He stresses the need for black/Hispanic dialogue ("cross-fertilization") on these two issues in order to promote greater understanding in each community of the other's perspective.

The legal issues surrounding bilingual education and their relationship to school desegregation are discussed in depth by Teitelbaum and Hiller (1977) and Roos (1978), who review the major cases related to the two areas and the precedents that have accumulated over the years. Consistently, they argue that the two mandates are compatible and feasible although their implementation at the classroom level may present difficult problems given the costs involved, administrative considerations, teacher certification, and other issues.

Orfield (1978a) gives a historical overview of how Hispanics have been subjected to segregation and other types of discrimination over the years. He highlights important issues, such as language and culture, and offers arguments against segregated bilingual programs, given their questionable efficacy and illegal status. He recommends avoidance of extremism in educational policies for Hispanics (that is, segregation) and urges that work be undertaken to find the most effective way of reconciling the educational needs of Hispanic children with school integration. In the same work, Orfield criticizes the transformation of goals by OCR from its early focus on integration to processes and policies which contain ambiguity and inconsistencies, promote polarization among groups, are subject to political pressures, and redefine basic objectives. As a specific example, Orfield highlights the "new definitions of discrimination" and, focusing on language (national origin), argues that federal bureaucrats appear to have gone beyond the mandate of the *Lau* decision in defining compliance requirements with Title VI of the Civil Rights Act. Inconsistencies and inverted or forgotten priorities are criticized for their adverse impact on prior integration/desegregation efforts by OCR and civil rights advocates.

In his 1978 report to the court as an expert on desegregation in the Los Angeles case, *Crawford* v. *Board of Education,* Orfield (1978b) raises the issue of whether Hispanics and other national origin groups (such as Asian-Americans) should be considered minorities for purposes of desegregation planning, since, arguably, they may not have been subjected to discrimination in the same way or as intensely as blacks. The provision of bilingual services as a component of desegregation planning is also addressed, and three potential areas of conflict are outlined: (1) scattering of linguistic minority children; (2) lack of sufficient (qualified) staff; and (3) unwillingness of Anglos to integrate bilingual classes, or the possible educational advantages of bilingual classes, even if they are racially identifiable or segregated, for all or part of the day. Orfield concludes his analysis by suggesting that apparent conflicts can indeed be resolved through proper planning and careful implementation, and ends by emphasizing the importance of Spanish as a language in Southern California, especially for Anglo children, in view of the changing demographic profile of the region.

Crain (1978) voices similar concerns in his report to the Los Angeles court. Citing studies and data related to reduced social distance and high rates of intermarriage of Hispanics with whites (vis-à-vis blacks) as indicators that Hispanics are subject to a lesser degree of discrimination than blacks, Crain views Hispanics as another immigrant group and conjectures that in 50 years they will be assimilated into American society, and thus will not be subject to any real discrimination.

As the only Hispanic expert to testify during these proceedings, Arias (1978) cautions against the enactment of a desegregation plan which would have deleterious effects on services and programs for limited-English-proficiency (LEP) children, and addresses the issue of how to classify Hispanics by suggesting that factors other than race or racial phenotypes, such as cultural and socioeconomic isolation, must be considered. She makes specific recommendations pertaining to (1) the assignment of LEP or non-English-speaking (NES) children so that a sufficient number of students and properly trained bilingual staff will be present at receiving schools, (2) the inclusion of the most isolated Hispanic schools in the selection of any desegregation remedy, and (3) effective remedies for racial isolation, such as magnet schools in which parents are actively involved and multicultural education is provided for students and staff.

In 1978, NIE commissioned three major studies on desegregation and its impact on bilingual programs (Carter and Segura, 1979; Noboa, 1979; Martin, 1979). Carter and Segura (1979) address problems of implementing bilingual education in several districts in California and Arizona and describe ongoing bilingual programs in desegregated schools. They argue that research on these issues has practical programmatic application in schools. No inherent conflict or contradiction is found between the *Lau* and *Brown* mandates, but caution is stressed against the confusion in directives to implement them, especially federal and state bilingual education directives. The authors see this confusion increasing, at least in California. Specifically, Carter and Segura urge that schools and districts of varying student bodies in differing geographic areas be studied since "there is no one model school, district, or community," and admonish that any study should include community perceptions or attitudes toward bilingual education and desegregation because they are especially pertinent.

Noboa (1979) analyzes desegregation trends among Hispanics across the country and reports findings of ethnographic studies of two cities (one on the west coast and one on the east coast) in which desegregation and bilingual education plans have been implemented. The dynamics of the interaction among individuals, groups, and communities in the desegregation process are presented in detail, along with such phenomena as ethnic cleavage and racial conflict, demographic shifts, and political power in the case studies. Based on his analysis of data collected by OCR between 1968 and 1976 on elementary and secondary schools throughout the country having enrollments of 3000 students or more and at least a 5 percent Hispanic population, Noboa highlights the finding that Hispanic segregation trends did not change significantly, while figures for blacks indicated significant improvement. In a more intensive analysis of triethnic communities, nearly half the districts studied showed that Hispanics became more segregated after the implementation of school desegregation plans.

Martin (1979) focuses on concerns of migrant children and how desegregation has affected them. His study is primarily a compilation of facts and a cursory review of the major cases and related issues on desegregation and bilingual education. Its usefulness in helping to answer questions related to these topics is limited.

To date, there has been only one study which focused on the impact that a proposed race desegregation plan might have on bilingual education programs in a school district. This study (Noboa and Fernández, 1981) analyzes an OCR feasibility plan developed in 1979 for the desegregation of the Chicago public schools and the impact it would have on Hispanic and other national origin minority group children. Taking into account that a predominantly black school zone was excluded from the plan, a principal finding of the study is that Hispanic schoolchildren would bear a disproportionate burden of being bused if such a plan were to be implemented. Another significant finding of this analysis suggests that a disorganization and dismantling of existing bilingual programs, especially non-Hispanic-language programs, would occur, since not enough students would remain in any one school to justify such programs under Illinois state bilingual education law.

According to Schofield's (n.d.) review of the research on the effect of desegregation strategies on intergroup relations between Hispanics and whites and blacks, very little is known. She mentions a few studies which indicate that whites might be more positive toward Latino students than blacks. One study (Jacobson, 1977) indicates that this seems to be true for teenagers, and two studies indicate that this holds for elementary students as well (Gerard et al., 1975; Green and Gerard, 1974). White students were more likely to choose Mexican-American students as friends and work partners than they were to choose blacks.

Several studies attempt to examine the effect of cognitive learning strategies on measures of acceptance of white and black students. A few of these studies include Mexican-American pupils (Blaney et al., 1977; Gonzáles, 1979b). Some of the data indicate that positive interactions have occurred between whites and Mexican-Americans as a result of these strategies. In addition, some researchers indicate that Mexican-American students may be culturally oriented to cooperative learning strategies, enhancing the potential of these techniques for intergroup relations (Kagan, 1977; Knight and Kagan, 1977). In summary, Schofield notes that there are too few studies to be able to say much about the impact of desegregation on intergroup relations among whites, blacks, and Hispanics, and that more research is definitely needed.

Individual case studies have also been conducted, such as those by Haro (1977) of Los Angeles, and Báez et al. (1980) of Milwaukee. These focus on the political processes related to the Hispanic community's participation in school desegregation and bilingual education planning and implementation in these cities.

In conclusion, research on the relationship between bilingual education and desegregation and on the impact of desegregation on Hispanics has been undertaken only in the last few years. Given the fact that over 1000 studies have been conducted on race desegregation, it is clear that Hispanics have only recently become visible in urban desegregation planing. There is a need for research examining all aspects of the situation — Hispanic participation in political and legal processes, the degree to which Hispanic segregation may be increasing, the impact of desegregation plans on bilingual programs, and the outcomes of desegregation in terms of achievement and intergroup relationships of Hispanic students, both those limited in English and those who are English-proficient. Case studies of districts and schools as well as larger-scale comparative studies are also needed.

DISTRICTWIDE ISSUES

The planning, adoption, and implementation of a race desegregation plan in a district with a heterogeneous population including Hispanics present unique challenges to those communities. The following is a list of the major issues that emerge in these districts; each of these issues will be discussed below.

(1) fixed ratios of students and staff

(2) identification of Hispanic students and staff

(3) assignment of Hispanic students and staff

(4) resegregation

(5) LEP versus non-LEP students

(6) access to educational programs and services

(7) human relations programs

(8) white flight

(9) exemptions of Hispanic students from the desegregation process

(10) funding

(11) monitoring

(12) community input and participation in the desegregation process

(13) timing of the desegregation process

FIXED RATIOS OF STUDENTS AND STAFF

The use of agreed-upon ratios based on districtwide percentages of students and staff represented in the student body or in the work force to assess the level of desegregation on a school-by-school basis is a common practice in desegregating districts. A deviation of plus or minus 10 percent to 15 percent (and sometimes more) is allowed in most desegregation plans. In districts with small concentrations of Hispanic students and staff, the mechanical application of these fixed ratios can result in a scattering of the student population previously concentrated in some schools to schools throughout the district. This may prevent even the minimal concentrations necessary in order for a viable bilingual education program to exist in the receiving school, thus depriving LEP students of needed services.

Dispersal of staff throughout the district, in order to avoid exceeding particular ratios, may result in some bilingual programs not having the necessary staff to function adequately. In addition, the inflexible use of the Singleton ratios in some districts has limited the number of Hispanic staff allowed in buildings where the majority of the student body is Hispanic, while allowing some schools to remain without any Hispanic staff. For example, if the percentage of Hispanic staff in a hypothetical district is 7 percent of the total staff, and a deviation of plus or minus 10 percent were allowed, some schools might have no Hispanic staff, while others could have a maximum of 17 percent. The implications of such a ceiling, even in districts or schools with a high percentage of Hispanic students, are not favorable toward increasing the number of Hispanic staff in those districts.

IDENTIFICATION OF HISPANIC STUDENTS AND STAFF

Hispanics have been classified differently in desegregation plans across the country. For example, they have been grouped under the broad label of "minority," along with other groups such as blacks, Asian-Americans/Pacific Islanders, and Native Americans, in some plans, while in others they have been labeled "nonblack" or even "white." In a few cases they have been accorded separate identification as Hispanics, and planning has proceeded along triethnic lines. The implications of each classification vary by district. Abuses have occurred, such as when Hispanics labeled as "white" were sent to all-black schools to desegregate those schools, a practice that has been held consistently to be illegal by the courts and OCR. However, planning for desegregation will vary significantly depending on how Hispanic students and staff are classified.

ASSIGNMENT OF HISPANIC STUDENTS AND STAFF

The assignment of Hispanic students is often carried out without regard to their linguistic and cultural needs. Hispanic students usually come from homes in which a language other than English is spoken. Some of these children have limited proficiency in English, but there are many whose command of the language allows them to function in an all-English curriculum. The assignment of Hispanic students often does not take language needs into consideration. Consequently, Hispanic students may not be clustered in sufficient numbers ("critical mass") in schools and classrooms to allow special assistance (bilingual instruction or ESL) to be provided.

Staffing is also affected by assignment patterns in which Hispanic teachers equipped to address the needs of LEP students are not placed in schools according to the linguistic needs of the students, but rather are assigned by seniority or by fixed ratios.

It has been argued that the dispersal of minority students so that very few students end up in any one school is unwise. The isolation of students in any given school building has been a concern of both desegregation planners and scholars. Assignment of Hispanic and other minority students should distribute them in numbers sufficient to allow them to have social support systems and peer relationships with members of their own ethnolinguistic group. In addition, changes in the curriculum, such as new courses, activities, and materials that highlight social/cultural dimensions of Hispanics, will require that a minimum number of students be present in certain schools. Suggested minimum percentages for any one racial/linguistic group in any school range from 10 percent to 20 percent.

RESEGREGATION

Although clustering for instructional purposes is permissible under ESAA guidelines and the principle has been incorporated into many Title VI (*Lau*) compliance plans, there are instances of Hispanic students being enrolled in segregated or "racially ethnically identifiable" classes so as to produce long-term isolation. There are conflicting federal and state policies which account in part for this isolation. The primary one is the mandate to concentrate services on students with the greatest needs (LEPs). Although both Title VII (ESAA) and some state guidelines allow a percentage of non-LEP students to participate in bilingual programs paid for by federal and state funds, reimbursement is usually tied to the number of LEP students served in each classroom. There is, therefore, a disincentive to include non-LEP students, white or black, in these programs, since extra local monies would be needed. Desegregation goals, which promote a more diverse mixing of students in schools and classrooms, are thwarted by funding formulas supported by state and federal guidelines.

LEP AND NON-LEP HISPANIC STUDENTS

The number of Hispanic students eligible to receive special assistance under *Lau* due to limited English proficiency varies from district to district, and can, in some cases, exceed 50 percent of all Hispanic students. However, in urban areas, where 85 percent of the Hispanic population lives, the number of LEP Hispanics often falls below 50 percent. Nevertheless, there are no special services or programs earmarked for the non-LEP population, which frequently accounts for the majority of the Hispanic students in a district. Available compensatory services should be provided to these children, if needed, in a manner that recognizes their cultural and linguistic characteristics by staff trained to work with this population.

ACCESS TO EDUCATIONAL PROGRAMS AND SERVICES

Little or no attention is usually paid to the linguistic and cultural needs of Hispanic students in the selection and location of magnet schools or specialty schools. Consequently, they are excluded quite frequently from effective participation because no attempt is made to accommodate them in planning these schools.

The use of magnet schools which focus on language (language academies, immersion schools) as a tool for desegregation has been tried in several cities with varying degrees of success (for example, in San Diego, Milwaukee, and Cincinnati). The issue of whether there is a market for bilingual education among non-LEP white and black students seems to depend on whether the program is viewed as an enriching experience or simply as another compensatory effort to remediate "deficiencies." The recent history of bilingual education, coupled with issues pertaining to the inferior status accorded the Spanish language in the United States, seems to hinder rather than help promote this educational approach. Also, if these magnets are placed within Hispanic *barrios,* as has been the case in several districts, this may defeat their purpose of attracting students to a wide variety of racial and ethnic groups.

HUMAN RELATIONS

Desegregation planning usually includes training in human relations for staff and students. The input of Hispanic staff into the design and implementation of these special programs is usually limited or nonexistent. As a result desegregation issues are addressed in terms of black/ white relations, in spite of the usual references to "multicultural education" and "cultural pluralism."

WHITE FLIGHT

The response of desegregation planners to this phenomenon has been to try to prevent it by relieving whites of some of the burden of desegregation while necessarily increasing the burden on other groups, including Hispanics. There is little or no research on how whites react to having their children attend schools with Hispanic students, as opposed to with black students. It would be important to look at a number of factors in order to try to answer this question: (1) residential patterns over time; (2) size and history of Hispanic and black populations in that community and white perceptions of both groups; and (3) socioeconomic levels of Hispanics in that community.

EXEMPTIONS OF MAJORITY HISPANIC SCHOOLS
FROM THE DESEGREGATION PROCESS

Courts have generally frowned upon the practice of excluding Hispanic students or exempting certain schools with high Hispanic enrollments from the desegregation process. The rejection by the court of a comprehensive education plan (Cárdenas Plan) which would have left certain heavily Chicano schools in Denver out of the desegregation plan marked the first time that a clear directive was issued. However, in

Boston the court approved a plan in which one predominantly Hispanic school was allowed to exceed the maximum ratio set for all schools in the district. There have been instances in which more than one school has been exempted from the desegregation process, as happened in Milwaukee, where four schools with high Hispanic enrollment were excluded from the ratios required in the desegregation plan. In Minneapolis, Native American groups requested in 1979 that a school with a high enrollment of Native American students be exempted from compliance with court-ordered ratios, but their request was denied by the court.

Reactions to these exemptions are varied. In some quarters, they are viewed with resentment, since it appears that a specific group is receiving special privileges. Others, for reasons of administrative convenience, may agree with the decision, especially if very few Hispanic students are enrolled in that city or school district. Perhaps the most negative reaction may be that exemptions, especially those granted upon request of a particular racial ethnolinguistic group, are seen as a symbol of opposition to the desegregation process and thus perceived to be based on questionable motives, including racism.

FUNDING

The potential for conflict over budgetary allocations related to programs to provide services to Hispanic students (such as bilingual instruction) and to black students should be avoided through separate allocations for each program. Additionally, affirmative action efforts for Hispanics, which are often limited to the hiring of bilingual teachers and an occasional administrator, should be expanded to include all levels of administration and services.

DESEGREGATION MONITORING

An efficient monitoring process requires that a mechanism be established to systematically collect and, where necessary, generate adequate data on students in the district. Hispanic students are often ignored by researchers and evaluators in school districts, who tend to collect data according to black and white racial categories, with Hispanics usually relegated to "white" or "nonblack." Recent efforts by OCR to collect data on Hispanic students in their biennial national survey of schools have begun to include data on Hispanics and other language minority students related to services they receive, suspensions, expulsions, and other indicators, such as special education needs.

COMMUNITY INVOLVEMENT IN DESEGREGATION

The effective, ongoing participation of the community in the planning for and implementation of school desegregation is recognized to be an essential component of any successful plan. Yet, even in cities in which they make up a sizeable constituency, Hispanics are often excluded from regular participation in the desegregation process. School districts fail to facilitate the involvement of Hispanic parents, some of whom do no speak English well, and do not provide translators at meetings of parent groups. Notices from school are not usually translated into a language or written on a level that is understandable to parents and interested persons in the community. Staff support to assist parent advisory groups in their work is not readily available, generally speaking, nor are nontraditional approaches used to attract more parent participation (such as meetings held in the community at times, places, and dates which are most convenient to parents).

TIMING OF THE DESEGREGATION PROCESS

Factors related to timing of implementing desegregation plans may have a bearing on Hispanic students and staff. In districts that have had long histories of involvement in bilingual education for Hispanic students, the development of a race desegregation plan can be accomplished with adequate planning so as not to jeopardize bilingual programs. However, when districts that have implemented desegregation plans are faced with the prospect of having to establish programs to serve LEP Hispanics, the process may be a bit more difficult: The proposed clustering of students for instructional purposes may well require altering assigned attendance patterns and transportation routes. This is often perceived by advocates of desegregation, who are frequently ignorant about the goals and current practices of bilingual education and in some cases may even be hostile to the concept, as a form of resegregation. Fears are raised about the possible competition of scarce resources among various groups, such as Hispanics and blacks. The basic compatibility between race desegregation and program/services for Hispanic students is downplayed, and the resulting negative repercussions are soon noticeable in the community.

IMPLEMENTING BILINGUAL PROGRAMS
IN DESEGREGATED SCHOOLS

Research and experience in implementing desegregation have identified certain key variables as important if the social and learning environment of schools are to be satisfactory for all students and staff. These same variables are important for schools implementing bilingual programs and race desegregation, but language and cultural diversity and the needs of bilingual staff add complexity.

Most researchers and educators involved in implementing school change, including desegregation, stress that change is a process, not a momentary event, and that time is needed for staff and students to understand what is desired and to become comfortable with new expectations. Unfortunately, desegregation has been seen too often primarily from the political, legal, and community perspectives, which stress the mixing of bodies at certain specified times, usually in the midst of a high level of conflict. Evaluation of its impact has often been in terms of numbers and achievement, usually within the first year of a desegregation plan. This hardly gives the staff and students sufficient time to take care of the building-level needs critical to successful implementation. General school climate issues, positive staff attitudes and expectations, changes in the curriculum, and informative and effective home-school relationships are not easy to implement during times of stress and goal unclarity and dissension.

When language and cultural differences are added to this setting, another area of possible conflict is present. Students, parents, and staff are likely to reflect the broader societal disagreement about the importance of recognizing and developing linguistic and cultural characteristics that students bring with them to school. Misunderstanding and competition for attention and resources are increased.

What are some of the characteristics of effectively desegregated schools? How does the existence of linguistic and cultural diversity and the simultaneous implementation of bilingual education and other programs/services for Hispanic students complicate the process of desegregation? The following characteristics are most often mentioned:

(1) fairness of rules throughout the school

(2) human relations training for staff

(3) leadership from the principal

(4) coordination of services

(5) strategies to inform parents and to develop trust between parents and school staff

(6) reexamination of grouping practices which might produce long-term isolation of students

(7) modification of curriculum materials to be more inclusive of the racial and ethnic linguistic mix of the students and staff and to eliminate biased materials

(8) strategies to raise teachers' expectations about achievement of minority pupils

These factors will be discussed briefly in terms of possible modifications for schools with both bilingual education and desegregation.

FAIRNESS OF RULES

The issue of fairness and equity of rules and regulations is particularly important in desegregated schools, so that control can be maintained and conflicts resolved based on individual behaviors, rather than allegations of general unfairness to a segment of the school population. It is not going to be helpful for good relationships if students claim that teachers or administrators unfairly discipline them due to their membership in a particular racial or ethnic group. Suspensions of students from any one group which are perceived as excessive will feed underlying conflicts and provide an issue for those who wish to prove that desegregation and/or bilingual education is not working. Norms against racial or ethnic name-calling need to be clear to all, although this kind of behavior often continues without teachers being aware of it. In a desegregated school, everyone is supposed to at least "get along" and "be polite," and those with the power (teachers and administrators) are expected to "be fair."

The existence of bilingual education in a desegregated school means that there is greater linguistic and cultural diversity within the building. This may mean misunderstandings about what is important to each group, how they prefer to interact with one another, and how they show respect or anger. Cultural groups show anger, friendship, and respect in different ways. Misunderstandings can lead to charges that teachers or students are "unfair." For example, if students who have limited English skills speak their home languages, some students or staff may find this upsetting and try to stigmatize the students. These students may in turn show anger or withdrawal. It is important that the principal and staff be aware of the different behaviors and attitudes of students toward linguistic and cultural diversity and that they try to create a climate of respect and understanding.

HUMAN RELATIONS TRAINING FOR STAFF

Staff relationships can be observed by students. Students are aware that some people seem to be isolated from others, even if they may not know why. They can observe the power dynamics between teachers and aides and know who is really in charge. If only the aides, and none of the teachers or administrators, are Hispanic, this tells them something about their group and their program. If linguistically and culturally different staff members are marginal to the rest of the school, students are likely to feel that they and their programs are also not valued. Isolation or stigmatization of bilingual staff seriously affects the implementation of bilingual programs and should be avoided.

Given the racial and ethnic stratification of our society, it is likely that the staff in a racially desegregated school with a bilingual program have had limited contact with others from the various groups involved. While some Puerto Ricans live in *barrios* near black inner-city areas, other Hispanics in a school may have had very little interaction with blacks. Differences among various Hispanic groups should also be addressed. It cannot be assumed that they have had experiences with other Hispanics or knowledge about each other's history, language varieties, and cultural values. Without some planned assistance in how to learn about and adjust to differences among student groups, conflicts or isolation can take place among staff members. In triethnic or multiethnic settings, it is important that staff retraining and human relations efforts address *all* groups present in the setting. It may be necessary to have consultants familiar with specific ethnolinguistic groups brought into the school so that human relations training programs are not implemented only as a black-white effort (Guskin et al., forthcoming).

Underlying staff conflicts are likely to exist in any school. Everyone is not expected to love one another, or even seek out other staff equally in order to share ideas, feelings, or gossip. Some teachers like to stay to themselves. However, it is important to know if a teacher is doing so because of personal preference or because he or she is feeling unwelcome. Principals know that there will be subgroups within the staff, and that some people are loners. While principals should respect the wishes of staff, at the same time they should try to see that all staff members are treated fairly and feel welcome. They may need help in understanding and respecting differences due to language and culture, just as they need help with racial issues.

THE PRINCIPAL AS LEADER

Many researchers and practitioners mention the key role principals play in implementing desegregation. They set the climate for a desegregated school; they should seek additional resources, allocate them fairly, and provide educational leadership to staff members who may be implementing new units of programs. They also need to relate to the central office staff, both in terms of procedures and programs and in terms of supervision. In addition, principals must help students resolve conflicts and help parents and community members understand and support the school. All of these functions are critical for the successful implementation of bilingual programs within a desegregated school.

One of the key problems that emerges when bilingual programs are instituted in schools is the jealousy of nonbilingual staff toward paraprofessional staff and other resources that are needed to implement the program. The principal needs to make it clear why resources are allocated the way they are. Teachers who have not taught in bilingual classrooms may not be aware of the tremendous heterogeneity that usually exists in terms of language proficiency of the students and their past educational experiences. Since this tends to be the rule, not the exception, materials and aides are key to their ability to meet the needs of such diverse student population (Guskin et al., forthcoming).

Supervision of bilingual program staff is a major issue, since there are few bilingual principals, and many do not feel that they know enough to supervise bilingual staff. As in some other programs, bilingual supervisors are usually provided from the central office, even though it is clear that the principal is always the one in charge of what happens in the school, and any conflicts must be resolved with his or her help. Often, especially in large school districts, there are few bilingual central office staff members available to provide regular and consistent supervisory services. Bilingual teachers complain about feeling isolated, especially if the central office program staff is small, and there are members of the local school staff who are vocal in their opposition to the program. The few supervisors in the central office find themselves very busy, given teacher recruitment and turnover and the need to orient and support new teachers who may or may not have received appropriate training in how to assess language proficiency, teach bilingually, or select appropriate materials for the diverse student population they are teaching.

Research on educational innovation has indicated that it is critical for teachers not only to be willing to work hard to implement new programs but also to have continuous support so that they understand very clearly what is expected of them and get feedback on the development of their own competencies (Gross et al., 1971). Principals can play a critical role in this process, but very often give up their leadership role by saying that it is the responsibility of the central office staff to take care of the bilingual program. In an effective desegregated setting many staff may be trying out new ways to structure their classrooms to equalize the status of black, white, and Hispanic students, to introduce new social studies units, or try some team teaching. Principals should include the bilingual staff and the nonbilingual staff in an effort to reward new approaches and to facilitate the sharing of successful practices. It may require a greater effort on their part to learn about bilingual education so that they feel comfortable and knowledgeable. Principals need not be bilingual, but it helps social relationships if they show some desire to learn the language spoken by many of the people in the school and by the parents of the students.

COORDINATION OF SERVICES

In contemporary urban schools many special services are provided to students who are not performing at grade level. For example, they may be eligible for Title I services if they have scored below a certain cutoff score on an achievement test. In addition, they might be provided with social work services, or the services of a psychologist or speech therapist. Some of these people are present as part of the school staff, while others only spend part of the week at the school or come when a student is referred. The issues of coordination, assessment, and correct placement of bilingual students are complex. Students participating in bilingual programs come from a variety of home and school situations. For example, a student with little prior schooling may arrive at the end of the year from a rural Mexican town. That child may not read or write in Spanish or English, but age might indicate placement at the fourth grade level. What services are needed? If that student was not tested in September due to late enrollment, he or she is ineligible for Title I assistance. Besides, the Title I teacher may not be bilingual and the child may not speak any English. Assessment may be made for possible special educational needs, but perhaps that student's problems merely stem from a lack of schooling. Who will administer those tests, and what tests are appropriate? The child might be given a language proficiency test, but that may be postponed until the next year. English as second language services are also needed, so that oral English can be developed. Districtwide competency tests given to fourth-grade pupils for promotion purposes would clearly be inappropriate for this student.

Assessing and placing students in appropriate settings should involve the parents of those students. If the parents do not speak English, efforts should be made to find bilingual personnel and translators. Principals who are unable to communicate with the parents of these students will have additional problems. Community members, many of whom may have experienced the frustrations of misplacement, may not trust that appropriate decisions will be made. Implementing bilingual education in a desegregation context puts greater demand on the principal and the staff to gain the trust of the community and the parents.

STRATEGIES TO INFORM PARENTS AND BUILD TRUST

In a desegregated school with an Hispanic population it is essential that procedures for communication with parents in Spanish be adopted. This is likely to be needed for Hispanic students who speak mostly Spanish, as well as for those who are bilingual, for the parents may only speak Spanish even if the student knows English. There are several situations for which this is necessary. For example, when parents register their children for school, someone must be available to explain to them in a language they understand not only the forms needed but their options for placement. If bilingual education is an option, it is critical that the person speaking to them indicates that this does not mean that the student will be in a Spanish-only classroom environment. If the child is likely to be eligible for Title I services, or needs to be tested by a psychologist, the parents need to understand these things and know what they mean for the education of the child. If the white or black principal or teacher cannot communicate with the parent or does not believe in bilingual education, this leads to community concern that the parent may not be properly informed.

When a parent needs to be informed about a student's progress, this must be done in a language the parent understands. If someone other than the teacher is providing this information due to the teacher's lack of proficiency in Spanish, there should be some safeguards about what needs to be communicated, and confidentiality must be maintained. Report cards should be available in Spanish.

Students may become ill and someone may have to call their parents. The lack of a bilingual person in the office of the school often leads to some difficulty. Also, students may not tell their parents when they are performing poorly, or may not tell their parents about placement decisions. The use of aides for translating, calling parents, and informing them may not always be adequate. It removes them from the classroom, and they may not have had enough training to handle some of the more difficult questions related to placement.

Sometimes teenagers do not adequately share information about options available to them with their parents. They may need bilingual education services or Title I services, but because of peer pressure they may not choose these programs. Counselors must be able to communicate directly with parents about the options available to Hispanic students. If such issues are not addressed, community members may suspect that the district does not wish to provide services to these students.

Some Hispanic parents may have limited trust in school staff members who are not of the same cultural background. This may be due to their own experiences in school or their own lack of experience and comfort in relating to members of other groups. Hispanics can relate well to black or white principals and teachers, but school personnel need to be aware that extra efforts are needed. Hispanics, like most parents, often wish to let school officials do their jobs without interference. However, issues that cause conflict are bound to emerge in newly desegregated schools. Principals and staff cannot assume that trust exists; they must work to build it.

Hispanic parents can be informed about what is happening at the school through newsletters and regular parent meetings. If the school staff do not wish to produce a newsletter, perhaps the district can publish one to be distributed through the schools. If Hispanics are not attending the school PTA, efforts should be made to gain their interest and participation. Perhaps a separate advisory group for parents limited in English would need to be established, or a translator provided.

On a districtwide basis, a parent advisory group can provide information to Hispanic parents about new program options and school policies. This group should be representative of the district as a whole and should provide information to Hispanic parents about new program options and school policies. In addition, this group should provide training to parents to make them effective communicators about school matters. It is to be expected that not all parents have the time to participate, but those who wish to do so should be encouraged and trained. If there are citizen groups concerned with effective school desegregation, the parent advisory group can provide representatives to such bodies. These citizen groups would provide an opportunity for cooperative experiences for Hispanics with whites and blacks.

If Hispanic parents are adequately informed, efforts are made to build trust, and positive experiences exist regarding trying to solve school-related problems jointly with whites and blacks, this will affect the desegregated students also. They will see that their parents and community members are not isolated or stigmatized. Schools will "belong" to them and their parents in a more meaningful way, and they may be more motivated to increase their performance in school. To do well in school implies that one perceives potential benefits. While unemployment and poverty may still dampen aspirations, positive role models of parents and community leaders trying to improve schools will help foster the belief that better performance in school may indeed be a means to a better future.

REEXAMINATION OF GROUPING PRACTICES

Desegregation planners wishing to avoid segregation of pupils within a desegregated school may fear that bilingual programs will necessarily increase segregation and unequal status. This does occur in some situations, but there are a variety of curriculum models that limit the isolation of limited-English-speaking students.

First of all, it should be clear that ability grouping itself is not a problem; the use of ability grouping to segregate students for long periods of time, and the potential that grouping practices have for the creation of unequal status, are what causes the problems. Most teachers use ability grouping in the teaching of reading, and students may be moved from one group to another as they advance in reading level. Students are aware of differences in ability and, as long as these differences are not clearly associated by grouping with only one race or ethnic group, this is an acceptable teaching practice.

Second, it is likely that Hispanic students who are limited in English will be in the lower achievement groups and may be isolated due to their language ability in an all-English curriculum, no matter what the racial and ethnic mix of the students in the classroom. This is also a kind of stigmatizing "permanent track," for, without extra help, they will continue to fall further behind.

Third, the existence of a bilingual program in a school enhances the status of the non- or limited-English speaker and could produce some positive results in how such students are perceived. These students may perform quite well in their mother tongues, thereby dispelling any perception on the part of their peers or teachers that they are unintelligent, or unable to learn how to read.

There are a variety of organizational models used to implement a bilingual program. The choice of organizational model depends on staff availability and training, classroom space, available materials, the proficiency levels of students, and the school's desire to enhance both integration and the bilingualism of students. There are always compromises when choices are made, and some of these will be mentioned below.

The most integregated bilingual program in a desegregated school is a program which involves everyone within the school to some extent. This avoids stigmatizing the program. Those students who do not know Spanish would be learning it and would have an opportunity to interact with native speakers; the same would be true for those who do not know English. This assumes that everyone values learning two languages, no matter what their initial language ability, or racial or ethnic background. It also assumes that the staff of the school would know how to teach languages both to native speakers and to those learning a second language.

Another approach might be to separate the native speakers from the nonnative speakers for a certain period of time, until the nonnative speakers gain enough fluency to learn effectively together with the native speakers. This would allow the instructional staff to deal with a narrower range of abilities initially, but would enhance language acquisition and integration as well. Meanwhile, students could relate to each other informally and in music, art, and gym, thereby providing opportunities for social relationships. In a transitional mode. the native speaker would be placed gradually in the monolingual classroom and the English speakers would not learn Spanish. In a two-way bilingual model, both groups would learn English and Spanish.

If only LEP students are provided with bilingual education, it becomes more difficult to avoid stigmatization and isolation no matter what the organizational model. Some programs provide a resource room, to which students come for additional help. This model, often called the "pull-out" approach, may provide for greater integration, but poses numerous problems. Teachers do not like to have students taken out of their classrooms due to the need to coordinate with other teachers. The resource teacher may not be able to handle the needs of the students who may be at various grade and proficiency levels, the students going to the resource teacher could be stigmatized, and the instruction provided may be closer to tutoring than to the development of a sequential curriculum. If students are very limited in English, they may be spending long periods of time in the room because they are unable to understand English-only instruction.

Some programs provide a half day of instruction in one language and another half day in the other. This requires coordination and a team teaching approach to be effective. It would also be advisable for teachers to observe student performance in both settings. As a recent study by

Moll et al. (1980) has indicated, teachers who do not see the performance of students in their native tongue may underestimate their abilities. Again, this type of program could be planned to enhance language learning in both groups or as a program primarily for limited-English students.

The key variables in any model are teacher proficiency in both languages, knowledge about the background of the students, and attitudes toward bilingual education and integration. Teachers cope with great diversity in their classrooms. Having aides and materials is critical, but so is the motivation and knowledge of the teacher, as well as the support that teacher is getting from other teachers and administrators. Teaching bilingually in a desegregated setting can be exciting and challenging, but the teacher will be working extra hard and will need to feel that people care and that help is available if needed.

MODIFICATION OF CURRICULUM MATERIALS

Many desegregation specialists have written about the need to review materials in terms of bias against blacks. In a desegregated school with Hispanics, it is important to do more than this because of the lack of inclusion of Hispanic cultures and history in most published materials.

Teachers need special training in the culture and history of all the Hispanic groups in the United States. They need to be familiar with the differences that exist within the Hispanic population as well as with the many similarities. Such training is needed even if the teacher is Hispanic. Supplementary materials on Hispanics are needed in both English and Spanish for students and staff members. These could be kept in the school library and the librarian trained about their use. Throughout the school, from time to time, the bulletin boards and displays should show some reflection of the ethnic and racial mix of the student body. If only the bilingual classrooms recognize the linguistic and cultural identity of Hispanics, these students may become isolated from the rest of the school.

Some staff members may wish to develop units on culture dealing with intergroup relationships within the Hispanic community, as well as relationships among Hispanics, blacks, whites, and other groups. Students could bring items from home to display and discuss. At some point, parents could be invited to come to special events.

Integration of Hispanic students in desegregated schools means that their identity is respected and their status enhanced within those settings. Their limited language proficiency in English is likely to stigmatize them, so that special efforts must be made to overcome this by positive means of support and their routine inclusion in school activities. The bilingual classroom should not be the only place they feel comfortable about being Hispanic if the desegregated setting is meant to integrate these students effectively.

In addition to cultural materials, a greater range of language materials are needed. Because students in bilingual programs are at so many different levels of proficiency in both languages, adequate materials are required in the classroom. Nothing is more frustrating to a bilingual teacher than to be unable to teach effectively because of a lack of materials. The teacher cannot be expected to create sufficient materials in two languages. Lack of materials may indicate to the teacher that no one really cares about these students.

STRATEGIES TO RAISE TEACHER EXPECTATIONS

An important concern in education in the last decade has been the way in which teacher expectations get translated into low academic achievement for pupils. Many studies have been conducted on this subject (for example, see Brophy and Good, 1974). Some have examined how language differences based on race and class can trigger lower teacher expectations (Guskin, 1970). Very few studies have looked at teacher expectations and behaviors as a result of having limited-English-speaking Hispanic students in a classroom. In one study on this topic, Laosa (1978) found that the language proficiency of the students became an increasingly important variable as the students progressed from kindergarten to the higher grades. Teachers were less likely to provide appropriate academic feedback to these students in the higher grades, perhaps because of expectations that they would not understand. As students progress into the higher grades, teachers have less training and patience to teach them beginning skills. LEP students must face the demands of an increasingly difficult curriculum, often without adequate depth in vocabulary and writing skills. They may be seen by teachers and some of their peers as "dumb," and become alienated from school. If the students can read and write in two languages, and if these skills are valued, their deficiencies in English are less likely to produce negative expectations about their basic intellectual capacities.

Some desegreated schools can provide an advantage to Hispanic students in that teachers are often concerned about demonstrating that achievement of minority students can improve. They may be more willing to deal with basic reading skills and have more extra resources to do this throughout the school year, and not only at the lowest grade levels. If teachers take pride in the progress of second language learners, their expectations may rise and achievement may also improve.

CONCLUSION

This chapter has presented some information on the growing size of the Hispanic population and its predominantly youthful, urban, and bilingual profile. Selected recent studies and meetings addressing the issue of the implementation of desegregation and bilingual programs in districts with Hispanic populations have been reviewed. Recommendations for consideration in the planning of race desegregation have been made, with issues presented from both districtwide and school building level perspectives. The implementation of desegregation and bilingual education can be compatible, if care is taken to consider the needs of Hispanic students throughout the planning and implementation process.

Many research questions remain. More information is needed about both the process and outcomes of desegregation in triethnic cities and schools. The perceptions of parents, students, and staff from different ethnic groups, as well as their behaviors in interaction with one another, should be the focus of future studies. In addition, regional and intragroup diversity should be taken into account. Previous desegregation research can provide guidance, but since Hispanics have usually been left out of these studies, it does not provide an adequate data base. It is also possible to improve on past research by emphasizing what occurs in districts and schools over time.

The 1980s may be a decade of dwindling resources and increasing resistance to issues of education equity. Both race desegregation and bilingual education have served minority populations as symbols of hope for better education of their children and a fair share of America's resources. Both movements are battle-weary and scarred by years of court cases, problems of implementation, and white resistance. There are those who feel the fight has been lost and quality segregated education may be all that minority pupils can hope for. As the white population leaves the cities for the suburbs, and now for smaller towns, the problems get more difficult. However, black and Hispanic students are going to school in increasing numbers, and the nation needs to educate them so that they can become productive citizens.

Hispanics and blacks know that a single approach will not solve all the problems they face. They desire quality education as well as integrated education. It is clear that for many years to come segregated education will continue. If there is an opportunity to implement both race desegregation and bilingual education in a school district, positive efforts should be made to reconcile any differences of opinion that exist.

These reforms do not solve all problems, but they do provide something to strive for and they express a hope that schooling will be improved for these students.

NOTES

1. This figure is based on the 1978 Current Population Survey. The 1980 census reveals that Hispanics have increased in number by 61 percent over the 1970 census totals, and now constitute 14.6 million persons, or 6.4 percent of the total U.S. population (U.S. Department of Commerce News, 1981).

2. 1980 census totals will in all likelihood reveal significant population increases for Hispanics in all these states.

3. For example, Hispanic enrollment in the Los Angeles public schools in 1980 was 43 percent; in Chicago, it is approaching 20 percent.

CASES

BRADLEY v. MILLIKEN (1975) 402 F. Supp. 1096 (E.D. Michigan)

BROWN v. BOARD OF EDUCATION (1954) 347 U.S. 483

DELGADO v. BASTROP INDEPENDENT SCHOOL DISTRICT (1948) Civil Action No. 388 (W.D. Texas, June 15)

GONZALEZ v. SHEELY (1951) 96 F. Supp. 1004 (D. Arizona)

HERNANDEZ v. DRISCOLL CONSOLIDATED INDEPENDENT SCHOOL DISTRICT (1975) 2 Race Rel. L. Rep. 329 (S.D. Texas, January 11)

KEYES v. SCHOOL DISTRICT NO. 1, DENVER, COLORADO (1973) 413 U.S. 189

KEYES v. SCHOOL DISTRICT NO. 1, DENVER, COLORADO (1975) 521 F. 2d 482 (10th Cir.)

LAU v. NICHOLS (1974) 414 U.S. 563

MENDEZ v. WESTMINISTER (1946) 65 F. Supp. 544 (S.D. California), aff'd 161 F. 2d 744 (9th Cir., 1947)

ROMERO v. WEAKLEY (1955) 131 F. Supp. 818 (S.D. California)

ROSS v. ECKELS (1972) 486 F. 2d 649 (5th Cir.)

TASBY v. ESTES (1976) 412 F. Supp. 1192 (N.D. Texas)

REFERENCES

ARIAS, B. (1978) "A report to the Honorable Judge Paul Egly: the desegregation plan's impact on services to limited and non-English speaking students." Presented to the Superior Court, State of California, County of Los Angeles, Case No. 822-854, November 6.

BAEZ, T. A., R. R. FERNANDEZ, and J. T. GUSKIN (1980) Desegregation and Hispanic Students: A Community Perspective. Rosslyn, VA: National Clearinghouse for Bilingual Education.

BLANEY, N. T., C. STEPHAN, D. ROSENFIELD, E. AARONSON, and J.
  SIKES (1977) "Interdependence in the classroom: a field study." Journal of Educa-
  tional Psychology 69, 2: 121-128.
BROPHY, J. E. and T. GOOD (1974) Teacher-Student Relationships: Causes and
  Consequences. New York: Holt, Rinehart & Winston.
CARDENAS, J. A. (1975) "Bilingual education, segregation, and a third alternative."
  Inequality in Education 19: 19-22.
CARTER, T. P. and R. D. SEGURA (1979) Workable Models of Bilingual Education in
  Desegregation Settings: An Exploratory Study of Arizona and California. Sac-
  ramento: California State University.
CASTELLANOS, D. (1978) "Bilingual education versus school desegregation: recon-
  ciling the conflict." (unpublished)
Center for National Policy Review, Catholic University (1977) Trends in Hispanic
  Segregation, 1970-1974 (Vol. 2). Washington, DC: National Institute of Education.
CRAIN, R. L. (1978) "Report to the Honorable Judge Paul Egly." Presented to the
  Superior Court, State of California, County of Los Angeles, Case No. 822-854,
  November 14.
FERNANDEZ, R. R. and J. T. GUSKIN (1978) "Bilingual education and desegrega-
  tion: a new dimension in legal and educational decision-making," in H. Lafontaine
  et al. (eds.) Bilingual Education. Wayne, NJ: Avery.
FOREHAND, G., M. RAGOSTA, and D. A. ROCK (1976) Conditions and Processes
  of Effective School Desegregation. Princeton, NJ: Educational Testing Service.
GARCIA, G. F. (1976) "The Latino and desegregation." Integrated Education 14, 5:
  21-22.
GERARD, H. B., T. D. JACKSON, and E. S. CONOLLEY (1975) "Social contact in
  the desegregated classroom," in H. B. Gerard and N. Miller (eds.) School Desegre-
  gation. New York: Plenum.
GONZALEZ, A. (1979) "Classroom cooperation and ethnic balance." Presented at the
  annual meeting of the American Psychological Association, New York, September.
GONZALEZ, J. M. (1979a) Bilingual Education in the Integrated School. Rosslyn,
  VA: National Clearinghouse for Bilingual Education.
———— (1979b) "State of bilingual education." Presented at the Title VII Management
  Institute, Washington, D.C., November.
GREEN, J. A. and H. B. GERARD (1974) "School desegregation and ethnic at-
  titudes," in H. Fromkin and I. Sherwood (eds.) Integrating the Organization. New
  York: Macmillan.
GROSS, N., J. GIACQUINTA, and M. BURNSTEIN (1971) Implementing Organi-
  zational Innovations. New York: Basic Books.
GUSKIN, J. T. (1970) "The social perception of language variation: black and white
  teachers' attitudes toward speakers from different racial and social class
  backgrounds." Ph.D. dissertation, University of Michigan.
————, S. ARVIZU, E. HERNANDEZ-CHAVEZ, and C. VALADEZ (forthcoming)
  Bilingual Education Community Study. Washington, DC: National Institute of
  Education.
HARO, C. M. (1977) Mexican/Chicano Concerns and School Desegregation in Los
  Angeles. Los Angeles: University of California, Chicano Studies Center.
JACOBSON, C. (1977) "Separatism, integrationism, and avoidance among black,
  white and Latin adolescents." Social Forces 55, 4: 1011-1027.

KAGAN, S. (1977) "Social motives and behaviors of Mexican-American and Anglo-American children," in J. L. Martinez, Jr. (ed.) Chicano Psychology. New York: Academic.

KNIGHT, G. P. and S. KAGAN (1977) "Development of prosocial and competitive behaviors in Anglo-American and Mexican-American children." Child Development 48: 1385-1394.

LAOSA, L. M. (1978) "Inequality in the classroom: observational research on teacher-student interaction." Aztalan International Journal of Chicano Studies Research 8, 2 & 3.

MARTIN, T. (1979) The Interface Between Desegregation and Bilingual Education as It Affects Hispanic Migrant Children. Raleigh, NC: Association of Farmworker Opportunity Programs.

MOLL, L. C., E. ESTRADA, E. DIAZ, and L. M. LOPES (1980) "The construction of learning environments in two languages." Presented at the annual meeting of the American Anthropological Association, December.

National Center for Educational Statistics (1980) The Condition of Education for Hispanic Americans. Washington, DC: Government Printing Office.

——— (1978) The Children's English and Services Study. Washington, DC: Government Printing Office.

——— (1976) Place of Birth and Language Characteristics of Persons of Hispanic Origin in the United States. Washington, DC: Government Printing Office.

——— (1975) Survey of Income and Education. Washington: DC: Government Printing Office.

National Institute of Education (1977) Conference Report: Desegregation and Education Concerns of the Hispanic Community. Washington, DC: Government Printing Office.

NOBOA, A. (1979) Trends in Segregation of Hispanic Students in Major School Districts Having Large Hispanic Enrollment (Vol. III-A). New York: Aspira of America.

——— and R. R. FERNANDEZ (1981) An Analysis of the Regional DHEW Office of Civil Rights Feasibility Study and Its Impact of Special Language Programs for Hispanic Students in the Chicago School District. Austin: University of Texas, Chicano Research Center.

ORFIELD, G. (1978a) Must We Bus? Segregated Schools and National Policy. Washington, DC: Brookings.

——— (1978b) "Report to the Honorable Judge Paul Egly." Presented to the Superior Court, State of California, County of Los Angeles, Case No. 822-854, November 14.

ROOS, P. D. (1978) "Bilingual education: the Hispanic response to unequal educational opportunity." Law and Contemporary Problems 42, 4: 111-140.

ST. JOHN, N. H. (1975) School Desegregation: Outcomes for Children. New York: John Wiley.

SALINAS, G. (1971) "Mexican Americans and the desegregation of schools in the southwest." El Grito 4, 4: 36-39.

SCHOFIELD, J. W. (n.d.) "A note on desegregation which includes Hispanics." (unpublished)

TEITELBAUM, H. and R. J. HILLER (1977) "Bilingual education: the legal mandate." Harvard Educational Review 47: 138-170.

U.S. Department of Commerce (1979) Persons of Spanish Origin in the United States: March 1978. U.S. Bureau of the Census, Current Population Reports, Series P-20, No. 339. Washington, DC: Government Printing Office.

U.S. Department of Commerce News (1981) February 23, page 1.

U.S. Office for Civil Rights (1978) State and National Summaries of Data Collected by the 1976 Elementary and Secondary Schools Civil Rights Survey. Washington, DC: Government Printing Office.

URIBE, O. (1978) Bilingual Education in Desegregation Settings: A Research Agenda. Washington, DC: National Institute of Education.

VALDIVIESO, R. and R. SWIERCZEK (1978) National, Regional, and District Population and Segregation Trends Among Hispanic Students: 1970-1974. New York: Aspira of America.

6

GOING TO COLLEGE AND
GETTING A GOOD JOB:
THE IMPACT OF DESEGREGATION

JAMES M. McPARTLAND

JOMILLS HENRY BRADDOCK II

The ways different groups understand the potential benefits of school desegregation may be of great importance to future progress in the area. This chapter calls for new ways of thinking about why desegregated schooling can have worthwhile consequences. We argue that instead of concentrating only on how school desegregation may *improve people* by increasing student test scores or reducing prejudice and stereotypes, emphasis should be placed on how desegregated schooling can *open opportunities* for career success by reducing specific barriers that frequently exclude minorities from fair competition. We shall suggest that such a change in emphasis can significantly affect how various audiences evaluate school desegregation, including parents who are making school choices for their children and public officials who are developing policies to cope with major social problems.

AUTHORS' NOTE: This work was funded in part by National Institute of Education Grant NIE-G-80-0113. The opinions expressed in this chapter do not necessarily reflect the position or policy of the Institute, and no official endorsement should be inferred.

THE NEED FOR A BROADER RATIONALE

The belief that segregated schools exclude minority students from learning environments needed for optimal individual development provides the foundation for most legal and political rationales for school desegregation. It begins with the argument in the Supreme Court's 1954 *Brown* decision that segregation negatively affects the "hearts and minds [of minority children] in a way unlikely ever to be undone." And, although many subsequent desegregation cases have concentrated on the intent of school or housing policies in local areas, an interest by the courts in the effects on student learning has usually also affected the remedies prescribed. Similarly, when political spokesmen disagree about future directions for school desegregation policies, their arguments usually include differences of opinion about the impact of school desegregation on student test scores and attitudes.

A broader rationale for thinking about school desegregation policies is suggested by recent research studies of the sources of unequal adult attainments. This rational may generate a deeper understanding by relevant audiences of the long-term impacts of desegregation.

There is a growing awareness in the research community that race, sex, and age differences in career success are not fully explained by differences in human capabilities. Although the studies are still in their early stages, the research indicates that inequalities in educational and occupational attainments are also sustained by specific structural barriers in labor markets, organizations, and firms (Baron and Bielby, 1980; Stolzenberg, 1978; Jencks, 1980). These structural barriers involve not only overt discrimination, in which selection officials withhold positions from qualified minorities, but also include a variety of formal and informal practices that unintentionally but effectively prevent minority access to promising opportunities (McPartland and Crain, 1980). Thus, public policies that eliminate differences in the distribution of skills and training among different population groups would still leave significant inequities in adult success, due to the continuing influences of structural exclusionary barriers that work against minority opportunities. Desegregation policy deliberations should also take advantage of these research developments, by considering the possible links among school desegregation, various exclusionary processes, and long-term adult outcomes.

In the realm of public opinion and political support, various important audiences have had trouble with the limited rationale for school desegregation based on individual student improvement. A broader justification concerning ways in which desegregation may break down the exclusionary barriers to equal opportunities should contribute to more helpful discussions among these groups.

Many minority spokesmen have found unattractive or unconvincing the idea that the purpose of desegregated schooling is to improve minority student achievement (Hamilton, 1973). They reject the implications of this idea that minority students need to sit in classes with whites to learn, and that no all-minority school can provide an optimum learning environment. As a consequence, minority opinion leaders are more comfortable arguing for school desegregation on the basis of constitutional rights (students should not be prevented from attending any particular public school because of their race) or from the perspective of power politics (minority students can get funding for first-rate educational facilities only if there are whites in their schools who can make effective demands on government officials). Any new evidence that desegregation is tied to the structure of career opportunities, even if racially isolated schools can do just as good a job in teaching academic skills, would generate a useful basis for further discussion of the issue among minority parents and opinion leaders.

Similarly, problems arise with majority public opinion when school desegregation is defended primarily on the basis of raising minority student achievement. Under these terms, school desegregation policies can be judged as giving special compensatory advantages to minorities at the expense and inconvenience of other citizens (Glazer, 1975). Further debate with this focus is unlikely to produce a broader consensus on the importance of school desegregation. On the other hand, there is deep feeling in this country for the goals of equal opportunity and fair competition. Thus, a better understanding of conditions that inhibit equal access to career opportunities is especially useful for constructive public policy debates. In particular, public discussions about school desegregation policies could be significantly enriched with new information showing how desegregation may open adult opportunity structures, which are otherwise only available to whites, to minorities.

State or federal agencies and policy makers concerned with employment inequities and discrimination do not usually propose solutions to reduce the unintentional exclusionary processes embedded in labor market and organizational structures. These agencies ordinarily are more concerned with reducing overt or intended discrimination in the labor market by establishing and enforcing fair employment practices. Racial segregation of schools is seldom considered part of the problem by public officials concerned with equalizing adult career opportunities. A broader understanding of the role of desegregation in providing minority access to adult opportunities could gain the attention of public agencies and officials concerned with employment issues, who rarely consider segregation as directly relevant to their concerns.

DESEGREGATION AND THE STRUCTURE OF OPPORTUNITIES

Although researchers have conducted only a few direct studies of the possible links between school segregation and the structure of opportunities, it is useful to consider some specific examples of conditions in labor markets and firms that may place minorities at an unfair disadvantage. These examples indicate some of the major current directions in research on structural determinants of adult success, and argue that public policies are insufficient when restricted to the improvement of minority employment qualifications because exclusionary barriers remain that restrict equal access to opportunities. Where it exists, direct and indirect evidence will be cited to suggest that school desegregation plays a role in differential opportunity structures.

THE STRUCTURE OF THE LABOR MARKETS

The first insight to be drawn from recent research is that the chances of occupational success differ among several distinct labor markets or types of work. No longer are researchers thinking that there is a single general labor market in this country or a single career process by which an individual's educational credentials and human talents become translated into occupational prestige, income, or employment stability. Instead, different segments of the labor market or different occupational types are now being identified in which the chances of career success or the importance of education are generally not the same.

Evidence is accumulating that black workers are overrepresented in a restricted range of types of occupations, and that these so-called traditional fields of work offer less income payoff for each additional year of educational attainment than other occupational fields where blacks are underrepresented (see, for example, Gottfredson, 1977; Marshall, 1974; Piore, 1977; Kallenberg and Sorensen, 1979; Wilson, 1978; Wright, 1978). The separation of black and white workers into different types of occupations cannot be adequately explained by racial differences in educational attainments and the educational requirements of different fields of work: One study estimates that educational factors account for less than half of the existing differences in racial distributions across fields of work (Braddock et al. 1981). The studies indicate that income gaps will remain between many black and white workers, even if differences in educational attainments are lessened, as long as minority workers continue to be disproportionately relegated to a restricted set of labor markets and fields of work. A Congressional Budget Office (1977) study of income differences found major black-white differences across occupational categories net of region, sex, and educational levels, and concluded: "Before the large part of the overall (racial) income disparities is removed, the occupational distributions, and particularly the distributions within subcategories of the major occupational groups, must be equalized" (see also Kluegel, 1978).

The analysis of segmented labor markets that has received most attention is the notion of a dual labor market used to distinguish the sector of lower-level unstable jobs from the sector of upper-level career ladder jobs available in the economy. According to this view, blacks and other minority workers are more often channeled into the lower-level sector of jobs, which neither offers high pay and sustained employment nor leads to dependable career lines (see, for example, Beck et al., 1980; Spilerman, 1977; La Gory and Magnani, 1979).

Some other studies of multiple labor markets have used typologies of occupations based on job requirements, characteristics of job occupants, and the regularities of movement of workers among jobs (Gottfredson, 1977; Gottfredson and Joffe, 1980). These studies provide a clearer picture of the types of occupations in which minority workers are over- or underrepresented, and the income consequences of such concentrations. Black workers are found much more frequently than similarly educated whites in "social" occupations, such as education and social service jobs. For example, among the most highly educated workers in 1970, 47 percent of black men were in "social" occupations, compared with 19 percent of white men of similar age and education. And black workers are greatly underrepresented in "enterprising" occupations, such as business management or sales, and in "investigative" occupations, such as scientific work: For highly educated workers in 1970, 12 percent of black men, compared with 39 percent of white men, were in enterprising occupations; 12 percent of black men, conpared with 21 percent of white men, were in investigative occupations. Further study has also revealed that the income returns for increased education are much less for the occupational types in which blacks are overrepresented than for those in which blacks are underrepresented: An additional year of education is associated with an additional income of $200 to $300 per year in social occupations, $400 to $600 in investigative occupations, and about $1000 in enterprising occupations (Gottfredson, 1978a). Thus, the separation of blacks and whites into different segments of the occupational structure is a factor with important income implications, as blacks are channeled more toward fields that require extensive education for a high income but which pay off less for increases in educational attainments.

Is there reason to believe that school segregation contributes to continued racial separation in types of work, and that desegregation would produce a more rapid movement of minorities into fields that have frequently been closed to them in the past?

There is good evidence that the racial divergences in occupational expectations develop during the secondary school ages. At the college level, student choices of major fields show the same patterns of black over- and underrepresentation described above. A recent study of elementary and secondary student aspirations for different occupational types indicates that racial differences usually first occur during the junior high and senior high school ages. Data from the 1976 National Assessment of Career and Occupational Development show that the occupational expectations and values of black and white students are similar at elementary school age, but diverge toward the end of high school to match traditional race and sex stereotypes and continue to diverge after initial employment (Gottfredson, 1978b). Comparisons of the major fields of 1974 college students also demonstrate the continuing racial differences in occupational aspirations (Thomas, 1978). Among four-year undergraduates, blacks major in education, social sciences, and social work at higher rates than whites; they major in natural or technical sciences at lower rates than whites. The racial differences in major fields at the graduate levels of higher education follow the same pattern, and the differences are even larger (Institute for the Study of Educational Policy, 1976; Thomas, 1981).

The only analyses currently available on the relationship between occupational outcomes and school desegregation have been based on data collected in a 1966 retrospective survey of black adults, most of whom had completed their elementary and secondary schooling before 1960. The study analyzed approximately 300 cases from the original sample of 1624 black adults who had attended northern high schools and who reported their current jobs in 1966 (Crain, 1970). It was found that black men from desegregated schools were more likely to hold nontraditional jobs in sales, crafts, and the professions (33 percent) than those who attended segregated schools (21 percent).

Further work is needed to better understand why opportunities for minorities to move into certain labor market segments and occupational career lines are restricted, and to determine with more current data whether school desegregation helps to interrupt the processes that direct many minorities into the traditional and less promising directions. National longitudinal data sets have recently become available for these purposes, so we can expect improved research knowledge on these points. At this time, it is clear that the processes channeling minorities into a restricted range of careers are a very important source of income inequalities, and that these processes exist apart from differences in educational credentials and other relevant individual employment capabilities. Also, based on the limited research available, it seems reasonable to expect that school desegregation may be able to interrupt these processes for minority students and produce a wider range of career choices and opportunities.

THE STRUCTURE OF FIRMS

A second consideration derived from recent studies is that a firm's personnel selection practices and reward systems can affect the opportunities for different workers to find jobs and establish stable careers (Baron and Bielby, 1980; Thurow, 1975). These practices may limit the access of potential minority applicants to formal and informal networks of information, contact, and sponsorship through which many jobs and promotions are obtained (Becker, 1979). In other words, structures may be in place that unfairly limit the chances of minorities to know about and apply for job opportunities for which they are qualified. The claim can be made that segregation of schools limits the equal access to useful networks of information and sponsorship, and thus contributes to an exclusionary barrier to equal opportunities.

Research is currently establishing the importance of networks of opportunity for adult career success, especially informal social ties that can provide job information and employment sponsorship (Lin et al., 1981). There is less firm evidence that blacks and other minorities are frequently deprived access to the more effective networks, but some indirect research results imply that they are (Becker, 1979).

Similarly, there is a growing awareness that firms vary in the internal practices that influence how individuals enter specific jobs and receive promotions, but at present there is limited direct evidence on the specific variations and how they differentially affect whites and minorities (Baron and Bielby, 1980). Nevertheless, some research does support speculation that minorities are at a distinct disadvantage regarding networks of opportunity and internal practices of firms, and that desegregation may help to penetrate some of these barriers.

There is very little evidence on the effects of segregation in limiting access to important informal networks of opportunity. Some indirect evidence, however, suggests that this is a promising area for future research.[1] Most of this evidence comes from a study of 434 personnel managers of the largest employers in 15 major cities conducted in 1967 by Rossi et al. (1974) for the National Advisory Commission on Civil Disorders. In this study, each personnel manager reported the number of blacks among the last 20 individuals who applied for work and among those who were hired at 3 broad skill levels (professional and white-collar, skilled workers, and unskilled workers). This information was related to other data about each firm and about each city's labor supply, including the firm's personnel recruitment practices, the racial composition and size of the work force in the firm and the city, city differences in industrial composition, and the degree of concurrent school segregation and racial educational differences in the city.

The authors reasoned that the past employment practices of a firm (as measured by the percentage of blacks in the current work force) could be used as a variable to indirectly assess the importance of social networks of opportunity in the job recruitment process and the willingness of that firm to admit blacks in the hiring process. According to the authors, if the current racial composition of a firm is the best predictor of the rate of recent black application, we would have indirect evidence that the social networks through current black employees provide an important recruitment channel to reach potential new black applicants. If a firm's current racial composition is the best predictor of the rate at which black applicants have been recently hired, it could be inferred that a firm's evaluation of blacks as potential employees is more positive after it has had some experience with blacks in its work force. If current racial composition is the best predictor of both the rate at which blacks had recently applied and the rate at which black applicants were recently hired, it could be argued that both disadvantages of informal networks for blacks and racial preferences of firms for their employees can account for employment outcomes that discriminate against blacks. This study finds that the proportion of blacks in a firm's current work force is an important predictor both of the likelihood that blacks had recently applied for work and of the fact that black applicants were recently hired, even after all other measured characteristics of the firm and the city (including racial composition of the city) were taken into account. The result was particularly strong for professional and white-collar applicants and hiring; in those occupations, the current percentage of blacks in the work force accounted for more variance than any other measured characteristic of the firm or city. Yet, without time series data on rates of black employment, applications, and hiring in different firms, it is difficult to view the reported correlations as good evidence that social network mechanisms are actually operating to affect the employment access of minorities.

An analogous result has been obtained by Becker (1980) in his recent study of racial segregation in places of work. Becker used the Equal Employment Opporutnity Commission survey of the racial composition of firms to calculate an index of the segregation of employment across firms for nine occupational levels. He found that the racial composition of an establishment's work force in one occupation is strongly related to its racial composition in other occupations, particularly for occupations within the blue-collar and white-collar subgroups.

Although the Rossi et al. (1974) data from personnel managers include direct measures on the recruitment channels used by firms and on the concurrent level of school segregation in each city, results using these measures were not consistent and strong in explaining differences of black application and hiring rates at each occupational level. The reported use of specific recruitment channels did not relate to minority rates of application or employment, but the authors point out that the available data do not indicate which channel was actually used by the black applicants or employees. The degree of school segregation in each city also fails to be significantly related to the rates of application or hiring of blacks by firms at any occupational level. However, this is not a test of the long-term effects of school segregation on occupational opportunities for blacks, because the measure was not of the school desegregation experiences of those blacks presently in the work force, but of the segregation of students still in school who resided in the same city as the firms whose employment practices were being studied. The only research that links the school desegregation of blacks to their own later life employment success is the retrospective study conducted in 1966 for the U.S. Commission on Civil Rights (1968; Crain 1970). Although the sample size was small in this study and covered an earlier historical period, the study shows a positive effect of earlier school desegregation on present black income and job status. This study also suggests that black adults who had attended desegregated schools had developed a more useful social network for job referrals and had a better knowledge of specific job opportunities (Crain and Weisman, 1972).

THE PERPETUATION OF SEGREGATION
AND PERCEPTIONS OF OPPORTUNITY

A third implication of recent research is that segregation tends to be perpetuated across stages of the life cycle and across institutions when individuals have not had sustained experiences in desegregated settings earlier in life. Contributing to the social inertia that sustains segregation over time is the fact that segregated experiences may influence minority students' perceptions of opportunity.

Studies based on recent longitudinal data show that school desegregation affects the movement of minority students into desegregated settings after high school graduation. Comparing the adult behavior of blacks who had attended segregated or desegregated schools, it has been shown that those from earlier segregated school settings are more likely at later stages in their lives to be in segregated colleges and segregated work groups, while whose who graduated from desegregated schools are more likely to enter desegregated colleges and work groups. The phrase *perpetuation of segregation* has been used to characterize these processes.

The evidence on the effects of earlier school desegregation on attending desegregated colleges is drawn from studies that included statistical controls on factors such as the students' region, social class background, college admissions credentials (high school grades and test scores), and residential proximity to alternative colleges (Braddock and McPartland, forthcoming; see also Braddock, 1980). Using national longitudinal data from over 3000 black students who graduated from high school, these studies find both direct and indirect effects of earlier school desegregation on attendance at desegregated colleges.

In the South, where a large number of both predominantly black and predominantly white two-year and four-year colleges are available, elementary-secondary school desegregation directly affects black student enrollment at desegregated colleges. The rate of black student attendance at *some* colleges was about the same for those from segregated or desegregated elementary and secondary schools, but the choice of a *desegregated* college was significantly higher for those with earlier experiences in desegregated schools before high school graduation. This effect on the choice of a desegregated college was especially strong for students entering four-year institutions.

In the North, both majority black and majority white two-year colleges are widely distributed, but almost all four-year institutions are majority white. A direct effect of early desegregation was found among northern black students who entered two-year colleges — the enrollment rates at desegregated institutions were significantly higher for those who came from desegregated elementary and secondary schools. Direct effects could not be assessed for four-year college students, because almost all four-year institutions in the North are desegregated — there are no segregated options for black four-year students to choose. However, studies of northern students did reveal a significant positive impact of early school desegregation on whether a black high school graduate enrolled at all in a four-year college: Black students from northern desegregated elementary and secondary schools were significantly more likely than black students from segregated schools to attend some four-year college, after controlling for family background and college qualifications (see also Crain and Mahard, 1978). Thus, desegregated elementary and secondary schools are creating a greater proportion of blacks who enroll in desegregated colleges than are created by segregated elementary and secondary schools. In other words, there is an indirect effect for northern blacks of early school desegregation on attendance at desegregated four-year colleges, due to the direct positive influence on enrollment at some northern four-year college.

Preliminary evidence also indicates that earlier experiences in desegregated schools affect the likelihood that blacks will be members of desegregated work groups as adults. Tabulations from a 1979 follow-up survey of a national sample of black adults who were college freshmen in 1971 show that individuals from desegregated high schools are significantly more likely than segregated high school graduates to be working in a desegregated work group.[2] These studies are preliminary and require careful statistical controls to more firmly establish the direct relationship between school desegregation and employment desegregation, but they provide the first available investigation of this relationship and are based on a large sample of students with similar educational attainments.

Some other studies also suggest that students who attended desegregated schools are more likely to function in desegregated environments in later life, and that this relationship may be due in part to the influence of desegregated schooling on minority students' perception of opportunities. An earlier study based on a 1966 retrospective survey of adults reported that both black and white adults who attended desegregated schools were more frequently found to live in desegregated neighborhoods, to have children who attended desegregated schools, and to have close frineds of the other race than did adults of both races who attended segregated schools (U.S. Commission on Civil Rights, 1968). The same data provide evidence that northern blacks from desegregated schools have a stronger sense that occupational opportunities are available to them (Crain and Weisman, 1972). Other studies have also pointed to the effects of school desegregation on black students' sense of personal efficacy (Coleman et al., 1966) and on desegregated college students' perceptions of fairer opportunities to get a good job (McPartland and Crain, 1980).

In our view, the strongest direct research evidence of the long-term effects of elementary-secondary school desegregation available at this time pertains to the perpetuation of segregation. Minority students who have experienced desegregation earlier in their lives are found to be moving more often and more successfully into desegregated settings as adults. It will be important to extend future research to examine other important measures of adult accomplishment and participation, including income attainment and involvement in political and civic activities and leadership.

SCHOOL DESEGREGATION AND PUBLIC POLICY

Experience in recent decades has taught us that the problems of racial inequalities in adult life are deeply complex, and public policies aimed simply at reducing gaps in human capabilities and eliminating overt discrimination will bè painfully slow at best in dealing with the

problems. Recent research helps us understand some of the complexities, and reveals specifically that structural barriers exist which
restrict minority opportunities even though no individual or organization
may be intentionally imposing these restrictions. Put another way, we
are beginning to learn that "discrimination" is a poor word to characterize the continuing exclusionary barriers, because unequal opportunities frequently are embedded in structural processes and inaccurate
perceptions that go beyond bad intentions or selfish judgments (Alverez
et al. 1979; Crain and Weisman, 1972; Feagin and Feagin, 1978). The task
for public policy is to incorporate this perspective into effective programs that deal with the true complexities of unequal opportunities and
exclusionary processes.

Segregation of schools may be related to the structure of opportunities; desegregation may be a viable public policy alternative if
viewed in the long run and in the context of inequities of adult life. We
already have some evidence that current progress in planned school
desegregation programs is an investment for the future, in the sense that
graduates of desegregated schools are more likely as adults to freely
choose desegregated colleges, neighborhoods, places of work, and
schools for their children, reducing the need for future public policies in
these areas. More generally, there is some reason to believe that school
desegregation may be linked to equal access for minorities to the structural opportunities for adult success. Desegregation may help penetrate
the continuing exclusionary barriers that channel blacks in less promising directions, limit their access to useful networks of information and
sponsorship, or create special burdens that foreclose consideration of
potential opportunities. The task for research is to more carefully define
and study specific structural barriers to equal opportunities, and to
investigate the possible linkages of desegregation to these structural
factors. As this work proceeds, it would be useful to broaden discussions of problems of adult inequities beyond the concentration simply on problems of overt discrimination and differences in human
capabilities, which can only account for a limited part of the problem, to
include an awareness of structural barriers that limit opportunities.
Likewise, public policies such as school desegregation should be considered for their potential effects not only on improving student learning
but also on opening opportunities.

NOTES

1. The following discussion is largely drawn from McPartland and Crain (1980:
114-115).

2. Personal communication from Kenneth C. Green, Higher Education Research
Institute, Los Angeles, California.

REFERENCES

ALVAREZ, R., K. G. LUTTERMAN, and Associates (1979) Discrimination in Organizations. San Francisco: Jossey-Bass.

BARON, J. N. and W. T. BIELBY (1980) "Bringing the firms back in: stratification, segmentation, and the organization of work." American Sociological Review 45: 737-765.

BECK, E. M., P. M. HORAN, and C. M. TOLBERT (1980) "Industrial segmentation and labor market discrimination." Social Problems 28: 113-130.

BECKER, H. J. (1980) "Racial segregation among places of employment." Social Forces 58: 761-776.

——— (1979) "Personal networks of opportunity in obtaining jobs: racial differences and effects of segregation." Presented at the annual meetings of the American Educational Research Association, San Francisco, April.

BRADDOCK, J. H. (1980) "The perpetuation of segregation across levels of education: a behavioral assessment of the contact hypothesis." Sociology of Education 53: 178-186.

——— and J. M. McPARTLAND (forthcoming) "Assessing school desegregation effects: new directions in research," in R. Corwin (ed.) Research in Sociology of Education and Socialization (Vol. 3). Greenwich, CT: Jai.

BRADDOCK, J. H., M. P. DAWKINS, and J. M. McPARTLAND (1981) Black Participation in the American Occupational Structure: Alternative Strategies for Measuring Over- and Under-Representation. Baltimore: Johns Hopkins University, Center for Social Organization of Schools.

COLEMAN, J. S., E. Q. CAMPBELL, C. J. HOBSON, J. M. McPARTLAND, A. M. MOOD, F. D. WEINFELD, and R. L. YORK (1966) Equality of Educational Opportunity. Washington, DC: Government Printing Office.

Congressional Budget Office (1977) Income Disparities Between Black and White Americans. Washington, DC: Government Printing Office.

CRAIN, R. L. (1970) "School integration and occupational achievement of Negroes." American Journal of Sociology 75: 593-606.

——— and J. M. McPARTLAND (1980) "Minority employment opportunities: preliminary analysis of effects of school and college desegregation." Presented at the annual meetings of the American Educational Research Asociation, Boston, April.

CRAIN, R. L. and R. E. MAHARD (1978) "School racial composition and black college attendance and achievement test performance." Sociology of Education 51: 81-101.

CRAIN, R. L. and C. S. WEISMAN (1972) Discrimination, Personality and Achievement. New York: Seminar.

FEAGIN, J. R. and C. B. FEAGIN (1978) Discrimination American Style. Englewood Cliffs, NJ: Prentice-Hall.

GLAZER, N. (1975) Affirmative Discrimination. New York: Basic Books.

GOTTFREDSON, G. D. and R. D. JOFFE (1980) An Evaluation of Mobility-Based Occupational Classifications for Placement of Job Applicants. Baltimore: Johns Hopkins University, Center for Social Organization of Schools.

GOTTFREDSON, L. S. (1978a) "An analytical description of employment according to race, sex, prestige, and Holland type of work." Journal of Vocational Behavior 13: 210-221.

——— (1978b) Race and Sex Differences in Occupational Aspirations: Their Development and Consequences for Occupational Segregation. Baltimore: Johns Hopkins University, Center for Social Organization of Schools.

————— (1977) A Multiple-Labor Market Model of Occupational Achievement. Balti-
    more: Johns Hopkins University, Center for Social Organization of Schools.
HAMILTON, C. V. (1973) "The nationalist vs. the integrationist," pp. 297-310 in N.
    Mills (ed.) The Great School Bus Controversy. New York: Teachers College Press.
Institute for the Study of Educational Policy (1976) Equal Educational Opportunity for
    Blacks in U.S. Higher Education: An Assessment. Washington, DC: Howard
    University Press.
JENCKS, C. (1980) "Structural versus individual explanations of inequality: where do
    we go from here?" Contemporary Sociology 9: 762-767.
KALLENBERG, A. L. and A. B. SORENSON (1979) "Sociology of labor markets."
    Annual Review of Sociology 5: 35-379.
KLUEGEL, J. R. (1978) "The causes and cost of racial exclusion from job authority."
    American Sociological Review 43: 285-301.
LAGORY, M. and R. J. MAGNANI (1979) "Structural correlates of black-white
    occupational differentiation: will U.S. regional differences in status remain?" Social
    Problems 27: 157-169.
LIN, N., J. C. VAUGHN, and W. M. ENSEL (1981) "Social resources and occupa-
    tional status attainment." Social Forces 59: 1163-1181.
McPARTLAND, J. M. (1978) "Desegregation and equity in higher education and
    employment: is progress related to the desegregation of elementary and secondary
    schools?" Law and Contemporary Problems 43, 3: 108-132.
————— and R. L. CRAIN (1980) "Racial discrimination, segregation, and processes of
    social mobility," in V. T. Corvello (ed.) Poverty and Public Policy: An Evaluation of
    Social Science Research. Boston: G. K. Hall.
MARSHALL, R. (1974) "The economics of racial discrimination: a survey." Journal of
    Economic Literature 12: 849-871.
PIORE, M. J. (1977) "The dual labor market," pp. 93-97 in D. Gordon (ed.) Problems in
    Political Economy. Lexington, MA: D. C. Heath.
ROSSI, P. H., R. A. BERK, and B. K. ERDSON (1974) The Roots of Urban Discon-
    tent: Public Policy, Municipal Institutions, and the Ghetto. New York: John Wiley.
SPILERMAN, S. (1977) "Careers, labor market structure, and socio-economic
    achievement." American Journal of Sociology 83: 551-593.
STOLZENBERG, R. M. (1978) "Bringing the boss back in: employer size, employee
    schooling, and socio-economic achievement." American Sociological Review 43:
    813-828.
THOMAS, G. E. (1981) Black Students in Higher Education: Conditions and Experi-
    ences in the 1970s. Westport, CT: Greenwood.
————— (1978) Equality of Representation of Race and Sex Groups in Higher Education:
    Institutional and Program Enrollment Statuses. Baltimore: Johns Hopkins Univer-
    sity, Center for Social Organization of Schools.
THUROW, L. C. (1975) Generating Inequality. New York: Basic Books.
U.S. Commission on Civil Rights (1968) Racial Isolation in the Public Schools (Vols. I
    and II). Washington, DC: Government Printing Office.
WILSON, W. J. (1978) The Declining Significance of Race. Chicago: University of
    Chicago Press.
WRIGHT, E. O. (1978) "Race, class, and income inequality." American Journal of
    Sociology 83: 1368-1397.

PART III

**THE DEMOGRAPHICS
OF DESEGREGATION**

7

UNDERSTANDING WHITE FLIGHT
AND DOING SOMETHING ABOUT IT

CHRISTINE H. ROSSELL
WILLIS D. HAWLEY

In the last five years, the school desegregation policy debate has been characterized by a reversal of the traditional roles of advocates and opponents. Desegregation advocates are now on the defensive and opponents on the offensive. The issue probably most responsible for this is white flight from school desegregation. The possibility of its occurrence has caused judges to be reticent in finding fault and prescribing remedies, and has dimmed the ardor of former desegregation advocates. But both the inevitability of white flight from desegregation and the impotence of public policy to deal with it have been overstated in the public debate. In this chapter, we summarize what is known about the effects of school desegregation on the racial composition of school districts and identify a range of alternative policies which might reduce racial isolation and retard "white flight."

DESEGREGATION IN CONTEXT

THE SUBURBANIZATION OF WHITE AMERICA

The term *white flight* was originally used to characterize the phenomenon of middle-class, white suburbanization that has occurred since the 1950s. The suburbanization trend is a function not just of "push" factors, but also of "pull" factors. Indeed, the research suggests that the pull factors — the greater space, greenery, lower-cost family housing, low tax rates, federal suburban housing loan policies, and changes in production and transportation in the suburbs — are more important than such push factors as central-city crime and increasing minority populations (Katzman, 1978). The initial, large, middle-class suburbanization that occurred because of these "pull" factors in turn worsened the problems of the central cities, causing still more middle-class families to leave (Bradford and Kelejian, 1973). Thus, middle-class suburbanization resulting from pull factors contributes to middle-class flight because of push factors. This suburbanization trend would have characterized all races were it not for job discrimination and suburban housing discrimination against minorities.

If the problem is not so much one of "flight" as of relative attractiveness, the comparative advantage of the suburbs could presumably be changed by federal incentives. Possible incentives range from housing and school tax benefits to urban renewal programs. We discuss these below in the context of school desegregation policy. At the present, most federal policies provide disincentives to living in the central city (see Orfield, 1979; Taylor, 1979).

WHITE ENROLLMENT TRENDS: AN OVERVIEW

The term *white flight* has most recently — and erroneously — been used to describe the decline in central-city white public school enrollment. Most of this decline is a function of the secular suburbanization trend discussed above, and the declining birthrate. All races have had declining birthrates since 1957, although the white birthrate is the lowest and its decline the greatest. The difference between black and white birthrates, however, has decreased each year (National Center for Health Statistics, 1975). In fact, birth expectations of young black women are almost the same as those of young white women and the birthrates of the two groups should converge in the future (U.S. Bureau of the Census, 1975).

The declining birthrate has implications for school enrollment, both public and private. School populations of all races have declined nationally since 1973. For whites this has meant an annual decline of almost 1 percent since 1968. The annual decline is now almost 3 percent. The black school-age population, on the other hand, continued to increase (except in 1972) and did not begin to decline until 1975. School population racial percentages can fluctuate dramatically from year to year. Most recently, however, they exhibit a trend of less enrollment decline each year.

Table 7.1 shows the percentage enrollment change for whites, blacks, and Hispanics, broken down by public and private enrollment. The public school enrollment decline for whites has been greater than the private school enrollment decline, but not dramatically so. For blacks and Hispanics, we see a large increase in private school enrollment until 1978, when it begins to decline, probably as a result of economic conditions as well as the declining birthrate.

Because of these factors, we can expect for most northern central-city school districts a "normal" (that is, with no desegregation) percentage public school enrollment decline of at least 4 percent to 8 percent annually, and for most northern suburban school districts, an annual public school white enrollment decline of about 2 percent to 4 percent (see Rossell, 1978a; Farley et al., 1979). Some southern countywide school districts, because they benefit from northern migration to the South, have stable or increasing white enrollment, in spite of the national decline in birthrate.

The percentage white enrollment decline, however, does not necessarily tell us anything about the racial balance of a school district, since that is affected by minority enrollment as well. Table 7.2 shows the total population percentages, by race, in central-city and suburban metropolitan areas, and in nonmetropolitan areas for 1960, 1970, and 1975. These data indicate that, although the decline in proportion white is greatest in the central city, it is declining in the suburbs of metropolitan areas as well. Moreover, although the proportion minority is increasing at a faster rate in the central cities, it is also increasing in the suburbs of metropolitan areas.

The "normal" change in the white percentage of school enrollment in northern central-city school districts should be a decline of 2 percentage points annually. For most northern suburban school districts we would expect a reduction of less than 1 percentage point annually. This should also be true for the South. As Table 7.3 indicates, those areas of the United States experiencing white outmigration, such as the Midwest and the Northeast, are also experiencing black outmigration. Areas experiencing white inmigration, such as the South and the West, are also experiencing black inmigration. The result of all this movement is that, in terms of racial balance, ultimately the North may not be as disadvantaged vis-á-vis the South, and the cities vis-á-vis the suburbs, as it appears when one examines only white enrollment change.

Trends in racial balance over time suggest that public schools are also less advantaged vis-á-vis private schools than we would expect from

TABLE 7.1 Percentage School Enrollment (K-12) Change, 1968-1978

	1968	1969	1970	1971	1972	1973	1974	1975	1976	1977	1978
White											
Public		1.8	0.2	0	4.4	-0.8	-0.8	-1.2	-1.0	-2.8	-3.2
Private		-8.5	-1.5	-5.5	0	-5.4	-0.4	1.7	-5.6	3.9	-0.2
All		0.6	0.2	-0.3	-2.6	-1.3	-0.7	-0.9	-1.5	-2.1	-2.9
Black											
Public		1.8	1.3	3.5	-4.7	-1.5	4.3	-0.5	0.2	-0.6	-1.5
Private		5.0	8.1	-10.9	11.1	-2.5	-18.3	14.7	15.0	7.8	-7.5
All		2.0	1.6	3.1	-4.1	-1.5	3.4	0	0.7	-0.3	-1.8
Hispanic[a]											
Public		4.5	4.3	4.1	7.5	-4.9	10.1	4.1	-2.9	-6.3	1.1
Private		17.3	14.7	12.8	12.3	-3.4	47.2	-16.3	-11.3	30.4	-19.0
All		5.2	5.0	4.7	7.9	-4.8	13.1	2.0	-3.6	-3.4	-1.0

SOURCE: U.S. Bureau of the Census (1979a: Table 1).

a. Data on Hispanic enrollment are not available for 1968-1971, so they were estimated from a linear trend analysis of the 1975-1972 period. Since white enrollment dropped sharply in 1972, when Hispanics were counted separately for the first time, we assume they were included in the white enrollment for 1968-1971. Hence, after estimating the Hispanic enrollment for 1968-1971, that estimate was subtracted from the white enrollment for those years.

TABLE 7.2 Racial Percentages in the Metropolitan and Nonmetropolitan Areas, 1969-1975

	Racial Percentage			Change in Racial Percentage		
	1960	1970	1975	1970-1960	1975-1970	1975-1960
Blacks and Other Minorities						
Metropolitan areas	11.5	13.2	14.6	1.7	1.4	3.1
Central city	17.6	22.2	25.2	4.6	3.0	7.6
Suburbs	5.4	5.6	6.6	0.2	1.0	1.2
Nonmetropolitan areas	11.3	10.2	9.5	-1.1	-0.7	-1.8
Whites						
Metropolitan areas	88.5	86.8	85.4	-1.7	-1.4	-3.1
Central city	82.4	77.8	74.8	-4.6	-3.0	-7.6
Suburbs	94.6	94.4	93.4	-0.2	-1.0	-1.2
Nonmetropolitan areas	88.7	89.8	90.5	1.1	0.7	1.8

SOURCE: U.S. Bureau of the Census (1977: Table 1/9).

TABLE 7.3 Net Intercensal Migration, by Region, 1940-1985

	South	Northeast	Midwest	West
Blacks (in thousands)				
1940-1950	-1,599	463	618	339
1950-1960	-1,473	496	514	293
1960-1970	-1,390	612	382	301
1970-1975	14	-64	-52	102
Whites				
1960-1970	1,806	-520	-1,272	2,269
1970-1975	1,791	-1,240	-1,145	594

SOURCE: U.S. Bureau of the Census (1972, 1979b: Tables 8 and 9).

examining white enrollment alone. Table 7.4 indicates that the proportion white in the public school system has actually shown less decline over the 1968-1978 time period than in the private school system. If we examine the 1972-1978 time period (when Hispanics began being counted separately), the decline in proportion white in the public school system has been -1.7 percentage points, compared to -1.3 percentage points in the private school system. In short, the trends that characterize the public school system also characterize the private school system.

TABLE 7.4 School Enrollment (K-12) Racial Percentages, 1968-1978

	1968	1969	1970	1971	1972	1973	1974	1975	1976	1977	1978	1978-1968	1978-1968 [a]	1978-1972 [b]
Public														
White	80.1	80.0	79.7	79.1	80.0	80.3	79.2	78.9	78.8	78.7	78.3	-1.8	-6.8	-1.7
Black	14.9	14.9	15.0	15.4	14.3	14.2	14.7	14.8	15.0	15.3	15.5	0.6	1.3	1.2
Hispanic	5.0	5.4	5.3	5.5	6.0	5.5	6.0	6.3	6.2	6.0	6.2	1.2	1.4	0.2
Private														
White	93.5	92.3	91.4	91.1	90.2	90.0	88.9	89.4	88.8	87.5	88.9	-4.6	-6.8	-1.3
Black	4.3	4.8	5.2	4.9	5.4	5.6	4.5	5.1	6.2	6.3	5.9	1.6	1.7	0.5
Hispanic	2.3	2.9	3.3	4.0	4.4	4.5	6.6	4.8	5.0	6.2	5.1	2.8	2.9	0.6
All														
White	81.1	81.3	81.0	80.3	81.8	81.2	80.2	79.9	79.8	79.6	79.4	-1.7	-7.0	-2.4
Black	13.5	13.8	13.9	14.3	13.5	13.4	13.7	13.8	14.1	14.3	14.5	1.0	1.5	1.0
Hispanic	4.6	4.9	5.1	5.3	4.7	5.4	6.1	6.3	6.1	6.0	6.1	1.5	1.4	1.4

SOURCE: U.S. Bureau of the Census (1979a: Table 1).

a. Data on Hispanic enrollment are not available for 1968-1971, so they were estimated from a linear trend analysis of the 1975-1972 period. Since white enrollment dropped sharply in 1972, when Hispanics were counted separately for the first time, we assume they were included in the white enrollment for 1968-1971. Hence, after estimating the Hispanic enrollment for 1968-1971, that estimate was subtracted from the white enrollment for those years.

b. The estimate of change compares only blacks to whites, thus ignoring Hispanics, for whom data were not available.

Determining the decline in white public school enrollment resulting from school desegregation requires isolating the impact of policy from these long-term demographic trends. The analytical question addressed by the research on the relationship between school desegregation and white flight is this: In any given school district, how much does school desegregation add to the already declining white enrollment?

FROM RESEARCH TO POLICY:
A THEORETICAL BRIDGE

We synthesize a substantial body of empirical research in this chapter, but that research is less than definitive on many issues of importance to the development of public policy. Theory may serve as a bridge between research and practice, facilitating the interpretation of research findings and thus the development of policy recommendations. What is needed is a theory of white flight from desegregation that (1) defines the conditions that result in flight from desegregated schools and (2) provides some basis for reducing or eliminating such flight.

Obviously, many whites flee from desegregation because they are prejudiced, but this explanation by itself explains too little. Racism permeates our entire society, but only a minority of whites actually flee when a school district desegregates. Moreover, surveys indicate that individual racism is only weakly related to one's intention to leave a desegregated school system (McConahay and Hawley, 1977; Giles et al., 1976).

Hirschman (1970) has developed some concepts that provide a way to think about the white flight problem. If we take some small liberties with Hirschman's ideas, we can postulate that people will consider "exit" from the public schools when they perceive that the costs of seeking another option (private schools or suburban public schools) are lower than the cost they experience, or expect to experience, by staying in the public schools. In other words, exit occurs when the benefits of a move from the public schools outweigh the costs. The costs people experience are both economic and psychological, and it is perceived cost, rather than objectively measured costs, that shape behavior.

When schools are desegregated, many parents believe that the ratio of costs to benefits changes. These beliefs appear to be based on one or more of five assumptions:

(1) The quality of education their children are receiving is declining or will decline.

(2) Their children will be subjected to greater physical violence or emotional harassment.

(3) Their children will be exposed to and probably influenced by values concerning academic achievement or social and sexual behavior that are not in the children's interest.

(4) They will lose influence over their children's education.

(5) Their property values will decline, either because the value placed on the schools in their neighborhood will decline or because others will flee from desegregation, creating a "buyers' market" for real estate.

The decision to act on an assessment that desegregation will increase the costs and decrease the benefits of sending one's child to public school does not depend wholly on the net costs people attach to sending their children to desegregated schools in the city in which they now live. It will depend also on:

(1) *Loyalty.* Hirschman's (1970) concept refers, in this case, to the public schools. Loyalty leads some people who believe that desegregation will weaken the quality of education to stay in the city public schools. These people, particularly if they are middle class, are likely to become activists for school reform (in Hirschman's terms, they engage in "voice" and are "quality consumers"). If the "voice" they express is not responded to, these consumers may eventually exit.

Unfortunately, communities in which costs are perceived to be the highest often experience the greatest protest. As a result, school officials may spend all their time responding to opposition to desegregation rather than to educational improvement, thus encouraging the "quality consumers" to leave. Ironically, "loyalty to the public schools" may cause people who could afford private schools in central cities and who like living in the city to move their residences to suburbia in order to enroll their children in "quality" public schools.

(2) *Options.* Whether one can exit depends on the availability of private schools and suburban options. In Florida, for example, where all public schools are countywide and there has been no highly developed parochial school system, we would expect exit to be minimal. In the mid-Atlantic states and in some parts of the Midwest, where parochial schools have underutilized capacity and where suburbia is easily accessible and socioeconomically heterogeneous, we would expect much greater flight.

(3) *Ability to Pay for Options.* Exit from the public schools involves private school or residential relocation costs. One reason that studies often find a weak or negative relationship between favorable attitudes toward desegregation and willingness to stay in desegregating schools (McConahay and Hawley, 1977) is that those most opposed to desegregation often have low incomes or, if they are southerners, belong to a religious faith for which there is no developed parochial school

system. Such individuals are likely to feel trapped by desegregation and to engage in voice. When one is opposed to desegregation and without exit options, voice is likely to be manifested as protest against desegregation itself. Since busing is the tangible instrument through which desegregation imposes costs on opponents, it is likely to be the symbol of opposition to the larger school changes about which these persons are concerned.

This theory would be more instructive in helping to understand the magnitude of white flight from desegregation and the kinds of policies that will minimize flight if we knew more about the factors that account for exit, voice, and loyalty among the different elements of the population. Nevertheless, we believe that the framework just outlined facilitates a research-based identification of a range of policy options that might well reduce white flight. In general, such options should do one or more of four things: increase the costs of exit, decrease the costs of staying, increase the loyalty of consumers, and/or increase the responsiveness of school systems to "voice."

We do not systematically assess the costs and benefits or the political feasibility of the options we suggest here. Such an effort is impossible with the available data. Moreover, we recognize that some of the ideas offered here are, within the present context and in their present form, clearly impractical. But, given the sense of hopelessness many policy makers express in considering what might be done about the white flight problem, it seems desirable to extend the potential policy agenda as far as possible. Some notions that seem unreasonable at this time may, in the hands of others and in other settings, become practical policy alternatives.

CHARACTERISTICS AND CAUSES OF WHITE FLIGHT

THE MAGNITUDE OF WHITE FLIGHT: IMPLEMENTATION YEAR

Virtually all of the research on school desegregation and white flight indicates that school desegregation significantly accelerates white flight in most school districts in the year of implementation *if* it involves mandatory white reassignments (see Rossell, 1978a; Coleman et. al., 1975; Armor, 1980b; Farley et al., 1979). The magnitude of white flight is a function of three factors: the white proportion of enrollment in the district, the proportion of whites reassigned to formerly black schools, and the proportion of blacks reassigned to white schools. The first two factors are the most important. Racial tolerance appears to have progressed to the point where black reassignments into white schools (that is, one-way busing) do not significantly increase white flight from the receiving school except in school districts above 35 percent black. Even in those school districts, the effect of black reassignments is one-third to one-half that of white reassignments to formerly black schools (see Rossell, 1978a; Rossell and Ross, 1979).

Rossell (1978a) and Giles et al. (1976) find that there is a threshold effect in white flight produced by the black proportion of enrollment in the school or school system. At 30 to 35 percent black there is an additional increment in white flight, and again at 40 percent black, but there is little increase between these points. Whites apparently do not make fine distinctions between varying levels of proportion black.

It is estimated that — on the average — for every 20 percent of whites reassigned to formerly black schools in city school districts, the percentage white enrollment decline will increase in that year by an additional 9.6 percentage points annually over the predesegregation year percentage white enrollment decline in districts with over 35 percent black enrollment. In districts below 35 percent black, white enrollment will decline by an additional 4.7 percentage points. The average desegregation plan (about 30 percent of blacks reassigned, 5 percent of whites reassigned, reduction in segregation of 30 percentage points) implemented in districts above 35 percent black results in the percentage white enrollment decline increasing by an additional 8 percentage points above its predesegregation percentage white enrollment decline. Thus, if a 35 percent black school district has a predesegregation percentage white enrollment decline of 4 percent, it can expect a 12 percent white enrollment decline in the year it implements the above plan. In districts below 35 percent black, such a plan would usually result in an additional 5 percentage point increase above its predesegregation percentage white enrollment decline.

In county school districts (usually southern), the loss is about half that of city school districts (usually northern). The magnitude of white enrollment loss, however, is greater in southern districts. All other things being equal, northern countywide districts have less white flight than southern countywide districts, and northern city school districts have less white flight than southern city school districts.

RESIDENTIAL FLIGHT OR PRIVATE SCHOOL FLIGHT?

In determining the impact of school desegregation, it is important to distinguish enrollment losses due to white flight out of the desegregating school district from those due to transfers of whites from public to private schools within the district. We know from school enrollment data, shown in Table 7.5, that the proportion of white students enrolled in public schools has actually increased from 1968 to 1978. From 1972 to 1978, there has been only a small change (although the signs are now reversed). Hence, at least nationwide, there has been no wholesale abandonment of the public school system, as some observers have claimed.

Because there has been no nationwide abandonment of the public school system, however, does not mean there will be no flight to private schools when a particular school district desegregates. Unfortunately, most of the comparative aggregate analyses of the effect of desegregation on white enrollment are unable to separate white flight characterized by the transfer of students to private schools from that characterized by the movement of families outside the district. There are, however, five case studies of four school districts that distinguish the two phenomena through survey sampling techniques or a housing market analysis.

In these districts it appears that there has been little residential relocation in response to school desegregation. Three of the studies are of two countywide plans (Lord, 1975; McConahay and Hawley, 1977; Cunningham et al., 1978), so this finding should not be surprising. We would expect large metropolitan school districts to have less residential outmigration in response to school desegregation, if only because the costs of moving are so high — finding housing outside the district is difficult, and the distance from one's work place is greatly increased. The two studies of central-city school districts — Orfield's (1978) study of Los Angeles and Estabrook's (1980) analysis of Boston — also indicate more white flight to private schools than to the suburbs. Orfield found little suburban white flight in his analysis of the Los Angeles housing market in 1978. Los Angeles, however, is geographically one of the largest central-city school districts in the United States. Estabrook's analysis of Boston — a much smaller school district in geographic size — indicates that, of those white middle-class neighborhood residents who took their children out of the public schools during the two-year implementation of desegregation, 55 percent transferred them to parochial schools, while 45 percent moved to the suburbs. Boston's greater white flight to the suburbs may also be attributed to its low rate of home ownership, since renters are more likely to move to the suburbs than homeowners who have to sell their houses.

The fact that most white flight is to private schools, at least in these districts, is encouraging. Private school flight should be less damaging to

TABLE 7.5 Private and Public Proportions of White School Enrollment (K-12) 1968-1978

Schools	1968- 1978	1972- 1978	1968	1969	1970	1971	1972	1973	1974	1975	1976	1977	1978
Public	1.6	-0.5	86.6	87.8	87.9	88.4	88.7	89.1	89.1	88.8	89.2	88.5	88.2
Private	-1.5	0.5	13.3	12.2	12.1	11.5	11.3	10.9	10.9	11.2	10.8	11.4	11.8

SOURCE: U.S. Bureau of the Census (1979a: Table 1).

a community than suburban flight, in part because the possibility of returning to the public schools is much greater, but also because these individuals will remain part of the community and presumably a part of whatever social change occurs. Moreover, flight to private schools has no negative effect on the tax base of the desegregating community, although it may diminish overall political support for school taxes and bonds.

FACTORS AFFECTING THE EXTENT OF WHITE FLIGHT

We have noted that the busing of whites to formerly black schools accelerates white flight more than does so-called one-way busing, and that white flight is greater in districts with more than 35 percent minority students. Other characteristics of the district and the desegregation process also appear to affect the extent of white flight from desegregation. These include the race of minority students with whom whites are being desegregated, the timing of the plan, the geographic scope of the district, and the age of the children being bused.

There are two case studies which contradict each other with respect to whether there is a difference in the white flight produced by white reassignment to Hispanic schools in contrast to white reassignment to black schools. We would expect less white flight from Hispanic schools, simply because, in almost all areas of social and economic life, Hispanics are less discriminated against than blacks. For example, Hispanics have significantly higher levels of residential integration with whites than do blacks and also tend to have higher income levels than blacks, despite having lower educational levels.

In Denver, the white flight from black schools was almost three times greater than the white flight from Hispanic schools (Rossell, 1978a). In the first year of the Los Angeles plan, however, there seemed to be greater white flight from Hispanic schools than from black schools when busing distance and other factors were controlled (Rossell, 1980). Los Angeles, however, may be an unusual case. The student assignments were announced so late that many white parents did not know if their children would be reassigned to black schools or Hispanic schools. Alternative schooling may have been found in anticipation of their children being reassigned to black schools. In addition, the continual influx of new Mexican immigrants and the media publicity surrounding gang warfare among Mexican-American youths may also distinguish the Los Angeles situation from others.

There is little anticipatory white flight the year before implementation of a desegregation plan only because whites typically are not given enough warning (Rossell, 1978a). The average desegregation order comes down some time during the year before implementation. The court order would have to be decided at least a year and a half before desegregation (which occasionally does happen) for it to produce anticipatory flight in the year before desegregation.

Countywide school districts have half the white enrollment decline of city school districts because the costs of movement to the suburbs are increased the greater the number of surrounding suburbs included in the plan (Rossell, 1978a; Farley et al., 1979; Armor, 1980b). In addition, the costs of staying are decreased because countywide school districts have lower minority enrollments and thus need less white reassignment to desegregate their minority student populations.

There is, in general, greater white flight produced by elementary than by secondary school desegregation reassignments (Rossell, 1978a; Rossell and Ross, 1979; Massachusetts Research Center, 1976). White parents are much more reluctant to allow their younger children to be bused across town to minority schools than their older children, although research indicates that the younger children are best able to adjust to their newly integrated situation. An exception to this finding is seen in Los Angeles, where junior high schools had greater white flight than elementary schools, but this is probably because grades 1-3 (which have the greatest white flight) were excluded from the plan, as were grades 9-12.

THE LONG-TERM IMPACT OF DESEGREGATION ON WHITE ENROLLMENT

There is still substantial disagreement over the long-term effect of school desegregation on white flight. Research that uses cross-sectional multiple regression to analyze postimplementation annual changes in white enrollment finds no long-term negative effect in most districts (Coleman et al., 1975; Rossell, 1978a; Farley et al., 1979). That is to say, short-term implementation losses appear to be compensated for by less than normal postimplementation losses. The problem with these analyses is that they average effects across school districts. A subsample analysis by Rossell indicates that the school districts least likely to make up their implementation year losses by less than normal postimplementation losses are big city school districts with minority white school populations (see also Rossell and Ross, 1979; Armor, 1980b).

There are three possible reasons for less than normal postimplementation losses in many school districts: (1) School and hous-

ing available in a metropolitan region are limited; if the slack is taken up
in one year by greater than normal usage, there will be nothing available
in future years for the "normal" population use, hence that usage will be
reduced; (2) after the controversy subsides, many parents who put their
children in public schools may find that income constraints take precedence over their fear of desegregated schools; and (3) citywide plans
may stabilize some racially changing neighborhoods by reducing and
stabilizing the minority school population (see Schnore and MacRae,
1975).

BLACK FLIGHT FROM DESEGREGATION

There has been almost no research conducted on the determinants of
black flight from desegregation. Rossell and Ross (1979) find black flight
to be associated with factors similar to those associated with white flight,
but only at the high school level. Black reassignments to white high
schools in Boston resulted in approximately 20 percent not showing up,
on the average, every other year since the first year of implementation.
At the elementary school level, there is very little black flight in any year.

A POLICY AGENDA

The remainder of this chapter identifies several policy options that
might be adopted or encouraged by local, state, and federal government.
These policies involve the design of desegregation plans, improving
public information, facilitating full metropolitan desegregation, encouraging the desegregation of housing, providing financial incentives
for voluntary desegregation, enhancing the perceived quality of desegregated schools, and desegregating schools on the basis of work place
and work needs.

POLICY OPTIONS FOR
LOCAL SCHOOL DISTRICTS AND COURTS

Voluntary plans. Voluntary plans do reduce white flight, but for
school districts with more than 30 percent minority enrollment, they
produce almost no desegregation (Rossell, 1979; Larson, 1980). Hence,
if one's goal is actual desegregation, a voluntary plan is not a feasible
option for most big city school districts. Desegregation plans, while they
may include such voluntary options as magnet schools, must be mandatory if they are to substantially reduce racial isolation.

Mandatory plans with a voluntary magnet school component. The problem with mandatory plans, of course, is that they produce extensive flight in the implementation year. Since we can estimate that, on the average, white reassignments produce almost three times the white flight of black reassignments, whites should not be *randomly* assigned to black neighborhoods if one's concern is to maintain white enrollments.

One potentially effective option is a desegregation plan with a two-stage reassignment process. The first stage is voluntary and includes the creation of magnet school programs over a four- or five-month period in the preimplementation year. All magnet schools should be built in minority neighborhoods. Some of them should be "fundamental" schools, in order to counteract the image white parents have of black schools as unsafe and undisciplined. Surveys indicate that the single greatest educational concern of parents is school discipline (Golladay and Noell, 1978: 53). Badly deteriorating black schools and, if possible, the most isolated schools should be closed in favor of maintaining schools near the boundaries of black and white neighborhoods.

The first stage of the reassignment process would then begin with the magnet school reassignment. The evidence from Boston suggests that there are enough white parents who are willing to put their children in schools in black neighborhoods to racially balance them if these schools are publicized as superior schools, and *if* the alternative is mandatory reassignment to another desegregated school chosen by the school administration (Massachusetts Research Center, 1976; Rossell and Ross, 1979). It is important that this be done on an individual basis, rather than on a school basis, as in Los Angeles. There, schools were asked to volunteer for pairs and clusters, with the alternative being later mandatory reassignment. The problem with this policy is that when whole schools are asked to volunteer, rather than individuals, any given school may have enough parents who oppose this action and, as a result, withdraw their children, to effectively sabotage any chance of racial balance.

After white parents are asked to volunteer for magnet schools in minority neighborhoods, the additional seats in minority schools can be filled by mandatory reassignment of whites. Minorities can also be reassigned by the same process (that is, they can either volunteer for a magnet school or accept the school district's assignment).

Curriculum. To reduce the perceived costs of desegregation, magnet schools should be made part of any mandatory desegregation plan. It also seems reasonable to offer college preparatory and advanced academic courses in all secondary schools in order to keep the middle class in the public school system. Offering college preparatory courses in some schools (for example, magnets), but not others, can result in class and racial resegregation.

Implementation timing. Desegregation plans should not be phased in over a period of two or more years if at all feasible, since doing so tends to contribute to greater white flight than would be expected from the extent of reassignment (see Rossell, 1978a). That is to say, with a two-year plan, as in Boston, there will be greater white flight than would be expected from the first year's plan in anticipation of future reassignments. In short, the more warning people are given about desegregation, the more white flight results (see also Armor, 1980b).

Busing distance. Busing distances should be minimized in districts with the potential for the greatest white flight. Although some of the research (Giles et al., 1976; Pride and Woodard, 1978) finds no relationship between busing distances and white flight, other research analyzing big city school districts (Armor, 1980a; Massachusetts Research Center, 1976; Rossell, 1980) finds longer bus rides to be associated with lower white enrollment (except in magnet schools). Rossell (1980) also finds that the greater the busing distance and the higher the average socioeconomic status of the students in the white school, the greater the white flight. One important difference between the studies finding no white flight and those finding an effect is that the former are of county school districts and the latter are of city school districts. Furthermore, the Giles et al. (1976) study of Florida county school districts is of postimplementation years, while the Massachusetts Research Center (1976) study includes an implementation year. Rossell (1980) finds no relationship between busing distance and white flight in Los Angeles in the postimplementation year. Parents who are willing to have their children bused a certain distance, or who do not have the means to withdraw their children in the implementation year, seem not to withdraw them later because the bus ride is too long. This suggests that the apparent contradiction in the research may simply be the difference between types of school districts (county versus city) or between implementation year effects and postimplementation year effects. It seems reasonable to conclude, then, that minimizing busing distances will probably reduce implementation year white flight in those districts and those schools where flight is likely to be greatest.

Subdistricting. The evidence from an analysis of Boston's school system (which was divided into nine court-mandated subdistricts) suggests that it is inadvisable to draw inviolable subdistrict attendance zones, particularly when the only residential area included in a single subdistrict is a transitional one (Rossell and Ross, 1979). Racially changing neighborhoods are stabilized only if stable white neighborhoods are also included in the attendance zone. The advantage of a citywide plan with no subdistricts is that school authorities are able to redraw attendance zones and reassign students from all over the city whenever necessary to stabilize schools.

Providing incentives for housing desegregation. Desegregation plans should exclude residentially integrated neighborhoods from cross-town busing in order to give families an incentive to integrate neighborhoods, but it should be widely understood that the racial balance of those schools will be maintained by reassignments if necessary. Hence, if the proportion white enrollment declines in a school that is exempt from busing because of its integrated neighborhood, everyone should understand that additional whites will be reassigned in, or minorities reassigned out, to bring the proportion white up to a stable level. Unfortunately, there is no agreement about what such a level is, though most observers believe schools that are majority black will not usually hold whites. A half-and-half racial distribution might be stable if it is closely monitored. In triethnic districts, this standard could be relaxed if the Hispanic community involved is not very poor.

Public information. Since the greatest white flight occurs in most districts in the year of implementation, those who have fled are people who have never tried desegregation. Typically, these people do not know anyone who has experienced desegregated schools, yet they believe that the quality of their children's education will suffer when their schools are desegregated. The inevitable question arises: From what sources do they get their information? In most cases, the answer is the mass media. Although the media have a liberal reputation among those opposed to busing, researchers who have done content analyses (Rossell, 1978b; Stuart, 1973; Cunningham et al. 1978: 39) find the press tends to emphasize antibusing protest, white flight, and interracial conflict as a product of desegregation. In addition, Rossell (1978b) finds this negative coverage exacerbates white flight. That is, the greater the negative coverage of desegregation, the greater the white flight.

If the mass media serves as the source of information on the costs, benefits, and risks of desegregation, then it is important that the school districts (or a state agency) provide the newspapers with positive stories on desegregation and positive evidence on school performance, both before and after desegregation, and with press releases about new and innovative school programs. This is a full-time job which requires someone skilled in public information and marketing. Although the cost of maintaining such an office might be high, the benefits could be substantial.

As noted earlier, in many communities most of those who leave the public schools to avoid desegregation do not move out of the school district. School systems should maintain contact with these parents, identify their concerns, and provide them with programs and information that might attract them back to the public schools. Parent-teacher-student associations can play a major role in such recruitment efforts, but the school district should also maintain an office for this purpose.

Civic organizations, as well as school districts, should sponsor activities in minority neighborhood schools, with transportation provided, to familiarize white parents with these neighborhoods, and to dispel myths regarding the danger of passing through such neighborhoods and of attending formerly black schools.

It is important to constrain protest, if possible, because the available research suggests that protest demonstrations exacerbate white flight. Encouraging leaders to play a more positive role in desegregation controversies is one strategy frequently advocated as a way of shaping public reaction. There is no empirical evidence, however, that communitywide leadership has any influence on white flight and protest except indirectly, by contributing to the slant of newspaper and media coverage (see Rossell, 1978b). This may be due to the fact that desegregation is an issue area where there usually is no leadership from traditional leaders. The evidence suggests that if leadership activity is to be successful in minimizing negative reactions, the activity should be at the neighborhood level (see Hayes, 1977; Taylor and Stinchcombe, 1977). Thus, while it is clearly desirable to have communitywide leaders endorsing desegregation, pious announcements from afar about the need to obey the law are not likely to be very consequential, particularly when anti-busing leaders are actively influencing opinion and behavior at the grassroots level.

FEDERAL AND STATE POLICY OPTIONS

Facilitating metropolitan solutions. Metropolitan desegregation plans are more stable than city plans from every viewpoint. Nevertheless, the courts have been reluctant to order metropolitan plans except where there is a clear cross-district violation. Proving there is a cross-district violation is a laborious, time-consuming task which few plaintiffs or defendants have the resources to accomplish. This is an area where the Office of Civil Rights, in coordination with the Justice Department's Title VI unit, could play a useful role. Together, they could create a combined interagency investigation staff consisting of lawyers, demographers, sociologists, economists, urban historians, and other experts who could collect and analyze data on real estate practices, local housing regulations, unnatural patterns of residential growth, and other instances of discriminatory practices which involve collusion between the city and the suburbs to keep minorities in the suburbs.

A study by the President's Reorganization Project of general civil rights coordination problems at the federal level has produced tentative recommendations that would substantially strengthen the role of the Justice Department and establish a permanent civil rights staff within OMB to assure informed examination of civil rights performance in the annual budget review (Orfield, 1979). If this also included the interagency coordination described above, significant policy developments might result.

The federal government could provide matching funds to states or cooperating districts to support interdistrict transfer programs that have the effect of furthering desegregation in the participating districts. The 1978 revisions of the Emergency School Assistance Act allowed such expenditures, but since districts must choose between using funds for these purposes or for others of more immediate educational benefit to them, it seems unlikely that this option will be widely used. Moreover, Congress has made it unnecessarily difficult to qualify for such money (for instance, by requiring cooperation agreements to be excessively inclusive). As a result, the 1980 applications for ESAA funds by local agencies indicate no new interest in metropolitan cooperation. In 1980, Houston implemented, without federal support, a modest voluntary cross-district plan, but the amount of desegregation achieved by this plan is small. The National Educational Opportunity Act of 1979 sponsored by Congressman Preyer and others would establish a separate interdistrict program, but Preyer was defeated in the 1980 election, and no new sponsor for the bill has come forth.

Interdistrict transfer programs, however, will probably have to be actively advocated and brokered by state or federal agencies if they are to account for much desegregation. Nationally based agencies (such as the Education Commission of the States or the Title IV Desegregation Assistance Centers) could provide technical assistance to such efforts. On the basis of past experience, however, such assistance in itself will probably only reduce segregation by a few percentage points and should be seen as part of an array of programs aimed at stabilizing enrollments.

Housing and school desegregation. The need for school desegregation is largely a function of the fact that housing is segregated. Housing policies which encourage racially mixed neighborhoods would facilitate desegregation and reduce incentives for white flight. Orfield (1979: 42) notes that the housing and education sections of the Civil Rights Division of the Justice Department have been merged, and the Division is reported to be actively interested in combined school and housing litigation. If this is coordinated with the investigation of metropolitan collusion discussed above, we might see some successful northern metropolitan cases.

In Louisville-Jefferson county, the Kentucky Human Rights Commission (1977) was able to promote housing integration by an aggressive program of publicizing the school attendance zones that families could move into to keep their children from being bused, since children moving into opposite race neighborhoods were excluded from busing. Some white neighborhoods then began recruiting black families on their own, because neighborhood integrated schools were also excluded from busing.[1]

Taylor (1979) suggests that HUD should replicate the positive experience in Louisville by initiating an affirmative program to use Section 8 housing opportunities to residentially integrate school districts. Section 8 certificates are available to low- and moderate-income families to make up the difference between the amount representing 25 percent of their income and the amount of rent being charged. Section 8 guarantees are also available to builders in order to induce them to build low and moderate income housing by guaranteeing that enough families will be given Section 8 certificates to fill a certain proportion of the units and by subsidizing any vacant units (Bowers, 1980). Both of these programs could be used to enable minority families to move into white neighborhoods in school districts where integrated schools are excluded from busing (which gives whites an incentive to accept them). This would not necessarily entail additional expenditures because it could conceivably be accomplished by a more rational allocation of funds already expended.

Financial incentives for living in desegregating school districts. It seems reasonable to assume that an important reason that whites leave racially changing neighborhoods or schools, or desegregating school districts, is that they are concerned about the racial stability of their neighborhoods and schools and the decline in property values they believe will accompany desegregation. (The assumption that economic factors serve as an incentive for moving is reasonable because we know that a chance to make a profit on one's home as housing values go up is a major incentive for whites to move into inner-city minority neighborhoods undergoing urban renewal.) It follows, then, that one way to reduce white flight might be for the federal government to guarantee a fair market value for the homes of individuals living in integrated neighborhoods or having children in integrated schools. In effect, such a policy would be a federal assurance that desegregation would not increase the cost of sending one's children to public schools. In order that it not serve as a stimulus for additional white flight, however, there would have to be a stipulation regarding the minimum amount of time spent in the integrated school or neighborhood after desegregation.

Three years might be sufficient. Although this would entail new legislation, it would probably cost little if it (a) failed to stem white flight in the short run and (b) was a successful policy. Even if whites moved after three years to a more segregated school system, the costs of this policy would probably be small, since the depression of property values is greatest when white flight is greatest, which typically occurs right after desegregation. In general, the consensus among observers of desegregation is that property values tend to rise to normal levels by the third year of desegregation.

Providing financial incentives for voluntary school integration. Another possible option that might also stimulate voluntary integration is the provision of tax credits for those who have their children enrolled in integrated schools. This is, of course, an expensive option which would entail new legislation being passed by Congress. Congress, however, might be willing to pass such legislation if it were billed as a means of stimulating voluntary integration and thus freeing their constituents from "forced busing." The actual cost of this program might be offset by its impact on minority life changes and on the economic health of cities. Ultimately, the net expense might be no greater than the tax credits routinely given to business in order to encourage investment and to homeowners in order to encourage home ownership.

A less expensive variation on this idea would be to provide parents with a limited voucher that could be spent in either public or private schools *if* it resulted in increased desegregation. Since most parents believe that money improves schools, such a voucher might induce them to send their children to desegregated schools. At the same time, this would serve as an incentive for schools to recruit students whose attendance would reduce segregation, since they would also increase the school's budget. This program could be either a state or federal program, but it would entail new legislation.

ENHANCING THE PERCEIVED QUALITY OF PUBLIC SCHOOLS

A key assumption behind voluntary plans is that parents will be attracted to "quality" schools (magnets). One problem with this assumption is that educators and parents have different conceptions of educational quality and both, especially parents, have only vague notions about what accounts for quality education. Nevertheless, the adoption of policies that support programs and conditions parents value should reduce their perceptions of desegregation-related costs and increase the benefits they attribute to public schooling.

Maintaining smaller classrooms. One belief that almost all teachers and parents share is that small class size makes for better schooling.[2] Since enrollment in most school systems is declining and many teachers consequently face unemployment, a federal program aimed at retaining teachers in school systems that are desegregating could have positive educational consequences and might reduce white and middle-class flight.

Maintaining smaller schools. Smaller schools are most effective in achieveing desegregation and fostering integration for several reasons. First, whites usually overestimate the proportion of minorities in a given environment and, probably, the more nonwhites in that environment (that is, the larger the school), the more they overestimate. Thus, white flight might be reduced in smaller schools simply because the minority proportion will seem smaller and less threatening than in a larger school.[3] Second, one way that unfavorable stereotypes are repudiated is by personal experience. Students are more likely to have interaction with most of their schoolmates in a smaller environment. Finally, discipline, which parents perenially see as the biggest problem in the public schools (see Golladay and Noel, 1978: 53), is easier to achieve in smaller environments (Gottfredson and Daiger, 1979).

Consumer protection. It is probably safe to say that most parents who remove their children from public schools in the face of desegregation believe that the quality of education their children will receive in a private school is superior. To be sure, this belief may be a rationalization or a secondary consideration, but it no doubt makes both the decision and the bearing of the financial costs easier.

It seems likely, however, that parents overestimate the quality of private schools with respect to the cognitive development of their children and the resources available to facilitate these and other types of learning. White flight might be retarded, and white return facilitated, if schools of all kinds were required by states or the federal government to publish information about the range of resources (including teacher qualifications) and educational opportunities students have available to them, and individual student progress as measured by standardized tests. Some indicators on which the public schools might do better than private schools are pupil-teacher ratios, teacher salaries and qualifications, per pupil expenditures, and, perhaps, change in *individual* student scores over time. There is a belief among many parents that their children's achievement scores will go up in private schools and down in public schools. To date, there is no empirical evidence available that supports this belief.

Requirements for the publication of such information could be limited to instances where tax exemptions are involved and even then they would be hotly contested on constitutional (and other) grounds. Nevertheless, private schools have public responsibilities and it is in the national interest to provide parents with adequate information upon which to base their decisions about how to educate their children.

DESEGREGATING SCHOOLS ON THE BASIS
OF WORK PLACE AND WORK NEEDS

It is estimated that half the nation's children under age 18 have mothers in the labor force (Waldman et al., 1979). Other important ways in which desegregated schools might compete with private and suburban segregated schools would be to make themselves more attractive to these working mothers by providing all-day school activities until a parent comes home from work and/or by desegregating schools according to the parents' work places, rather than their homes.

The voluntary aspects of such programs may enhance their political feasibility. The all-day schools would probably increase educational expenses for a typical school district by one-fifth. On the other hand, if such a policy could be coordinated with Title 20 day care programs, the cost would be lower.

The idea of desegregating schools by linking student assignment to parents' place of work is intuitively attractive since work places are invariably more desegregated than residential areas. Moreover, parents may feel more secure in sending their students to desegregated schools if the schools are nearby. In addition, parental involvement might be more easily achieved, since many schools would be more accessible if desegregated by work place rather than by neighborhood.

The feasibility of this proposal, however, cannot be easily assessed from existing data, although it does seem possible to do such an analysis in principle. Combining existing data sets may provide some clues. One attractive aspect of this suggestion is the possibility of energy cost savings to families, schools systems, and the nation, since parents and children could commute together, rather than separately as they do now.

THE COST OF WHITE FLIGHT

Most of the policy options discussed here follow from the assumption that it is desirable and worth considerable expense to retain whites in desegregating cities and school systems. That assumption is very troublesome to some nonwhites. For this and other reasons, it deserves further examination, especially when a number of efforts to stem white flight may mean that some schools will remain segregated and that minorities will be required to accept a greater share of the busing burden.

The cost of white flight in terms of reduction in interracial contact can easily be estimated (see Rossell, 1978a; Coleman et al., 1975). Mandatory desegregation plans, in school districts above 35 percent black, have a greater net benefit (that is, more interracial contact opportunities) than voluntary plans, both in the short term and the long term, despite the fact that they have greater implementation year white flight. For every 20 percent of the district's blacks who are reassigned, there is likely to be a 12 percentage point increase in interracial contact. For every 20 percent of whites who are reassigned, a 10 percentage point increase in interracial contact is likely to occur (Rossell, 1978a). This increased interracial contact lasts for at least a decade or more, although during this time period the level of interracial contact will decline as long as the white proportion of enrollment is declining. If there is a one percentage point decline in the proportion white every year (as part of the long-term secular trend) and all the schools are racially balanced, a half percentage point decline in the level of interracial contact can be expected. This will occur in all school districts whether they are desegregated or not, but the desegregated school districts should always have greater levels of interracial contact since they started out much higher.

Although there is a net benefit from mandatory, extensive desegregation plans in terms of increased interracial contact, it is not clear what the effects of such plans are on the socioeconomic composition of the student or community population. The research evidence indicates that those most likely to withdraw their children from desegregated schools are those with higher income and higher education (Giles et al., 1976; McConahay and Hawley, 1977; Pride and Woodard, 1978; Lord, 1975; Rossell, 1980).

This is a problem, since the research suggests that school desegregation produces greater achievement gains for lower socioeconomic status students when the socioeconomic level of their classmates is higher. Furthermore, there is little evidence regarding the effects of white flight on the community property tax base or citizen support for public schools. The long-term implications of these possible negative impacts for the quality of desegregated education is uncertain.

In short, while there are ways to think more systematically about the issue, there is no empirical way to assess the costs of white flight to a school system or a community. What is involved is a question of values and, as white flight continues, the values that whites and minorities consider important may change. Some observers believe, for example, that the waning of minority support for desegregation in some areas is linked to the increased electoral power minorities have when whites leave the cities.

We have summarized the existing research on white flight and concluded both that desegregation does not always and inevitably lead to long-term changes in the racial composition of communities. Further research will no doubt clarify several issues that we now inadequately understand. We have also argued that there appear to be a number of initiatives that could be taken at all levels of government to reduce the exodus of white and middle-class students from the public schools. To be sure, some of the ideas presented here are inappropriate in some circumstances, and not politically viable in others. What we consider feasible, however, is often the product of how badly we want something and how many options we think we have. This chapter has tried to suggest that there is much more we could do to deal with desegregation-induced flight from public schools if we wanted to.

NOTES

1. Pearce (1980) concludes, after studying seven matched pairs of desegregated and undesegregated school districts, that school desegregation promotes housing desegregation.

2. A meta-analysis conducted by Glass and Smith (1979) supports this assertion. Classrooms that were smaller than 20 students showed increases in achievement with reductions in size.

3. This may be why Rossell (1980) found less implementation year white flight in Los Angeles when whites were reassigned to smaller minority schools than when they were reassigned to larger ones.

REFERENCES

ARMOR, D. J. (1980a) Exhibits presented to the Court in *Crawford* v. *Board of Education of the City of Los Angeles,* March.

——— (1980b) "White flight and the future of school desegregation," in W. G. Stephan and J. R. Feagin (eds.) Desegregation: Past, Present, and Future. New York: Plenum.

BOWERS, J. (1980) Personal communication, League of Women Voters, July 20.

BRADFORD, D. F. and H. H. KELEJIAN (1973) "An economic model of the flight to the suburbs." Journal of Political Economy 81: 566-589.

COLEMAN, J. S., S. D. KELLY, and J. A. MOORE (1975) Trends in School Segregation, 1968-1973. Washington, DC: Urban Institute.

CUNNINGHAM, G. K., W. L. HUSK, and J. A. JOHNSON (1978) "The impact of court ordered desegregation on student enrollment and residential patterns (white flight)." Presented at the annual meeting of the American Educational Research Association, Toronto, March.

DeVRIES, D.L., K.J. EDWARDS, and E.H. WELLS (1974) Teams-Games-Tournament in the Social Studies Classroom: Effects on Academic Achievement, Student Attitudes, Cognitive Beliefs, and Classroom Climate. Baltimore: Johns Hopkins University, Center for Social Organization of Schools.

ESTABROOK, L.S. (1980) "The effect of desegregation on parents' evaluations of schools." Ph.D. dissertation, Boston University.

FARLEY, R., T. RICHARDS, and C. WURDOCK (1979) "School desegregation and white flight: an investigation of competing models and their discrepant findings." Ph.D. dissertation, University of Michigan.

GILES, M., D. GATLIN, and E. CATALDO (1976) Determinants of Resegregation: Compliance/Rejection Behavior and Policy Alternatives. Washington, DC: National Science Foundation.

GLASS, G.J. and M.L. SMITH (1979) "Meta-analysis of research on class size and achievement." Educational Evaluation and Policy Analysis 1: 2-16.

GOLLADAY, M.A. and J. NOELL [eds.] (1978) The Condition of Education. Washington, DC: Government Printing Office.

GOTTFREDSON, G.D. and D.C. DAIGER (1979) Disruption in Six Hundred Schools. Baltimore: Johns Hopkins University, Center for Social Organization of Schools.

HAYES, J.G. (1977) "Anti-busing protest." Presented at the annual meeting of the North Carolina Educational Research Association, Charlotte, November.

HIRSCHMAN, A.O. (1970) Exit, Voice, and Loyalty. Cambridge, MA: Harvard University Press.

KATZMAN, M.T. (1978) The Quality of Municipal Services, Central City Decline and Middle-Class Flight. Cambridge, MA: Harvard University.

Kentucky Human Rights Commission (1977) Housing Desegregation Increases as Schools Desegregate in Jefferson County. Louisville: Author.

LARSON, J.C. (1980) Takoma Park Magnet School Evaluation. Rockville, MD: Montgomery County Public Schools.

LORD, J.D. (1975) "School busing and white abandonment of public schools." Southeastern Geographer 12: 81-92.

McCONAHAY, J. and W.D. HAWLEY (1978) Reactions to Busing in Louisville: Summary of Adult Opinions in 1976 and 1977. Durham, NC: Duke University, Institute of Policy Sciences and Public Affairs.

———— (1977) Attitudes of Louisville and Jefferson County Citizens Toward Busing for Public School Desegregation: Results from the Second Year. Durham, NC: Duke University, Institute of Policy Sciences and Public Affairs.

Massachusetts Research Center (1976) Education and Enrollment: Boston During Phase II. Boston: Author.

National Center for Health Statistics (1975) Vital Statistics of the United States, 1971: Natality (Vol. 1). Rockville, MD: Author.

Office of Education (1979) "Emergency school aid, notice of proposed rule making." Federal Register 44: 38364-38383.

———— (1978a) Title IV — Establishment of a New Title VI of the Elementary and Secondary Education Act of 1965, Public Law 95-561, 92 Stat. 2252-2268, November 1.

———— (1978b) "Desegregation of public education." Federal Register 43: 32372-32387.

ORFIELD, G. (1979) Federal Agencies and Urban Segregation: Steps Towards Coordinated Action. New York: Ford Foundation.

—— (1978) "Report to the Honorable Judge Paul Egly." Presented to the Superior Court, State of California, County of Los Angeles, Case No. 822-854, November 15.

PEARCE, D. (1980) Breaking Down the Barriers: New Evidence on the Impact of Metropolitan School Desegregation on Housing Patterns. Washington, DC: National Institute of Education.

PRIDE, R. A. and J. D. WOODARD (1978) "Busing plans, media agenda, and white flight: Nashville and Louisville." Presented at the annual meeting of the Southwestern Political Science Association, Houston, April.

ROSSELL, C. H. (1980) Is It the Distance or the Blacks? Boston: Boston University.

—— (1979) "Magnet schools as a desegregation tool: the importance of contextual factors in explaining their success." Urban Education 20: 303-320.

—— (1978a) Assessing the Unintended Impacts of Public Policy: School Desegregation and Resegregation. Washington, DC: National Institute of Education.

—— (1978b) "The effect of community leadership and the mass media on public behavior." Theory into Practice 17: 131-139.

—— and J. M. ROSS (1979) The Long-Term Effect of Court-Ordered Desegregation on Student Enrollment in Central City Public School Systems: The Case of Boston, 1974-1979. Report prepared for the Boston School Department.

SCHNORE, A. B. and C. D. MacRAE (1975) A Model of Neighborhood Change. Washington, DC: Urban Institute.

SLAVIN, R. E. (1977) Student Team Learning Techniques: Narrowing the Achievement Gap Between the Races. Baltimore: Johns Hopkins University, Center for Social Organization of Schools.

STUART, R. (1973) "Busing and the media in Nashville." New South 28: 79-87.

TAYLOR, D. G. and A. L. STINCHCOMBE (1977) The Boston School Desegregation Controversy. Chicago: National Opinion Research Center.

TAYLOR, W. L. (1979) Mounting a Concerted Federal Attack on Urban Segregation: A Preliminary Exploration. New York: Ford Foundation.

U.S. Bureau of the Census (1979a) School Enrollment, Social and Economic Characteristics of Students: October 1978. Current Population Reports, Series P-20, No. 335. Washington, DC: Government Printing Office.

—— (1979b) The Social and Economic Status of the Black Population in the United States: An Historical View, 1790-1978. Current Population Reports, Series P-23, No. 80. Washington, DC: Government Printing Office.

—— (1977) Social Indicators, 1976. Washington, DC: Government Printing Office.

—— (1975) Fertility Expectations of American Women: June 1974. Current Population Reports, Series P-20, No. 277. Washington, DC: Government Printing Office.

—— (1972) The Statistical Abstract of the United States. Washington, DC: Government Printing Office.

WALDMAN, E., A. S. GROSSMAN, H. HAYGHE, and B. L. JOHNSON (1979) "Working mothers in the 1970s: a look at the statistics." Monthly Labor Review 40: 102-110.

8

HOUSING PATTERNS AND
DESEGREGATION POLICY

GARY ORFIELD

The most severe contemporary problems of educational segregation, fiscal collapse, and declining confidence in public education are centered in large cities and their older suburbs. Very great progress has been achieved in the past generation in lowering the level of segregation of blacks in small cities and rural communities. Unfortunately, however, both blacks and the very rapidly growing Hispanic communities are highly dependent upon the great city school systems, particularly outside the South. More than a quarter century after *Brown* v. *Board of Education,* desegregation policies have had little impact on big cities, and a growing number of them are reaching the status of virtually all-minority enrollment without ever passing through desegregation.

Developing a set of policies that can successfully reduce segregation in these metropolitan centers and can prevent the spread of rapid ghettoization of large portions of their suburbs is extremely important for a number of reasons. First, of course, is the fact that millions of minority students will remain segregated, both by race and by class, without such a policy. They will be dependent upon central-city school districts with diminishing resources and political power. Second, these metropolitan areas are the center of American culture; it will be virtually impossible to move successfully toward an integrated society while most of the major white and minority leaders of government, communications, scholarship, education, and culture live in situations of intense segregation. Third, the cities have been the historic centers of violent racial unrest and are likely to be the focal point of future crises which will produce racial division. Fourth, there is no evidence that their housing will be desegregated in the foreseeable future on any substantial scale. Fifth, these cities are the principal recipients of Hispanic immigration and show disturbing signs of rapidly increasing separation into three separate societies, with problems of race and poverty overlaid by problems of language differences. Sixth, it is apparent that the problem of spreading ghettoization is one of the factors that inhibits needed investment in central cities and encourages the movement to the outer suburbs, which severely increases energy problems in a society which must conserve energy.

A STARTING POINT:
THE NATURE OF URBAN RACIAL CHANGE

The making of urban school desegregation policy has progressed a long way without any serious confrontation with the need to devise a general model of processes of urban racial change which incorporates the close relationship between school and housing policies. A number of the largest central cities in the United States are now in the midst of, or rapidly appraoching, implementation of major school desegregation plans after years of struggle.[1] Cleveland began desegregation in 1979, Los Angeles in 1978, St. Louis and Pittsburgh in 1980, and Chicago has signed a consent decree which will bring its plan before the court in 1981.[2] In Houston, the Justice Department asked the federal court to include the suburbs of the sprawling city in a desegregation plan and the issue is pending before the Court of Appeals.[3] In Atlanta a similar effort was summarily rejected by the Supreme Court in 1980, but an order has been issued for a city-suburban plan in Indianapolis in fall of 1981. In Seattle the local school board has successfully defended its desegregation plan from a state antibusing referendum and is now suing the state for cutting off funds for transportation. In St. Louis both the state and federal governments are under court order to devise school and housing plans including the suburbs. A number of the nation's other large cities have continuing school litigation and many operate their schools under widely varying court decrees. Courts continue to issue orders dramatically reshaping urban school systems.

The central difficulty is that there is neither a clear policy nor a clear image of urban reality that informs these cases. The results of litigation are often idiosyncratic and frequently show no serious analysis either by the court or the school district of the social structure of the urban community. Litigation concentrates attention on issues of guilt, not on analysis of social facts. Seldom do the courts deal with the nature of metropolitan housing segregation in designing a remedy. Often they either refuse to design a plan that affects more than a small fraction of the segregated children, or they design a plan that will predictably fail within a few years.

School desegregation litigation suffers seriously from the fact that it is both the only significant policy initiative now under way against urban segregation and it is simultaneously often carried out and implemented without any significant analysis of the demographics or housing patterns of the cities it is attempting to desegregate. To a certain extent, of course, some of the resulting problems are inevitable in areas where the policy is not made on a national basis, but is devised on a case-by-case basis and is intended not to produce the most stable or beneficial integration but to "remedy" proved constitutional violations.

Critics continue to claim that the schools cannot bear the full burden of the desegregation process and should not be expected to solve all social problems. Merely to state this is to recognize that it is self-evidently true. The problem is that the critics of the courts normally go on to conclude that the schools should do nothing and that the solution should come from some unspecified or unanalyzed change in some other sphere — the favorite candidates involve hopes of long-term changes in racial attitudes or vague hopes of housing desegregation or some kind of bootstrap compensatory education program.

This essay will start from a different first assumption — that school desegregation plans of some sort will be and must be expected. In the aftermath of the Supreme Court's decisions in the *Dayton* (1979) and *Columbus* (1979) cases it is apparent that serious litigation in any city is very likely to produce sufficient evidence to support a court order for districtwide desegregation. If one begins with that assumption, and it is certainly the only viable assumption for officials in cities now reaching or at the end of long legal battles, the real questions are how to achieve the maximum stable and beneficial desegregation with the least long-term costs to the city and its race relations. Obviously, if there are ways that might produce long-range benefits for the city reaching beyond school desegregation, every possible effort should be made to gain them. The courts are not likely to pay much attention to such considerations, at least within the traditional framework of the school desegregation case, but local officials, government agencies, and civil rights litigators planning strategies need to consider these possibilities. If there is to be a difficult and traumatic — one time only — reorganization of the most important part of local government, it is essential to the long-term values of the civil rights movement, as well as its long-term success and credibility, to produce a plan that has a reasonable probability of working.

When the Supreme Court decided *Milliken* v. *Bradley* (1974), its major metropolitan desegregation case, Chief Justice Burger's opinion noted that the Court had not considered evidence about the origin of housing segregation in metropolitan Detroit. The Court set a profoundly important policy for metropolitan America, limiting itself to an examination of school violations and legal theories. There was no analysis of the residential composition of the city and no consideration of the impact of the Court's decision on the future of neighborhoods and communities. Facing the conclusions of the lower federal courts that significant desegregation was impossible within the central city, the Supreme Court simply expressed its impatience that the impossible had not been accomplished already.

This essay is based upon two simple assumptions: First, that development of good urban school desegregation policies requires understanding characteristic patterns of urban racial composition and basic demographic trends. Second, that school and housing policies do have an impact on each other and that policy makers have an obligation to avoid unnecessary damage to existing housing and school integration and to attempt to maximize stable integration in the long run.

Obviously the task is complex, but there is surprising consensus on some of the important factual issues among researchers with fundamentally different value assumptions and research methodologies. The price of not facing up to these issues may be the production of plans that are doomed to certain failure from the beginning, that will produce great turmoil but little or no lasting desegregation. If lasting desegregation is the first essential precondition for obtaining the benefits of desegregation, there may be no significant benefits. The failure of plans has another consequence — it strengthens the belief that integration cannot be achieved and reinforces the view that the courts are not only acting arbitrarily but also futilely. If a court finds itself forced, by constitutional violations, to impose a major social change, it should not adopt a change that cannot work.

Development of a good approach to urban school desegration requires a clear understanding of the current pattern of segregation and a review of evidence on several key areas of research:

(1) the dynamics of urban racial change — the nature of the ghettoization process and the nature of existing residential integration;

(2) the history of educational ghettoization and its relationship to neighborhood transition;

(3) the development of Hispanic segregation;

(4) the impact of federal, state, and local politics on housing segregation;

(5) the prospects for housing desegregation; and

(6) the impact on residential stability of various forms of school desegregation plans.

ACCOMPLISHMENTS AND FAILURES: THE LOCUS OF CONTEMPORARY SEGREGATION

A simple review of the most recent statistics on levels of school integration is sufficient to show that the movement has had remarkable success where it first seemed impossible, and very little impact on the central cities, which were once the centers of civil rights liberalism. Contemporary segregation is worst outside the South, continuing a trend that first became apparent in 1970, and is concentrated in the large school districts. The worst patterns and the least progress are found in the school systems with more than 100,000 students.

There have been many more desegregation plans in the South than in the North and the typical southern plan involved a substantially greater reduction of segregation. In all regions segregation is higher now in metropolitan areas than in rural and small city areas, and it is higher in central cities than in the suburbs. School segregation is uniformly higher in the elementary grades than in the secondary grades and is extremely high in the elementary grades of the largest school systems (Taeuber and Wilson, 1979). (If the Crain and Mahard argument, in Chapter 3 of this

TABLE 8.1   Trends in School Segregation Between Whites and Total Minority Population, 1968-1976

School District Size	Non-South			South		
	1968	1976	Change	1968	1976	Change
2,500	17.5	15.7	−1.8	41.7	10.2	−31.5
2,500-4,999	26.6	21.5	−5.1	51.2	19.3	−37.9
5,000-9,000	32.5	24.3	−8.2	66.0	25.3	−40.7
10,000-24,999	37.6	29.9	−7.7	65.0	33.4	−31.6
25,000-100,000	51.7	39.2	−12.5	72.6	41.2	−31.4
100,000+	74.2	64.9	−9.3	74.3	45.6	−28.7
Total U.S.	28.3	24.8	−3.5	53.9	19.6	−34.3

SOURCE: Taeuber and Wilson (1979: Table 8).

volume, about the critical importance of early integration is correct, this suggests that the vast majority of big central-city blacks and Hispanics will miss virtually all the possible educational gains from the desegregation process.) The large school districts are very important to minority children. Almost half of black students (48 percent) and 60 percent of Hispanic students attend school in just 50 school districts in the United States (Taeuber and Wilson, 1979). Many are districts with only a shrinking minority of white students and many have never desegregated.

Among the largest districts, the most striking progress came in southern cities. In Savannah, Georgia, Charlotte, North Carolina, and Tampa, Florida, very sharp drops in segregation were reported. Tampa, Charlotte, and a number of the other large school districts of Florida virtually eliminated segregation, embarking on full metropolitan desegregation plans across entire counties. All in all, Taeuber and Wilson (1979) reported that among the 50 largest districts with substantial black enrollment, 27 showed significant declines in segregation levels, all but 6 of which were southern. For Hispanics only 3 large districts in the United States showed significant declines: Corpus Christi and Weslaco, Texas, and Denver, Colorado, the site of the first northern case decided by the Supreme Court. A number of the largest districts still had high segregation index levels: about 80 for black children and above 60 for Hispanic students. (The index number refers to the percentage of pupils who would have to change schools to achieve a fully integrated school system.)

The 10 systems with the largest black populations enrolled a total of approximately 1,700,000 black children and the 10 districts with the

TABLE 8.2   Black and Hispanic Segregation Levels in Ten School Districts with Largest Black and Hispanic Enrollment

District	Black Index		District	Hispanic Index	
	1968	1976		1968	1976
New York	64.3	70.5	New York	72.9	70.4
Chicago	90.1	92.0	Los Angeles	64.4	63.9
Detroit	76.6	63.2	Miami	57.2	53.6
Philadelphia	75.1	80.8	Chicago	64.8	65.0
Los Angeles	90.4	81.0	Houston	65.4	61.9
Washington	78.7	85.8	San Antonio	65.3	53.1
Baltimore	81.9	67.6	El Paso	68.1	59.2
Houston	91.7	77.1	Albuquerque	53.4	49.9
Memphis	95.2	56.3	Ysleta, Texas	59.4	62.0
New Orleans	83.4	75.8	Corpus Christi	70.6	34.0

SOURCE: Adopted from Taeuber and Wilson (1979: Table 12).

largest Hispanic concentrations had almost 900,000 Hispanic children. In 4 of the 10 districts, black segregation became more intense between 1968 and 1976, as it did in 3 of the systems with large Hispanic populations.

During this period the level of segregation remained very high and the number of whites continued to fall rapidly. By 1976 New York had 31 percent whites, Los Angeles 37 percent, Chicago 25 percent, Houston 34 percent, Detroit 19 percent, Philadelphia 32 percent, Baltimore 24 percent, Cleveland 38 percent, Washington, D.C., 4 percent, and St. Louis 29 percent. None of these figures were stable and all, except Washington's, would continue to decline in the coming years (Ravitch, 1981). During the 1978-1979 school year, for example, Chicago had only 21 percent, Los Angeles only 30 percent, Atlanta only 10 percent, and Houston only 31 percent.[4] In 1980-1981, Chicago had 18.6 percent white students as it faced desegregation, and St. Louis implemented a plan with 22 percent white enrollment. Projections showed that, given the normal trends established before any desegregation plan, the decline in these cities would continue until few whites remained.

THE POLICY DILEMMA

The courts and other policy makers confront the central difficulty that the largest number of segregated children and the most dramatic evidence of constitutional violations are concentrated in the central cities, where there are not enough whites to desegregate all of the schools and where that relatively small number is rapidly shrinking.

The existence of white flight, either the normal pattern of declining white enrollment or the special problem of accelerated initial loss of students following the implementation of certain kinds of desegregation plans, can be and has been used by the federal courts in a variety of ways. In the Supreme Court's *Milliken* decision, the court simply ignored the issue, assuming that a workable remedy was possible within the city of Detroit. The Court of Appeals (*Milliken* v. *Bradley*, 1973) had earlier concluded in this case that no workable remedy was possible within Detroit. The District Court (*Milliken* v. *Bradley*, 1975) which ultimately formulated the remedy concluded that it could desegregate only about a tenth of the students within the city. Justice Thurgood Marshall based his dissenting opinion in part upon his conviction that a plan limited to the city would simply speed up the loss of the minority of whites remaining.

In the Atlanta case, the local chapter of the NAACP and black school officials decided to drop litigation for a far-reaching busing plan in part because of a fear of accelerated white flight. When the decision was challenged by civil rights lawyers, the federal courts held that the "Atlanta compromise" was legal primarily because of the danger of white flight. The Atlanta school superintendent made white flight the central theme in his argument against an NAACP plan in the early 1970s which would have integrated slightly more than half of the district's enrollment. The compromise plan, supported by then Governor Jimmy Carter, dropped proposals for significant student integration, placing basic emphasis upon a promise to hire twenty more black administrators and allocate future administrative positions to blacks (Hadden et al., 1979).

The Atlanta compromise, however, seemed to achieve none of its major goals. Enrollment dropped from 151,000 in 1966 to 117,000 in 1971 and 76,000 in 1976, a decline of almost half in a decade. By the 1978-1979 school year the system was 90 percent black (Hadden et al., 1979). The extra administrators "increased Atlanta's administrative costs to well over the national average" for a period of years. The city has a very great concentration of poor children; all but five of its elementary schools meet the poverty level standards for the federal Title I program. Researchers reporting on an extensive study in 1979 found a "low level of community involvement" in policy making within the district, in spite of the increased number of important black decision makers (Hadden et al., 1979: 25, 87).

In spite of a new administration committed to achieving more equity within a framework of segregation, Clark College researchers found important inequities remaining in 1976. In Area 3, an area where almost half the schools remained predominantly white (the other areas all had less than one-sixth predominantly white schools), the class size was smallest, the total per student expenditures were highest, and the schools were least crowded. Achievement levels in this area were by far the highest in the system. Two of the other three areas did not have a single school achieving at the national norm level. The powerful Atlanta business community lost interest in the schools:

> Once integration was an accomplished fact, business lost interest in the schools. Since racial conflict no longer threatened economic growth, the community could simply cease to regard the schools as a variable relevant to the conduct of business in Atlanta. At the same time, people left the city altogether. In one year, 1971, the school system lost almost 45,000 children, or more than one-fourth of its enrollment [Hadden et al., 1979: 20].

After seven years in court, much of it with no action on the case, a lawsuit on metropolitan desegregation in Atlanta was tried in 1978. The

case, which offered massive evidence of intentional housing segregation, was rejected by the lower federal courts, whose decision was
summarily affirmed by the Supreme Court without hearing in 1980.[5]

The court in *U.S.* v. *Board of School Commissioners of Indianapolis*
(1971) came up with a very different approach. The presiding judge ruled
that white flight is a central reality and, therefore, it is essential to involve
the suburbs in a desegregation plan so that central-city whites will not be
forced to attend schools where the percentage of blacks is over the
"tipping point." The initial district court opinions identified the tipping
point as approximately 30 percent black. The district court ordered
one-way busing of black students to the suburbs and its decision was
sustained by the Court of Appeals in April 1980. Many other issues, of
course, are very important in this case — but it serves to illustrate the
judge's dilemma.

The court in Los Angeles found itself under an order from the
California State Supreme Court to achieve the maximum feasible desegregation, but to take care to minimize white flight (*Crawford* v. *Board
of Education of the City of Los Angeles,* 1976). A number of litigants in
the case, including the school district and the antibusing groups, claim
that this means that the courts must rely very largely on voluntary
procedures, reinforcing their argument with statistics on white loss
during the first year of a relatively small mandatory program for fourth
through eighth grades.[6] Civil rights plaintiffs have called for triethnic
desegregation within the city and eventually within the entire metropolitan area.[7] The court-appointed experts have reported that white flight
will be less in the metropolitan plan, a suggestion which helped spur a
move to amend the state constitution to forbid such an approach. The
California state courts have now sustained that amendment and ended
mandatory busing in Los Angeles until additional evidence of the constitutional violations of the city's board of education is produced.[8]

Among the other large school systems, Chicago has fought for years
for an entirely voluntary approach, defended as a way to minimize white
flight. It did not work and was not accepted.[9] Houston, the fifth largest
district, asked the federal court to release it from any obligation of
mandatory desegregation, largely on white flight grounds (Regan, 1979).
St. Louis and Omaha commissioned social science research on white
flight in unsuccessful efforts to forestall mandatory student reassignment
(Marylander Marketing Research, 1977; Taylor, 1979). In other words,
an issue which the Supreme Court assumed to be irrelevant in determining the proper reach of a desegregation plan in a metropolitan area turns
up constantly in litigation on big city desegregation plans. School officials fervently argue that the nature of the desegregation plan does affect

residential patterns, and judges frequently show, in one way or another, that they agree.

DYNAMICS OF URBAN RACIAL CHANGE

Although many people, including many policy makers, talk about cities and even individual neighborhoods as if urban communities are normally stable, the truth is that urban society has always been fluid and changing and that neighborhoods have long passed through cycles of fashionableness and high status followed by social and economic change and decay. Since World War I, sociologists have carefully observed and documented typical patterns of community change when race becomes salient. The basic patterns have been so clearly and repeatedly set out that a researcher from a half century ago would have little trouble understanding what was happening along the borders of expanding ghettos and barrios today. Designing sensible policies for school desegregation (and for housing desegregation) requires understanding both this underlying pattern and the special circumstances that affect the process now.

White suburbanization has been occurring for more than half a century, reflects a pattern that is found in many countries without racial conflicts, and is found in those American cities which have very few minority inhabitants. In 1956, Amos Hawley published *The Changing Shape of Metropolitan America: Deconcentration Since 1920.* He showed that suburbs in all regions had been growing rapidly throughout the twentieth century. His statistics showed that the population of the North and South had been deconcentrating since 1920, while western cities had been steadily spreading outward since 1900. As soon as transportation technology — the streetcar, the elevated railroad, and then the automobile — made it possible for large numbers of people to live away from the industrial center, decentralization took hold. Almost a fourth of urban residents lived in the suburbs by 1920, and the automobile produced an explosion of suburbanization in the 17 largest cities from 1920-1930 (Wood, 1958: 55-60). Canada, France, Britain, and Japan showed similar patterns, closely linked to transportation (Throns, 1972; Clark, 1966).

When modern urban sociology was born at the University of Chicago in the 1920s, the pioneering writers soon described the process of social and racial stratification through outward dispersion. Burgess

(1972: 119-120) summarized the trends in his 1925 article, "The Growth of the City":

> Encircling the downtown area there is normally an area in transition.
> . . . A third area is inhabited by the workers in industries who have
> escaped from the area of deterioration but who desire to live within
> easy access of their work. Beyond this zone is the "residential area" of
> high-class apartment buildings or of exclusive "restricted" districts of
> single family dwellings. Still further, out beyond the city limits, is the
> commuters zone — suburban areas, or satellite cities.

The "main fact" of growth, Burgess said, was "the tendency of each inner zone to extend its area by invasion of the next outer zone." In Chicago, for instance, "the present boundaries of the area of deterioration were not many years ago those of the zone now inhabited by independent wage-earners, and within the memories of thousands of Chicagoans contained the residences of the 'best families.' "

Concern for the loss of the white middle class was a fundamental justification for urban renewal and other early urban programs. Reading through the renewal plans prepared in any city, or the Congressional debates, it is clear that municipal leaders were searching for tools to stem the steady outward spread of "blight" and to hold or attract back the white middle class to the central cities. This was, for example, an important reason that urban renewal land, obtained by leveling low-income housing, was so often used to build upper middle class housing (National Commission on Urban Problems, 1968). The problems of suburbanization had been obscured in the cities by the collapse of housing construction during the Depression and then by the construction shortages and urban overcrowding of the war years. Once the war was over, however, white flight soon became a fundamental worry.

The concern is clearly expressed in Wood's (1958: 111-112) analysis of the 1950 census in his influential book, *Suburbia*:

> The suburbs are well on the way toward capturing the major share of
> the social and occupational classes which have always seemed best
> suited to the Anglo-Saxon political tradition. . . . The suburban popu-
> lation . . . is revealed as younger, more equally divided between men
> and women, and with a larger proportion of native white inhabitants. It
> contains a higher percentage of children, more married persons and
> many more family units. Its men are more regularly employed in more
> managerial skilled occupations, average suburban income is con-

siderably higher, and the majority of both men and women are better educated. If youth, a commitment to family life, relative economic well-being and education are helpful in organizing a community . . . then the suburb dwellers are clearly better off than their big city neighbors.

The basic research on this migration, including Rossi's (1980) important 1955 work, *Why Families Move* and Gans' (1967) classic study of the migration in the late 1950s to Levittown, New Jersey (the prototype tract suburb), showed that the primary concerns of the migrants did not relate to race. In fact, there was little racial contact in the highly segregated central cities. The migration was fueled by attractive prices, yards and facilities for children, the desire for space, very favorable financing for purchase of new homes, and a variety of other factors. Large blocks of land were available for development and it was possible to build new houses well within the economic reach of most Americans.

There is little evidence in the responses of movers, even in national and local studies during the past year, that either the schools or racial issues are central causes of this continued outmigration, though the migration is more rapid in cities with a higher fraction of black residents (Marans, 1979). It is apparent in surveys taken during this decade that the cities have become undesirable on many counts and that there is a strong affect not just for suburbs, but also for small towns and rural areas. Surveys from 1966 to 1974 found a continuing decline in the number of persons saying that they preferred to live in large cities, reaching only one-eleventh of the population in the later year (Sundquist, 1975).

A large national survey of public attitudes toward cities was conducted for the government by Louis Harris and Associates (1978a) to aid in the development of President Carter's urban program. The survey found that Americans are profoundly unsatisfied with cities as places to raise children (most believe they have become much worse in the last generation) and they perceive the schools very negatively:

> Americans are almost unanimous (82 percent) in rating large cities as the "worst place to raise children." Also, 62 percent rate large city public schools "worst"; 62 percent attribute the worst housing to the large city; 54 percent say the highest taxes are in the large city [Louis Harris and Associates, 1978a: 5].

> Further undermining the image of family life in the city is the widespread perception, voiced by 57 percent, that divorce rates are highest there. The large city is also viewed as a repository of social pathology. A near-unanimous 91 percent point to large cities as having the highest crime rates [p. 22].

Even city residents shared many of the negative images. A total of 54 percent said urban schools were the nation's worst, 57 percent said the housing was the worst, and 67 percent said the city was the worst place to raise children. Of all whites, 85 percent saw the city as the worst place to raise children, and 64 percent of blacks responded this way. Only 16 percent of blacks and 6 percent of Hispanics said that they preferred to live in an all-minority area (Louis Harris and Associates, 1978a: 24-25, 28, 124). During the 1970s, there was a striking alteration of historic patterns of metropolitan growth, as many of the nation's largest metropolitan areas, as a whole, began to lose population. In older central cities, rapid losses occurred. Between 1970 and 1976, for example, Cleveland lost 17 percent of its population, as did St. Louis (both cities had major school cases pending but not decided). Atlanta, Pittsburgh, Hartford, Buffalo, Newark, and Rochester all lost more than one-tenth of their people in 6 years.

The 1980 census showed dramatic changes in many cities. Chicago, which had almost two-thirds white residents in 1970, had less than half in 1980. New York City lost 10 percent of its population during the 1970s and about 30 percent of its white residents. Los Angeles became a city of minorities as the white population plummeted and the Hispanic totals skyrocketed. Los Angeles County as a whole, which includes the city and a great many suburbs — a total of 7.5 million residents, was changing very rapidly and had only 53 percent non-Hispanic whites (Anglos).[10] Although Atlanta has often been described as the most economically buoyant of the large southern cities, its statistics are similar. The city white population fell 102,625, while black residents increased by 27, 861. The Atlanta data showed that whites in the city had fewer children than those elsewhere in the metropolitan area and the Atlanta *Constitution* (April 13, 1981) reported a "flight from the city of families with children."

The Harris survey (1978a) showed a large potential for future outmigration both to the suburbs and to the suddenly growing smaller cities. Similar results were found in local research. A 1978 survey of residents of the cities and suburbs in northern New Jersey, for example, predicted a continued substantial decline in local central-city population. Only 18 percent of the people said they had preferred to live in central cities, while 54 percent preferred the suburbs and 25 percent preferred rural areas. Almost half (46 percent) of the present city residents expected their cities to become worse places to live during the next five years. Their principal complaints were deteriorated physical environments, social problems, crime, and the lack of safety. The researchers predicted that within 2 years a tenth of central-city residents could be expected to leave for the suburbs and 6 percent more to leave the state of New

Jersey. Of the existing suburbanites, less than 1 percent could be expected to move into a central city.

Although relatively few people said that they were leaving the cities mainly because of the schools, implications for the schools were very serious. The drastically falling birthrate meant, first of all, that enrollment was falling sharply nationwide. When this was added to the special problems of outmigration from the central cities and the aging of the white population in the older urban communities, the predictable losses were very large.

We are now in the midst of one of the most dramatic population changes in the history of American education. Administrators who had to cope early in their careers with the massive influx of millions of children from the post-World War II baby boom now find themselves in the midst of nasty battles over closing some of the schools constructed in the 1950s. The National Center for Educational Statistics summarized the facts in a 1978 report:

> Enrollments in regular elementary and secondary schools increased from 33.9 million in 1954 to a peak of 51.3 million in 1970. . . . Since then, enrollments have decreased to 49.3 million (1976) and are expected to decrease further to 44.5 million in 1983 and 1984. . . . These . . . decreases reflect the sharp decreases in the number of births since 1960 — from 4.3 million in 1960 to 3.2 million in 1976 [Frankel, 1978: 8].

In the 15 years after the 1954 *Brown* decision, the public schools gained more than 10 million elementary students, peaking at almost 37 million in 1969. During the next 7 years, however, the elementary enrollments fell 3.2 million and the experts predicted they would fall 2.4 million more by 1983, before beginning a gradual rise. Thus, during the early 1980s there will be an excess capacity of more than 5 million students in elementary grades. In the high schools, enrollment reached its peak in 1976 and was expected to decline steadily through 1986, a net decline of almost 16 percent (Frankel, 1978).

The declines are far more dramatic in many central city and suburban school districts because of the continued outmigration of young families, the rapidly rising number of unmarried and childless adults in central cities, and the aging of the population past childbearing age in many older urban and suburban communities. The skyrocketing cost of housing in many desirable suburban and central-city white areas also makes it increasingly difficult for families at early career stages with elementary age children to live there.

GENTRIFICATION AND THE CONDOMINIUM MOVEMENT

During the past several years there has been widespread attention given to the revival of American central cities through the renovation of older housing by young professional couples and, more recently, through the transfer of rental housing to higher status residencey by removing it from the rental market, upgrading the housing, and selling the units as condominiums. These discussions have earlier roots in the efforts of cities to replace slums with high-status apartments as part of their urban renewal programs of the fifties and sixties.

Although realtors have hailed the trends as the salvation of the cities and some minority group leaders have assailed them as a scheme to push poor minority families out of desirable urban locations, recent studies by HUD and the Bureau of the Census suggest that it is still a relatively modest movement, not nearly strong enough to counterbalance the continuing force of suburbanization, much less begin to significantly increase the central-city white population. A study of ten major cities for HUD (1979a) concluded in 1978 that there was a significant relative increase of the white population in only one city, Los Angeles. On closer examination it became apparant that this result grew out of a decision to count the rapidly growing Hispanic population as whites. Actually, the Hispanic and Asian populations in Los Angeles are growing rapidly but local demographic and school statistics show a continued sharp decline in the white proportion (Dembart, 1981).

An August 1979 analysis by Census Bureau expert Daphne Spain (1979) concluded that there are relatively few signs of a movement against the grain of the ghettoization process. In a study comparing the late 1960s to the mid-1970s by drawing data from the Bureau's Annual Housing Survey, she shows that the transfer of housing units from blacks to whites has risen only from 1.3 percent of total sales to 2.9 percent, still an extremely small part of the total market. In each period more than 5 percent of the sales were in the traditional pattern of change from white to black ownership. Thus, on the average, central cities had a modestly *higher* percentage of black-occupied residences each year, even in the 1973-1976 period. This trend continues even though there is now no net black immigration from the South. Only two things in the national statistics suggested that gentrificaiton was beginning to take hold. First, while the number of black-to-white transfers remained small, it was increasing. Second, in contrast to the normal filter-down transfer of housing from blacks to whites of lower status, which was observed in the

1967-1971 period, the more recent white purchasers had higher incomes and education levels than the black sellers.

Analysis of the 1960 and 1970 censuses showed that during the 10-year period more than 95 percent of U.S. housing units remained in the hands of the same racial group. There had been .5 percent black-to-white transfers and 3.7 percent white-to-black. In other words, transition in the ghettoization direction was more than 7 times as rapid as the opposite tendency. Between the 1967-1971 period and the 1973-1976 period, same-race sales declined from 90 percent to 86 percent in the central cities and from 96 percent to 92 percent in the suburbs (Spain, 1979). When HUD was directed by Congress to study gentrification, it reported in February 1979 that there was a low level of displacement involving only about 4 percent of the people who moved each year. The "in-movers tend to be young white professionals, single or with small families and with sufficient income to overcome neighborhood deficiencies in schools, security, recreation and shopping." Research on 18 large cities reported that typically fewer than 200 households were being displaced a year and that far more poor families were forced to move as a result of property owners abandoning or refusing to maintain their property than were pushed out by middle-class families (Reinhold, 1979; Washington Post, February 14, 1979: A2).

Gentrification is much more visible in some cities, particularly in Washington, D.C. Jacob (1979) of the National Urban League, reports that the capital's population is falling so rapidly that it will be smaller than 3 of its suburban counties in 16 years and it will probably be significantly whiter. "For the first time in a quarter century," he reported, "the number of whites moving into the District increased . . . while white flight tapered off." As the city's white population was stabilizing and beginning to climb, black suburbanization continued. "From 1970 to 1975," Jacob concluded, "53,000 blacks left D.C. for the deteriorating suburbs." The Urban League's survey of 9 areas under rehabilitation found that at least a third of the residents were being forced to move out, "most of them low-income renters forced out by rent increases, evictions and urban renewal." The newcomers were not using public schools.

The 1980 census showed, however, that claims of an imminent white takeover of central cities had been drastically overstated. The population distribution in Washington, D.C., remained stable from 1970 to 1980, approximately 70 percent black. Both blacks and whites were leaving the city at about the same rate as the city population dropped. Only two of the city's wards showed small increases in the percentage of white population (Washington Post, February 2, 1981, and February 22,

1981). Even in a city with an extremely active gentrification movement, in other words, the impacts on overall population trends were small and the substantial effects were felt in only a few neighborhoods. The white rise there was counterbalanced by white declines in other parts of the city.

The condominium movement can have the same impact in the rental housing market that the restoration movement has in the single-family home communities. It often does not result in the direct displacement of blacks or Hispanics, but it does shrink the rental housing market, producing increased competition and rising prices for the remaining units, and it raises the socioeconomic level of communities. So far, the most dramatic impacts of the change have been limited to sections of a few cities, most recently Chicago, which is undergoing a period known as "condomania." By the beginning of 1979 more than 30,000 units had been converted in the city, most of them in two North Side communities near Lake Michigan. One parochial school in the area reflected the changes when it reported that it had lost nearly a third of its largely Hispanic student body in a single year as the neighborhood upgraded. Some Hispanic families reported that they had been forced to move repeatedly, ending up on the western end of the city. Gail Cincotta, leader of the neighborhood-based Metropolitan Area Housing Alliance denounced the process: "The real estate speculators who are driving up property values and pushing the poor out of the city are the same type of people who disrupted neighborhoods 10 years ago with panic-peddling and blockbusting" (Page and Anderson, 1979). Chicago public schools, however, were still rapidly losing white students (*Chicago Tribune,* December 20, 1980).[11]

Both developments have important implications for public schools, because they tend to speed the depopulation of urban schools in the affected neighborhoods, as will the rapidly spreading practice of excluding children from large proportions of rental housing in white areas in some cities. The white inmigration is primarily young and childless. Renovated neighborhoods are frequently stopping points on the way to the suburbs for families with children, and there is a strong white suburbanization of families in their thirties (Long, 1975). The condominium movement often puts costs of former rental units far beyond the reach of young families — how many families with elementary school children can afford $100,000 plus high carrying charges for a three-bedroom apartment? Both the shrinkage of the rental market in the white areas and the discrimination against children in the units that remain available diminish the capacity of white families to live in the city and use the city schools. (There has been very little conversion of rental housing to condominiums in ghettos or barrios to date.) Most ghettos are now experiencing declines in population density. Continued outmigration of the more successful families and the lack of any white demand means relatively less demand within the old ghetto areas and less rapidly inflating prices and rentals within ghetto boundaries.

Obviously, there is a risk that the gentrification movement, if it becomes a serious force in more cities, may have many of the bad consequences of the urban renewal process, without even the saving grace of government relocation processes. The possibilities for integration through the return of whites may be lost through the displacement of the minority families who are equally necessary for integration. Similarly, the opportunity for increased school integration may be, and usually is, lost through the failure of the white newcomers to use the public schools. If the integrationist possibilities of this situation are to be realized, there must be conscious housing policies, particularly the location of scattered site subsidized housing in renovating neighborhoods, and positive policies to integrate the schools and make them attractive to the new professionals. San Francisco, Denver, Providence, and other cities already have small programs intended to permit some poor existing residents to stay and improve their homes. A larger effort with national support is needed (Reece, 1979).

GHETTOIZATION

The relatively small white return to big cities attracts a great deal of hopeful national attention, but it is still dwarfed by the continuing force of the ghettoization process. This process, since it effects relatively less affluent whites and is triggered by the search of young minority families for better homes and neighborhoods, has a much more immediate impact on the public schools. In Chicago, for example, the Chicago Urban League (1978) estimates that more than a thousand blocks began or compelted racial transition from 1970 to 1977. Year-by-year school enrollment statistics from the suburbs show that there are 9 separate areas in the suburbs now in relatively rapid racial transition, including communities as much as 30 miles from the Chicago loop.

The classic pattern of black ghettoization has been extensively documented in many cities since the 1920s. There is a cycle of white resistance, initial entry of blacks into an area on the edge of an existing ghetto or in a vulnerable community further out, panic peddling, sometimes racial violence, steering of minority families toward and white families away from a community, rapid transition of the local school population, and eventual incorporation into an expanding ghetto or barrio where only a declining number of aging whites remain. Urban geographers Sanders and Adams described the basic pattern in the 1976 book, *Black America: Geographic Perspectives:*

> Substantial structual changes take place not only at the edges of the ghetto, where territorial expansion is apparent, but also at the core of the established ghetto. Occasional leaps into noncontiguous areas of the inner city characterize ghetto territorial expansion, with simultaneous if less than spectacular accretions at the edge of the ghetto. This basic growth process forms cores of old age structure surrounded by "rims" of young population both within the main body of the ghetto and in the outlying areas of black residence. . . .
>
> 1. The ghetto begins to expand in contiguous fashion.
>
> 2. Noncontiguous ghetto "outliers" are established, and population numbers at the center of the ghetto fall.
>
> 3. Coalescence between the outlying areas and the main body of the ghetto follows. Further population depletions occur at the core of the ghetto and at the center of the "outliers" established in Stage 2. Ghetto contiguity is re-established.
>
> 4. . . . New "outliers" are formed and the process begins again [Sanders and Adams, 1976: 111-112].

These patterns are so deeply ingrained in the practices of the real estate industry and the expectations of the public that when the first black families enter a community near a ghetto, it is often widely assumed that it is only a matter of time before the community will become all black. The pattern is less dramatic for Hispanics, but, particularly for low-income Hispanics in the large cities, there is a tendency in the same direction.[12]

The cycle of change poses a fundamental problem for poor white areas near ghettos. A recent study of resistant neighborhoods in southwest Chicago documents the problem. The white residents in these neighborhoods perceived both a threat of violent racial tension and a real danger of losing their homes and neighborhoods:

> The heart of the Southwest Side is all white. But black families are beginning to move into blocks along the eastern edge. As this happens, white families move further west. It is not unusual to find white families that have moved two or three times to "escape" racial change. In the border areas where change is occuring, racial clashes flare up periodically. Black families . . . have been met with violence in the form of fire bombings and rock-throwing. Many white families, too, live with fear . . . for the safety of their children and their old people on once familiar streets [McCourt, 1977: 33].

The neighborhood groups attempted to control real estate through transactions through a housing referral service operated by the block clubs (McCourt, 1977). The service tried to counter what it saw as the realtors' practices of selling "almost exclusively to black families." The effort failed.

Between 1967 and 1972 the racial change was led by the local elementary schools, which went from an average of 10 percent black to an average of 80 percent black. The block groups defined the situation in the schools as a critical issue and the block clubs association presented demands to the Chicago Board of Education year after year for actions to redraw boundaries to prevent resegregation. The strategies included "presenting personal pleas to the Board at its monthly meetings, filing lawsuits, picketing the schools, and lying down in front of construction equipment which was being used to set up mobile classrooms." Local residents said that no one would act because of a self-fulfilling prophecy: "Everyone 'knows' that this community will soon be all black, so no one takes any action to prevent this from happening and then, in a few years, the area is all black" (McCourt, 1977: 41-42).

> Everyone on the Southwest Side faces . . . the possibility of moving.
> . . . The insecurity is due to uncertainty. . . . Residents of the
> neighborhood bordering on the black community know they will be
> leaving soon; those in the central area feel they will have to leave in
> three to five years; and even those living in the neighborhoods farthest
> west suspect that the South Side will be all black to its western bound-
> ary in ten years [McCourt, 1977: 57-58].

The people in the Southwest Side strongly felt that they were being singled out because of their lack of wealth and political power to bear a burden other communities would not share. Frequently the opponents of public housing for blacks in the Southwest Side, for example, argued that the only fair way to deal with the problem would be if "the public housing units were built throughout the city and the suburbs and not concentrated in working-class neighborhoods" (McCourt, 1977: 204).

An elaborate 1971 study of working-class white neighborhoods just outside Washington, D.C., boundaries showed the impact of a rapid outward black migration on white attitudes as transition approached. A year-long study by a resident observer concluded:

> It did appear that the residents were concerned about blacks competing
> for their jobs; about blacks moving into their neighborhoods; with
> safety on the streets and the muggings and robberies they associated
> with slums and lower income blacks; about their children being bused

to school in black neighborhoods; and about another possible "riot" as occurred in Washington in 1968. . . . Even more they resented the white people who were initiating social change and yet were unwilling to submit themselves to that change. In short, they felt that some upper-class whites were using working people as pawns for experiments in social change from which the working people had much to lose and little to gain [Zehner and Chapin, 1974].

The blacks and Hispanics who were coming were usually looking for things the whites feared losing. In a national survey, 52 percent of blacks and 50 percent of Hispanics said that the large city schools were the worst. More than a third of each group said that the suburbs had the best schools in the United States. Only one-fifth of the blacks, one-sixth of the Hispanics, and one-sixteenth of the whites felt that the friendliest people were in the big cities. Approximately one-fourth of each racial group said that they would consider moving if the schools became worse in the near future (Louis Harris and Associates, 1978b). If blacks or Hispanics moved, however, they triggered a cycle of expectations that produced a new ghetto or barrio. They had few real choices.

The ghettoization process does not usually trigger immediate flight of all whites from a neighborhood. Some communities experience a full-scale panic and a dramatically rapid change, but this pattern is rarely seen today. Sensitive research in Cleveland and in part of Chicago suggests that transition comes not from flight but from the inability of a neighborhood to continue to attract white families. In the United States the typical family moves every six years; the rate is more rapid in many cities. This means that if a neighborhood is to stabilize as an integrated community it must continually bring in new white, as well as minority, buyers and renters (Molotch, 1969; Guest and Zuiches, 1971).

Some research has suggested that whites stopped looking as soon as there was a significant minority population (Dudley, 1957). Recent studies by Schnare (1980) and Becker (1979) found a more complex pattern. Apparently a significant number of whites continue to move into integrated neighborhoods until the transition is well advanced. The basic problem is that minority families move in faster, thus gradually making the community more and more heavily minoirity, until virtually all whites stop considering it as a possible place to live. Becker (1979: 9) found that even in neighborhoods which were half black or Hispanic, one-third of the people moving in were white. Of course, as time passes, such a neighborhood will become increasingly minority, steadily attracting less whites until ghettoization occurs.

Becker (1979) reports that about one-fifth of the integrated communities had enough white inmigration to stabilize. Some of his findings suggest that the reason others did not stabilize was related to the schools. He found that 64 percent of the middle-class white families with school-age children who moved into these communities used public schools, in contrast to 80 percent in white areas, but that fewer families moved in and they were much more likely to rent than buy, avoiding long-term commitments. The most stable integrated neighborhoods were those with a good deal of housing for singles and groups other than families and areas with relatively high housing costs (Becker, 1979: 21-23). In other words, neighborhoods which had more of the characteristics of the gentrifying areas and less those of the normal communities had a better chance of achieving stability. Often integration was for adults only.

A basic problem in areas undergoing racial change is that the schools change much faster than the residential pattern of a neighborhood. Changing neighborhoods generally have older white families with relatively few children in school, but they attract young successful minority families with school-age children. In any case, minority families normally send a higher proportion of their children to public as opposed to parochial or private schools. This means that a 25 percent black neighborhood can easily have a 50 percent black school. Although many whites say they would accept a 50 percent black neighborhood, very few desire to enroll their children in an overwhelmingly black school, yet this is what they normally encounter in a community equally divided residentially.[13] Studies of community organizations working to stabilize family-oriented areas of racial change often show an intense focus on efforts to maintain stable integration and high quality in the local schools (Goodwin, 1979).

Ghettoization of the schools. Elementary schools are frequently key institutions in defining neighborhoods, but they are also the first institutions to pass through drastic racial transition. A 1978 study by Gifford of all of the public schools in Los Angeles found not one school in the city which had a substantial enrollment of both blacks and whites and which stabilized. All became virtually all-minority. The study found only a handful of relatively stable white-Hispanic schools in the vast city. The overwhelmingly dominant pattern was toward educational ghettoization. Normally the process was completed within a period of six years from its beginning.

A recent analysis of real estate marketing in fourteen metropolitan areas by Pearce (1980), of Catholic University, has shown that the nature of the desegregation plan in an area affects the way in which its housing is marketed. Her study of real estate ads and comments of brokers showed that in areas with metropolitan-wide school plans, plans which made all schools approximately similar in racial composition across the housing market, there was little mention of schools in real estate marketing. In other communities of the same size with desegregation plans limited to central cities or no significant desegregation efforts, schools were frequently mentioned and whites were steered away from areas of minority or integrated schools. References to schools by name in real estate ads virtually always referred to white schools.

Hispanic educational ghettoization. Though Hispanics encounter severe residential segregation in some cities, on the average they are significantly less segregated than blacks. In recent years segregation has seldom been a major issue in the Hispanic community except during desegregation cases, often brought by local blacks. For this reason, there has been little serious analysis of increasing evidence of spreading educational ghettoization in large city systems.

Change has been taking place very rapidly in the seventies and the contemporary Hispanic child today faces more separation from white culture and white children than in the past. In Houston, to cite one example, there were only 3 schools that were more than 90 percent Hispanic in 1970 (Houston Independent School District, 1979); 8 years later there were 11, covering a substantial fraction of the city.

Hispanic children today face a kind of isolation more characteristic of black children than Hispanic children in the past. In 1965 the average Mexican-American child was in an elementary school with more than half whites and a high school with three-fourths whites (Carter and Segura, 1979: 136). During the 1970s there was a steady drift toward more segregation in many central city school districts receiving increasing Hispanic migration. In Los Angeles, for example, the typical Hispanic student in the nation's largest Hispanic settlement in 1966 was in a school with 54 percent Hispanic children, 32 percent Anglo children, and 13 percent black and Asian children. By 1977 the school, on the average, had 64 percent Hispanics, 15 percent blacks and Asians, and only 20 percent Anglos (Farley, 1978). In Chicago, the principal locus of midwestern Hispanic settlement, the typical Hispanic child in 1967 was in a school that was one-half white children (50.1 percent) and only one-third Hispanic children (33.8 percent). In 1977, this child attended a school that had an average of 25.8 percent Anglos, 58.6 percent Hispanics, and 15.7 percent other minorities (Technical Assistance Committee on the Chicago Desegregation Plan, 1978: Table 5).

The trend toward gradually increasing segregation nationally was apparent early in a U.S. Commission on Civil Rights study (1971), which showed the number of Mexican-American children in predominantly minority schools rising from 54 percent in 1968 to 56 percent in 1972.

Statistics released by HEW in 1976 showed that the proportion of Hispanic children in segregated schools had risen slowly during the 1970s, while black segregation fell, and that slightly more Hispanics than blacks were in predominantly minority schools by 1974 (Center for National Policy Review, 1977). A 1979 report by Taeuber and Wilson contains data indicating that there has been no significant progress in desegrating Hispanic children in the 1970s, particularly in the large cities. It shows that even in districts with desegregation plans that reduced the racial isolation of blacks there was little impact on Hispanic segregation, with few exceptions.

If Gifford's data on Los Angeles is characteristic of the other major cities, it is apparent that a process of ghettoization with strong parallels with the black experience is emerging in urban centers. There are also an increasing number of urban schools with enrollments of both blacks and Hispanics, raising issues of integration between two minority groups, or triethic integration. Little research has been produced on these important trends, which deserve prompt and careful analysis.

MITIGATING TRENDS:
THE POSSIBILITIES OF FAIR HOUSING AND BLACK
SUBURBANIZATION

Social trends are seldom eternal. At some point declining birthrates level out and begin to rise. At some point, perhaps, the dynamic of housing and school ghettoization may be modified and a trend toward natural integration of schools and housing may develop. Some critics of civil rights policies claim that point has already arrived, that race has become a far less serious barrier to opportunity, and that civil rights policy makers are only making things worse by failing to recognize this healthy trend and insisting upon unnecessarily harsh policies which simple produce racial polarization.

The two principal hopes of those who believe natural integration is spreading are that the fair housing laws are beginning to take hold in the housing market and that the statistics on rapidly increasing black suburbanization represent a decisive breakthrough. Before considering drastic policies it is only logical to examine the available evidence on these points.

The federal fair housing law, and a powerful Supreme Court decision on fair housing, has now been the law of the land for thirteen years. Even before passage of the federal law, the majority of the nation's housing units were covered by state or local laws forbidding discrimination. The National Association of Realtors and other major industry organizations have adopted national policies supporting fair housing. Survey research shows that most white Americans believe that housing discrimination is a thing of the past.[14]

Unquestionably the law has made some difference. Open, blatant discrimination is far less common than in the past and there are many fewer communities that are totally white. A well-informed minority family that is sophisticated about housing practices, knows its rights, knows where to file a complaint, and has a long time to wait for the house or apartment has a good chance of obtaining housing. There are few such families. It is much more difficult today to defend the border of a white area adjoining a ghetto because most of the practices used earlier are illegal.

The overall record, however, offers little hope for significant residential integration. during the 1960s residential segregation levels actually increased on a metropolitan level (Schnare, 1980). In many cities almost 90 percent of the black households would have had to move to achieve a random population distribution, while few would have had to move to achieve complete racial separation (Municipal Performance Report, 1973). Even the impression of modest progress may have been due to the more rapid racial transition under way in central cities when the 1970 census was taken. (The standard measure — the dissimilarity index — is based simply on the racial composition of a city's census tracts at one point in time. Thus either a spread of stable integration or transition in broader range of communities may produce the same statistic. Calculations done on a metropolitan level suggest that overall segregation in the total urban housing market may well have increased during the sixties.)

It will not be possible, of course, to accurately measure all of the changes of the past decade until the detailed results of the 1980 census are available and analyzed. Probably the best available data, and the only source that offers year-to-year changes, are school enrollment statistics. These figures have many problems, since they exclude the majority of households who do not have school-age children as well as the tenth of students enrolled in private schools. They are, however, very relevant data for public school desegregation planners, and probably offer a reasonable reflection of the behavior of families with young children in those systems which have not implemented desegregation plans, or report the distribution of children by attendance area of residence as well as current school assignments. This means, of course, that it is possible to obtain some indication of trends in residential segregation of families by examining the trends in yearly desegregation indices of students within school districts. Recent studies of these trends show very little positive change during the 1970s in the Chicago and Los

Angeles metropolitan areas. They also show a continuing spread of virtually all-black schools and a consolidation of virtually all-Hispanic schools at the core of the barrios. The figures do show small gains in black residence in many areas and a good deal of dispersal of Hispanics in the suburbs (Farley, 1978).

Direct evaluations of fair housing programs have shown the enforcement programs to be weak and ineffective and have revealed strong continuing patterns of somewhat more subtle discrimination in housing. HUD itself has conceded the failure and Congress rejected new legislation providing enforcement power in 1980. A national effort to test the real estate market with 300 pairs of testers working in many parts of the country led to a July 1979 report which said that the typical black family attempting to buy a home could expect to encounter at least one instance of discrimination in 48 percent of the cases (HUD, 1979b). The level of discrimination for rental housing was reported to be higher. These levels were found in spite of the fact that the research did not attempt to evaluate discrimination in the form of racial steering or in often crucial matters of financing and mortgage terms. In mid-1976 a black New York *Times* reporter summarized the results of testing 22 brokers and management companies representing big landlords in Manhattan with the help of expert white testers:

> The black reporter encountered a variety of obstacles in both viewing and renting apartments, including being told apartments were not available when in fact they were, being quoted a much higher rental price than that for the white applicant and being subjected to more rigorous financial and business scrutiny than the white applicant. . . . There were no instances in which the black reporter received a set of apartment referrals identical to the white applicant, although in some cases the reporter indicated he was willing to pay much more in rent [Sheppard, 1976: 1].

There are numerous similar reports of local investigations.

The federal law was based on a serious misunderstanding of both the nature and depth of housing discrimination and the processes of ghettoization. Discrimination was conceived basically as a problem of individuals, individuals who faced relatively overt provable discrimination in attempting to buy or rent housing. The law assumed that investigations and conciliation by a small HUD staff could handle the problem, with the Justice Department on call to bring lawsuits in particularly difficult cases. Few resources were provided to enforce the law, less than two investigators per state, and the Justice Department completed less than two dozen cases per year nationwide in the first eight years of enforcement (Orfield, 1977). Each case consumed a great deal of time.

Even if housing discrimination were to disappear today, there would be powerful ongoing effects of the history of discrimination on both minority and white families. Minority families, for instance, often have limited knowledge of the housing market outside nearby neighborhoods and seldom desire to be the first nonwhite family in a neighborhood. Fears of violence, tension, and social isolation do not go away easily. Black families, according to several polls, tend to prefer integrated communities with substantial black populations. White families who say that they would accept residential integration without any objection tend to perceive a substantial black population not as a sign of stable integration but as a sign of impending transition (Farley et al., 1978). These expectations and self-fulfilling prophecies would tend to perpetuate a good deal of segregation even if overt resistance faded.

Unfortunately, overt resistance and even violence are not fading. A widely publicized series of more than 15 cross burnings and other incidents of violence and intimidation in suburban Long Island in 1979 were reminiscent of problems in many cities stretching back to the earliest days of ghetto formation (Feron, 1979). It does not require any complex research to imagine the impact on black parents with young children of firebombings and KKK activity against housing integration.

Even if families were welcome to move, the consequences past discrimination have a continuing impact on their ability to pay for housing today. If housing discrimination forced a family to remain in the rental market or buy a home in a deteriorating area, that family now faces vastly higher costs without the vastly increased equity that most white suburban families enjoy. Until 1972 housing purchase and rental prices rose less rapidly than average family income, and inflation was modest. After 1972, however, extremely rapid increases in housing purchase and operating costs began. During the next 4 years the average new home increased an average of 12.5 percent a year, operating costs rose 12 percent a year, and mortgage interest rates reached levels without precedent. The needed down payment skyrocketed and typical monthly payments rose 80 percent from 1972 to 1976 (Mayer, 1977). Inflation of housing costs was much worse in some of the largest metropolitan areas, particularly Los Angeles, San Francisco, and Washington, D.C. Inflation of this sort is a distribution of wealth to those who already own desirable property and a very large barrier to those who do not.

Suburbanization of minority families took place at a record rate in the 1970s. A 1979 study for HUD based on Annual Housing Surveys from

1974-1976 shows that "after 1970 black migration came to resemble white in being effectively directed toward the suburbs." The data also showed, however, that "black access to the suburbs remains less than white, and even suburban blacks are relatively constrained in moving to other suburban residences" (Nelson, 1979: 13). The large majority of metropolitan areas studied showed a net outward movement of blacks in the mid-1970s and there were particularly dramatic jumps in Washington, Baltimore, and Atlanta — cities with ghetto school systems. The black middle-class is leaving poor black cities and their schools.

During the 1960s suburbia was often described as an almost homogeneous area of virtually all-white occupancy which was a noose threatening to cut off opportunity to those trapped in the central city. Close students of suburbs, especially the early students of black suburbs, have always known this was a serious oversimplification. Research on black suburbanization during the sixties showed that a great deal of it was not a move toward integration, but expansion of traditional poor black settlements, extension of a growing ghetto into the suburbs, or the formation of a small new ghetto (Farley, 1970). Some of the black and Hispanic suburbanization of the seventies has clearly been of this character and is reflected in dramatically changing school enrollment figures. In Los Angeles the Watts ghetto has extended into suburbs to the south, and the East Los Angeles barrio has extended into eastern suburbs. The ghetto in northeast Washington has now extended far into Prince George's County, Maryland, and the largest suburban school district in the United States is experiencing rapid racial change. New York City ghetto patterns are affecting significant areas in the Long Island suburbs. In Chicago both the West and South Side ghettos now extend well into the suburbs: There is a set of suburban school districts with virtually all-black enrollment and nine other districts which are experiencing rapid racial change. One of the West Side suburbs is changing approximately a half percent a month in its public school enrollment (Davis, 1980). There are major efforts, particularly in the inner suburbs of Chicago and Cleveland, to attempt to stabilize some integrated communities before they are incorporated in the traditional ghettoization process. As minority migration to the suburbs continues this will be a central policy question.

HOUSING EFFECTS OF
SCHOOL DESEGREGATION APPROACHES

During the years since James Coleman's 1975 paper ignited a scholarly debate on the impact of urban desegregation plans on the decline in white enrollment, dozens of papers have appeared exploring the thesis that school desegregation produces substantial white flight. Both scholars whose personal values strongly support court-ordered desegregation and those who strongly oppose it have developed analytic techniques and examined the data. A number of leading researchers have been called into court to provide evidence on this issue. Judges who face recognized social scientists using the same sets of data to support radically different policies may be excused for wondering whether social science has anything to say about this important question.

Beneath the storm of controversy, however, a surprising agreement has emerged on some of the most important questions in the white flight debate. Virtually all of the major researchers now agree that implementation of a major desegregation plan in a central city with a high minority enrollment and surrounding white suburbs not included in the plan produces an accelerated white withdrawal from public schools. There is consensus that the acceleration occurs at least in the first year and the research results are sufficiently convergent that Farley (1978) was able to predict the results of the 1978 Los Angeles plan to the local court with remarkable accuracy.

There is a research consensus as well that the least white flight has been observed in urban school districts with full metropolitan desegregation plans, plans which put all children in predominantly white schools and leave no readily accessible all-white school districts to which to flee. Researchers differ widely in their personal attitudes toward metropolitan plans, but this finding is remarkably consistent.[15]

On other issues there is less consensus. Accumulating evidence suggests that the loss is accelerated considerably among white children transferred to schools in ghetto or barrio neighborhoods in big cities. There is heated disagreement on the question of long-term effects of desegregation plans. There is agreement, however, that most central cities will have few white students in the future, whether or not a desegregation plan doubles the loss rate for a year or two. There is some evidence that metropolitan plans will remove the concern of school ghettoization as a force in neighborhood transition and as a restraint on the inmigration of whites to renovating areas, thus easing the task of maintaining genuine residential integration. Other researchers argue that much of the flight is not actually flight from desegregation but from the kind of urban deterioration so evident in the surveys of current attitudes toward the cities (Louis Harris and Associates, 1978b).

Much work remains to be done. On the key issue, however, the evidence is relatively simple and clear. Plans limited to central cities will at least temporarily speed up to loss of white students. Plans incorporating the metropolitan area will hold students much more effectively.

PRINCIPLES FOR DESEGREGATION IN LARGE CITIES

The nation's largest cities are caught up in a spiral of spreading ghettoization and high and unyielding levels of segregation. The dynamic of racial change, with its powerful expectations, fears, and self-fulfilling prophecies, is still very powerful. It is essential that the judges and policy makers who participate in decisions which will be of great importance to hundreds of thousands of segregated children and to the future social and educational patterns of huge urban communities understand the long-term trends and underlying social forces that produce and sustain the spread of segregation.

Good basic information and understanding of the social forces at work cannot, of course, guarantee effective decisions. It can, however, make obvious the futility of some courses of action and put the judicially imposed changes in a context of ongoing social change. Anyone who travels from city to city studying or working on desegregation plans is struck by the common lack of any perspective on long-term local racial trends and any understanding of the experiences of other cities. For most of the critical decision makers, including the judge, local school administrators, local politicians, and the local media, the school case is a once-in-a-lifetime experience. It is extraordinarily complex, agonizingly protracted, and extremely tense, with great pressures brought to bear on all major participants. Controversy is inevitable, but there are a number of steps that may be useful in improving the quality of the decisions that are made.

Local trend data. All decision makers and the public should be provided with basic statistical information on school and housing segregation trends, both in the city and the metropolitan area. This data, which should be produced without attached policy recommendations, should include yearly desegregation indices for each minority group in the schools for at least a decade into the past and yearly statistics on the composition of the typical school attended by local black and Hispanic children. The location of overcrowding, double session, excess class space, and substitute teachers should be reported by school, with the school's racial composition. Local statistics should be examined for evidence of stably integrated school communities to be accorded special treatment in the plan and for an understanding of the typical resegregation cycles. Housing segregation statistics for the last three censuses and from any other special census or local survey should be presented both for the city and the metropolitan area.

Projections of the data presented would be the next useful step. Many discussions of desegregation plans are carried out on the assumption that enrollment will remain as it is the day of the court order (or the day the final briefs are filed). In a situation of long-term declining enrollments and spreading segregation it is surely best to begin planning with an expectation that these trends will continue (and perhaps temporarily accelerate). The projections will also have the benefit of separating the long-term forces from the separate impacts of the desegregation plan itself, speaking to a very common local problem in interpreting the first year of the desegregation process.

There are useful models of presentation of basic data to the courts in the reports of court-appointed experts Farley (1978) and Gifford (1978) in the Los Angeles school desegregation case. Both of those reports are primarily informational, setting a framework for policy decisions, and the statistics are cited by various parties advocating very different policies.

Courts and responsible officials should embrace the commonsense principle of "no further harm," prohibiting future housing decisions that will worsen school segregation and school desegregation plans that will destabilize existing integrated neighborhoods or feed the transition process just outside the existing racial boundary lines. This will require mapping of existing and past patterns of racial concentration in the schools and use of these maps to study the consequences of housing decisions for school racial composition.

Housing developers could be provided with maps showing where subsidized projects would be prohibited and where they would be given top priority. Stably integrated areas should be designated and guaranteed exemption from any busing out, a move that would create an incentive for the continued inmigration of families of both races that is essential to long-term stability.[16] Housing officials should be encouraged to aid communities that would be interested in subsidized housing or a major drive to increase residential integration; school officials and the courts should offer communities that succeed a guarantee of exemption from busing out.

Policy makers should adopt the position that inevitable changes should be examined carefully so that they are implemented in a way that aids the desegregation process. Every city and the great majority of suburbs face school closing decisions forced by the high cost of operating half-empty facilities with high fixed costs. These decisions and the resulting extensive redrawing of attendance boundaries should be integrated with desegregation planning and officials should be required to choose the course of action most likely to produce increased school integration. When facilities are closed and the sites become available, school and housing officials should be required to review the sites as possible locations for subsidized housing which would aid desegregation.

Supporting national policies would require HUD to consider the school segregation implications of its housing grants and to collect and publish racial statistics on its programs by metropolitan area. There is substantial evidence that some HUD programs are still being operated in ways that increase the burden on the schools.[17]

An urgent research priority for development of big city plans is a better understanding of triethnic desegregation. Substantial integration between blacks and Hispanics is taking place in some cities now and triethnic desegregation plans have been proposed. There is almost no well-developed research on the question of the relative value of this approach or the best way to carry it out.

The ultimate problem in the big cities, of course, is the fact that full desegregation is already impossible within city boundaries and that plans limited to the cities may increase the rate at which ghettoization of the entire city school system reaches its final end. Every possible effort must be made to involve suburban school districts in plans, efforts which include:

(1) special federal funding for voluntary metropolitan transfer plans

(2) consideration by the courts of a mandatory Wisconsin-type plan as part of a *Milliken II* order against a state government

(3) combined school and housing litigation to demonstrate the unavoidable historic and contemporary relationship between school and housing ghettoization and to produce a unified plan

(4) highest priority by private litigators, the Justice Department, and central-city school boards to obtain comprehensive metropolitan desegregation plans

A court-ordered school desegregation plan is major surgery for an urban society, something that normally happens only once in a city's history. Research cannot make this process easy or simple, but it may help to prevent decisions that will quite predictably fail. It cannot resolve fundamental legal questions about the appropriate reach of judicial power, but it can help to sort out the underlying trends in a community and focus the attention of policy makers on the basic issues essential to a successful resolution. Segregation in cities is a complex social and economic system with great power and in continual expansion. If integration policies are to counter and curb the consequences of the ghettoization process, the policy makers must first understand the facts and the long-term trends. The best surgeon cannot succeed without a careful and accurate diagnosis.

NOTES

1. For the best continuing report of developments in desegregation cases, see the regular feature, "Chronicle of Race, Sex and Schools," in *Integrated Education* magazine.

2. Cleveland and St. Louis desegregated under orders of federal courts, Los Angeles under a school board plan initially approved and then rejected by both the school board and the state courts, and Pittsburgh under state regulations. The consent order in U.S. v. Board of Education and the City of Chicago was filed on September 24, 1980, and promised the submission of a desegregation plan to the court by March 11, 1981.

3. Houston *Chronicle,* May 16, 1980. The Justice Department's effort to add 22 surrounding suburban school districts to the 24-year-old case was rejected by Federal District Judge Robert O'Connor, Jr., on June 10, 1980. The judge emphasized his interest in fostering voluntary interdistrict exchanges organized by the state education agency and left pending a motion for reconsideration (Ross and U.S. v. Houston Independent School District, 1980). Under President Reagan the Justice Department changed its position on the Houston case, leaving the appeal to private litigants.

4. Data are from annual enrollment statistics of each school district.

5. The Atlanta *Constitution* (September 25, 1979: 1) describes the action of the Fifth Circuit Court of Appeals in dismissing the case and the reaction of local officials and civil rights groups. The Supreme Court offered no explanation of its summary action in April 1980.

6. The most important witness for the Los Angeles Unified School District in the 1979-1980 trial of the Crawford case was David J. Armor of the Rand Corporation, who was employed by the school district to provide evidence and testimony on white flight and its threat to desegregation in the city. This work included a telephone survey to families in Los Angeles. It is reflected in Armor (1979a, 1979b).

7. "Petitioners' memorandum of points and authorities re definition of segregated schools," (Crawford v. Board of Education of the City of Los Angeles, 1976).

8. The reports of the eight appointed experts were filed in November 1978. Those of Robert Crain, Thomas Pettigrew, and Gary Orfield gave particular attention to the metropolitan issue. The demographic studies of Bernard Gifford and Reynold Farley showed that there was no stable natural integration and that the city would have a steadily shrinking white enrollment. The desegregation plan was rescinded as a result of action by the California Supreme Court on March 11, 1981 (Los Angeles *Times,* March 12, 1981; *School Law News,* March 27, 1981; 1-2).

9. See "Complaint and Consent Decree" filed in U.S. v. Board of Education of the City of Chicago (1980).

10. These figures are from the Chicago *Sun-Times* (April 12, 1981), the New York *Times,* (April 6, 1981), and the Los Angeles *Times* (April 6, 1981), respectively.

11. In fall 1980 the schools were 18.5 percent white, 60.8 percent black, 18.4 percent Hispanic, and 2.2 percent other.

12. One recent study of discrimination against Hispanics in the housing market was conducted by Hakken (1979). The most sensitive reflection of the rapid spread of residential segregation within some central cities is the rapid growth in the number of predominantly Latino schools.

13. The fact that new minority families are usually younger and more likely to use public schools magnifies their impact on school composition.

14. A Gallup poll (June 1980: 9) showed that 66 percent of the public said that blacks were treated the "same as whites" in their communities. A Harris survey (1978a: 5) found that only 23 percent of whites thought that blacks faced housing discrimination.

15. This finding is shared by active critics of court-ordered urban desegregation plans, including David Armor and James Coleman, and active supporters, including Thomas Pettigrew and Christine Rossell.

16. Such an exception is an explicit part of the Louisville and St. Louis court orders. A number of integrated neighborhoods were exempted at the outset of the Denver plan.

17. See Orfield and Fischer (1981), Fleisher (1979), and Orfield (1981a, 1981b).

CASES

COLUMBUS BOARD OF EDUCATION v. PENICK (1979) 99 S. Ct. 2941

CRAWFORD v. BOARD OF EDUCATION OF THE CITY OF LOS ANGELES (1976) 17 Cal. 3d 280, 130 Cal. Reporter 724

DAYTON BOARD OF EDUCATION v. BRINKMAN (1979) 99 S. Ct. 2971

MILLIKEN v. BRADLEY (1973) 488 F.2d 215 (6th Cir.)

MILLIKEN v. BRADLEY (1974) 418 U.S. 717

MILLIKEN v. BRADLEY (1975) 402 F. Supp. 1096

ROSS AND U.S. v. HOUSTON INDEPENDENT SCHOOL DISTRICT (1980) C.A. No. 10,444 (S.D. Tex.)

U.S. v. BOARD OF EDUCATION AND THE CITY OF CHICAGO (1980) C.A. No. 80 C 5124 (N.D. Ill.)

U.S. v. BOARD OF SCHOOL COMMISSIONERS OF INDIANAPOLIS (1971) 322 F. Supp. 655 (S.D. Ind.)

REFERENCES

ARMOR, D.J. (1979a) Deposition in Crawford v. Board of Education of the City of Los Angeles. October 8 and 26.

———— (1979b) Testimony in Crawford v. Board of Education of the City of Los Angeles. Reporter's daily transcript (Vols. 14-19), November.

BECKER, H.J. (1979) "Racially integrated neighborhoods: do white families move in? Which ones?" Presented at the annual meeting of the American Sociological Association, August.

BURGESS, E.W. (1972) "The growth of the city," in M. Stewart (ed.) The City: Problems of Planning. Baltimore: Penguin.

CARTER, T.P. and R.D. SEGURA (1979) Mexican Americans in Schools: A Decade of Change. New York: College Entrance Examination Board.

Center for National Policy Review. (1977) Trends in Hispanic Segregation, 1970-1974. Washington, DC: Author.

Chicago Urban League (1978) Where Blacks Live: Race and Residence in Chicago in the 1970s. Chicago: Author.

CLARK, S.D. (1966) The Suburban Society. Toronto: University of Toronto Press.

DAVIS, S.C. (1980) Letter to State Superintendent Joseph M. Cronin (Illinois) from the mayor of Bellwood, Illinois. February 11.

DEMBART, L. (1981) "L.A. now a minority city, 1980 census data shows." Los Angeles Times (April 6): 1.

DUNCAN, O. D. and B. DUNCAN (1957) The Negro Population in Chicago. Chicago: University of Chicago Press.

FARLEY, R. (1978) "A report to the Honorable Judge Paul Egly." Presented to the Superior Court, State of California, County of Los Angeles, Case No. 822-854, November 14.

———— (1970) "The changing distribution of Negroes within metropolitan areas: the emergence of black suburbs." American Journal of Sociology, 75.

————, H. SCHUMAN, S. BIANCHI, and D. COLASANTO (1978) "Chocolate city, vanilla suburbs: will the trend toward racially separate communities continue?" Social Science Research 7: 319-344.

FERON, J. (1979) "Incidents near city portend racial tension for 80's." New York Times (December 3): 1.

FLEISHER, R. (1979) "Subsidized housing and residential segregation in American cities: an evaluation of the site selection and occupancy of federally subsidized housing." Ph.D. dissertation, University of Illinois.

FRANKEL, M. M. (1978) Projections of Educational Statistics to 1986-87. Washington, DC: National Center for Educational Statistics.

GANS, H. J. (1967) The Levittowners: Ways of Life and Politics in a New Suburban Community. New York: Vintage.

GIFFORD, B. R. (1978) "A report to the Honorable Judge Paul Egly." Presented to the Superior Court, State of California, County of Los Angeles, Case No. 822-854, November 14.

GOODWIN, D. (1979) The Oak Park Strategy: Community Control of Racial Change. Chicago: University of Chicago Press.

GUEST, A. M. and J. J. ZUICHES (1971) "Another look at residential turnover in urban neighborhoods." American Journal of Sociology 77: 457-467.

HADDEN, S. G. et al. (1979) Consensus Politics in Atlanta: School Board Decision Making. Atlanta: Southern Center for Studies in Public Policy.

HAKKEN, J. (1979) Discrimination Against Chicanos in the Dallas Rental Housing Market: An Experimental Extension of the Housing Market Practices Survey. Washington, DC: HUD Office of Policy Development and Research.

Louis Harris and Associates (1978a) "A study of attitudes toward racial and religious minorities and toward women." Report prepared for the National Conference of Christians and Jews, Chicago, November.

———— (1978b) "A survey of citizen views and concerns about urban life." Report to HUD, February.

HAWLEY, A. (1956) The Changing Shape of Metropolitan America: Deconcentration Since 1920. New York: Macmillan.

Houston Independent School District (1979) Tables of school membership and maps. Submitted to the U.S. District Court.

JACOB, J. E. (1979) "The District: white in-migration, black exodus." Washington Post (May 2).

LONG, L. (1975) "How the racial composition of cities changes." Land Economics (August).

McCOURT, K. (1977) Working-Class Women and Grass-Roots Politics. Bloomington: Indiana University Press.

MARANS, R. W. (1979) "The determinants of neighborhood quality: an analysis of the 1976 annual housing survey." Report to HUD, March.

Marylander Marketing Research (1977) Results of the Los Angeles Unified School District Survey.

MAYER, N. S. (1977) Homeownership: The Changing Relationship of Costs and Incomes and Possible Federal Roles. Washington, DC: Congressional Budget Office.

MOLOTCH, H. (1969) "Racial change in a stable community." American Journal of Sociology 75: 226-238.

Municipal Performance Report (1973) "City housing." Municipal Performance Report (November): 16-18.

National Commission on Urban Problems (1968) Building the American City. Washington, DC: Government Printing Office.

NELSON, K. P. (1979) Recent Suburbanization of Blacks: How Much, Who, and Where. Washington, DC: HUD Office of Economic Affairs.

ORFIELD, G. (1981a) "The housing issues in the St. Louis case." Report to U.S. District Judge William L. Hungate, April 21.

——— (1981b) "Measuring equity requires measuring integration: the importance and methods of measuring the impact of housing programs." Report submitted to HUD, March.

——— (1977) "Desegregation and the cities: the trends and policy choices." Report to the Senate Committee on Human Resources, 95th Congress, 1st session.

——— and P. FISCHER (1981) Housing and School Integration in Three Metropolitan Areas: A Policy Analysis of Denver, Columbus, and Phoenix. Washington, DC: HUD.

PAGE, C. and M. ANDERSON (1979) "They lose as city blooms." Chicago Tribune (September 30): 1.

PEARCE, D. (1980) Breaking Down the Barriers: New Evidence on the Impact of Metropolitan School Desegregation on Housing Patterns. Washington, DC: National Institute of Education.

RAVITCH, D. (1981) "The evolution of school desegregation policy, 1964-1979," in A. Yarmolinski et al. (eds.) Race and Schooling in the City. Cambridge, MA: Harvard University Press.

REECE, B. A. (1979) "Preservation is not the enemy of the poor." Washington Post (February 10): E29.

REGAN, B. R. (1979) Testimony before U.S. District Court, June.

REINHOLD, R. (1979) "U.S. study finds displacement of poor in slums is minimal." New York Times (February 14).

ROSSI, P. (1980) Why Families Move (2nd ed.). Beverly Hills, CA: Sage.

SANDERS, R. and J. S. ADAMS (1976) in R. Ernst and L. Hugg (eds.) Black America: Geographic Perspectives. New York: Doubleday.

SCHNARE, A. B. (1980) Residential Segregation by Race in U.S. Metropolitan Areas: An Analysis Across Cities and Over Time. Washington, DC: Urban Institute.

SHEPPARD, N., Jr. (1976) "Racial discrimination found pervasive in rental of Manhattan apartments." New York Times (June 28): 1.

SPAIN, D. (1979) "Black-to-white successions in central city housing: limited evidence for urban revitalization." Presented at the annual meeting of the American Sociological Association, August.

SUNDQUIST, J. L. (1975) Dispersing Population. Washington, DC: Brookings.

TAEUBER, K. and F. WILSON (1979) Project Report 1: Analysis of Trends in School Segregation. Madison: University of Wisconsin, Institute for Research on Poverty.

TAYLOR, G. D. (1979) "Racial preferences, housing and systematic v. incremental effects: recent emphasis from an Omaha survey." (unpublished)

Technical Assistance Committee on the Chicago Desegregation Plan (1978) "Integration in Chicago." Report to the Illinois State Board of Education, May 11.

THRONS, D. C. (1972) Suburbia. London: MacGibbon and Kee.

U.S. Commission on Civil Rights (1971) "Ethnic isolation of Mexican Americans in the public schools of the Southwest," in Mexican American Education Study (Report 1). Washington, DC: Government Printing Office.

U.S. Department of Housing and Urban Development [HUD] (1979a) Interim Displacement Report (HUD-PDR-382). Washington, DC: Author.

——— (1979b) Measuring Racial Discrimination in American Housing Markets: The Housing Market Practices Survey. Washingotn, DC: Government Printing Office.

WOOD, R. C. (1958) Suburbia: Its People and Politics. Boston: Houghton Mifflin.

ZEHNER, R. B. and R. S. CHAPIN, Jr. (1974) Across the City Line: A White Community in Transition. Lexington, MA: D. C. Heath.

PART IV

**ORGANIZING SCHOOLS
FOR EFFECTIVE DESEGREGATION**

9

COOPERATIVE LEARNING
AND DESEGREGATION

ROBERT E. SLAVIN

Desegregation is in trouble. As a legal movement it has accomplished much of the task of bringing together black, white, and Hispanic children, although much still remains to be done in this area. Desegregation is in trouble not in the courts, but in the schools themselves. Early advocates of school desegregation expected that desegregation would lead to increased achievement for minority students, improved race relations, and several other outcomes (see Stephan, 1978). However, even the most sympathetic reviewers (for example, Crain and Mahard, 1978) point out that the positive effects of desegregation on minority achievement tend to be small, and can usually be attributed to quality education rather than to desegregation per se. Less sympathetic reviewers (such as St. John, 1975) do not see much of a positive trend at all. For race relations, the story is much the same; without special intervention, race relations do not tend to improve over time (Gerard and Miller, 1975; St. John, 1975; Stephan, 1978).

But desegregation is an opportunity, not a cure. Cook (1979), who participated in the deliberations that led to the famous Social Science Statement (Minnesota Law Review, 1953), which played a part in *Brown v. Board of Education* (1954), has pointed out that social scientists even then knew that desegregation must be accompanied by changes in school practices if the outcomes were to be optimal for positive relationships between black and white students.

The Social Science Statement was an appendix to appellants' briefs filed in the Supreme Court's school segregation cases, including *Brown,* in 1952. The Statement attempted to review the social science evidence then available to discuss the effects of segregation on black students. It was signed by 32 social scientists, including Gordon and Floyd Allport, Jerome Bruner, Isador Chein, Kenneth and Mamie Clark, Stuart Cook, Else Frenkel-Brunswik, David Katz, Otto Klineberg, David Krech, Robert Merton, Gardner Murphy, Theodore Newcomb, Arnold Rose, Nevitt Sanford, and M. Brewster Smith; in other words, the psychologists, sociologists, and other social scientists who were then or were to become the leaders of American social science.

Most of the Statement deals with the negative effects of segregation on the self-concept, aspirations, and personalities of black children, and with the possibility of negative effects on white children as well. Because the Statement was written in support of the plaintiffs in an adversary proceeding, it was predictably favorable toward desegregation and negative toward continued segregation. However, despite the overall prediction of positive effects of desegregation, it was cautious in predicting positive race relations in desegregated schools. At the time the Statement was written, school segregation was the law in 17 states and the District of Columbia (Cook, 1979), and was widespread outside of these states as a result of prejudice, housing patterns, and tradition. Thus, the social scientists had very little experience with school desegregation. However, they did have experience with desegregation in the armed forces, housing, and employment. This experience led the framers of the Statement to be optimistic, but cautiously so, in predicting positive race relations in desegregated schools. The most relevant portion of the Statement reads as follows:

> Under certain circumstances desegregation not only proceeds without major difficulties, but has been observed to lead to the emergence of more favorable attitudes and friendlier relations between races. . . . Much depends, however, on the circumstances under which members of previously segregated groups first come in contact with others in unsegregated situations. Available evidence suggests . . . the importance of consistent and firm enforcement of the new policy by those in authority. It indicates also the importance of such factors as: the absence of competition for a limited number of facilities or benefits; the possibility of contacts which permit individuals to learn about one another as individuals; and the possibility of equivalence of positions and functions among all of the participants within the unsegregated situation [Minnesota Law Review, 1953: 437-438].

Allport, in his classic book, *The Nature of Prejudice* (1954), made even more explicit the importance of the nature of interracial contact. He cited research that indicated that superficial contact could damage race relations, as could competitive contact and as could contact between individuals of different status. However, he also cited evidence to the effect that when individuals of different racial or ethnic groups worked to achieve common goals, when they had opportunities to get to know one another as individuals, and when they worked with one another on an equal footing, they became friends and did not continue to hold prejudices against one another. These principles became known as Allport's Contact Theory of Intergroup Relations.

It is now almost 30 years since the Social Science Statement was written, and more than 25 years since legally sanctioned segregation was struck down. How has American education responded to the warnings and suggestions made by the social scientists and elaborated by Allport and others so long ago?

A brief visit to virtually any desegregated secondary school will convince an impartial observer that the conditions outlined in the Statement are only minimally satisfied. Interracial or interethnic contact tends to be superficial. In the lunchroom, at the bus stop, on the playground, and in class, it is almost always possible to pick out a black group, an Hispanic group, an Asian group, an Anglo group. In the classroom, the one setting in which students of different racial or ethnic backgrounds are most likely to be at least sitting side by side, traditional instructional methods permit little or no contact between students that is not of a superficial nature.

Not only is interracial or interethnic contact superficial in the traditional school, but it is undeniably competitive. Blacks, Hispanics, Anglos, and others are in constant individual competition for good grades, for teacher approval, for places on school sports teams and cheerleading squads, and for other honors and privileges. Competition between individuals engenders suspicion and often hostility between them. In a competitive environment it is especially easy to perceive one's own frustrations and failures as somehow being caused by favoritism to the other group, or to otherwise blame them. Instances of settings that naturally lend themselves to interracial or interethnic cooperation are relatively rare. Team sports are the major exception to this, and it has been found that students who participate in interracial sports teams are far more likely than those who do not to have friends of a different race and to have positive racial attitudes (Slavin and Madden, 1979). Even though team sports involve competition with other teams, they create a condition of cooperation, support, and frequent interpersonal interaction within the team that transcends racial or ethnic boundaries.

It is unclear whether or not American schools provide for equal status contact across race lines. The research on which the equal-status criterion was based involved cases in industry in which it was found that contact between, say, white foremen and black workers did not lead to improvements in black-white relations (see Allport, 1954). By this standard, students in desegregated schools do have equal status, in the sense that their roles are equivalent. However, many have questioned the degree to which interracial contacts are of an equal-status nature in a society in which racial prejudice and low academic performance of black and Hispanic students makes interaction between majority and minority students inherently unequal. The work of Cohen (1972) and her associates documenting differences in participation in small-group activities between black and white students illustrates this inequality.

Thus, American schools only minimally meet the requirements of the Social Science Statement for interracial contact to lead to interracial harmony. The results of their failure to do so are readily apparent in many desegregated schools: racial tensions, racially homogeneous friendship groups, and, occasionally, racial violence (Dorr, 1972).

Despite the admonitions of the social science community in 1952, social scientists involved in desegregation did very little over the next quarter century to try to bring about in schools the conditions required for effective desegregation. Since the *Brown* decision, there has been an enormous outpouring of evaluative research on outcomes of desegregation (see St. John, 1975; Stephan, 1978; Cohen, 1975), but very little research in schools that evaluated programs that actually involve the cooperative, equal-status, intense contact described so long ago as precursors of positive relationships. As a consequence, the disappointing finding that race relations do not improve of their own accord in desegregated schools is hardly a disconfirmation of the Social Science Statement and the expectations for desegregation expressed in it, but is rather a confirmation of the fears expressed in the Statement about the outcomes of desegregation if the conditions of contact are not adequate. Contact theory itself has been supported and elaborated in laboratory studies (see Cook, 1978) and in correlational studies (such as Slavin and Madden, 1979), but only recently has field experimental research been done to actually implement the conditions of contact theory in classrooms and assess the results.

COOPERATIVE LEARNING

The major exception to the concentration on *documenting* outcomes of desegregation as opposed to *improving* them is the experimental research on cooperative learning strategies in desegregated schools. The term "cooperative learning" refers to instructional strategies in which students work in small, heterogeneous groups to master academic content. Cooperative learning methods are unique among various possible means of improving desegregation outcomes in that they explicitly use the strength of the desegregated school, the presence of students of different races or ethnicities, to enhance learning and intergroup relations outcomes.

The groups in which students work in cooperative learning settings are made up of students of different races, sexes, and levels of achievement, with each group reflecting the composition of the class as a whole in these attributes. The groups typically receive rewards, recognition, and/or evaluation based on the degree to which they can increase the academic performance of each of the members of the group. This is in sharp contrast to the interstudent competition for grades and teacher approval characteristic of the traditional classroom. Cooperation among students is emphasized both by the classroom rewards and tasks and by the teacher, who tries to communicate an "all for one, one for all" attitude. The structures of the various methods also attempt to ensure each student a chance to make a substantial contribution to the team, so that teammates will be equal both in the sense of role equality specified by Allport (1954) and in the sense of equal performance as a team member implied by Cohen (1972).

All of the cooperative learning methods are designed to be true changes in classroom organization, not time-limited "treatments." As such, they provide daily opportunities for intense interpersonal contact between students of different races. Also, when the teacher assigns students of different races or ethnicities to work together, this communicates unequivocal support on the part of the teacher for the idea that interracial or interethnic interaction is officially sanctioned. Even though race or race relations per se need never be mentioned (and rarely are) in the course of cooperative learning experiences, it is difficult for a student to believe that his or her teacher believes in racial separation when the teacher has assigned the class to multiethnic teams.

Thus, at least in theory, cooperative learning satisfies the conditions outlined in the Social Science Statement and by Allport (1954) for positive effects of desegregation on race relations: cooperation across race lines, equal-status roles of students of different races, contact across race lines that permits students to learn about one another as individuals, and the communication of unequivocal teacher support for interracial contact.

COOPERATIVE LEARNING METHODS

While the conditions of contact theory are not difficult to achieve in the laboratory, designing instructional programs that embody the principles of the theory and also accomplish the other goals of schooling is not so easy. For example, research on cooperative learning would be an academic exercise with little relevance to actual schools if the methods did not also improve student achievement, or if they were too expensive, too difficult, too narrowly focused, or too disruptive to school routines to be practical as primary alternatives to traditional instruction. As a consequence, features of cooperative learning methods other than the degree to which they are designed to improve race relations are of extreme importance.

There are three primary cooperative learning methods that embody the principles of contact theory, have been researched in desegregated schools, and have the practical characteristics outlined above: They are inexpensive, easy to implement, widely applicable in terms of subject matter and grade levels, easily integrated into the existing school without additional resources, and have been shown to improve achievement more than traditional instruction. Two of these methods were developed and evaluated at the Center for Social Organization of Schools of the Johns Hopkins University: Student Teams-Achievement Divisions, or STAD (Slavin, 1978a), and Teams-Games-Tournament, or TGT (DeVries and Slavin, 1978). These methods are both the most extensively researched of the cooperative learning techniques and are by far the most widely used in American schools. A third technique, Jigsaw teaching (Aronson et al., 1978), has also been evaluated in several desegregated schools and is widely used both in its original form and as modified and disseminated by the Johns Hopkins group (see Slavin, 1978b). These techniques, as well as less extensively researched and used methods, are described below.

STUDENT TEAMS-ACHIEVEMENT DIVISIONS

STAD is made up of five interlocking components: class presentations, teams, quizzes, individual improvement scores, and team recognition.

Class presentations. Academic material is initially introduced by means of a teacher lecture, audio-visual presentation, reading, or other activity.

Teams. Teams are composed of four to five students representing all levels of academic achievement in the class, all racial or ethnic groups, and both sexes. The major function of the team is to prepare its members to do well on individual quizzes that will follow the team practice session. After the class presentation, the team meets to study worksheets reviewing the material the teacher presented. Students within the teams usually quiz one another back and forth, work problems together, explain difficulties, and otherwise help one another master the material. Students are told that they are not finished studying until every one of their teammates completely understands the material. Note that students are *not* assigned roles as tutors and tutees; students are simply asked to learn together and to be responsible for one another's learning, and the cooperative studying is structured in such a way as to make it possible for students of all levels of ability to help any of their teammates master the material. This procedure emphasizes the equality of the teammates.

Quizzes. After approximately one class period of teacher presentation and one period of team practice, the students take individual quizzes on the material they have been studying. They are not permitted to help one another on the quizzes. This makes sure that each student has an individual responsibility to know the material.

Individual improvement scores. The quiz scores are translated into team scores by means of a system that rewards students for doing better than they have done in the past. Each student is given a "base" score based on past quiz scores. The "base" is the minimum the student is expected to achieve, and students receive points toward their team scores depending on how much their current quiz scores exceed their base scores. Scoring procedures ensure that no student can score higher than a student who gets a perfect score, regardless of the base, and the base score changes every two weeks to reflect changes in performance level (see Slavin, 1980a). The idea behind the use of the improvement score system is to put high scores within the reach of every student but to guarantee them to no one, and to equalize the potential contribution to the team score of each team member, so that no team member will be rejected as an automatic drag on the team score.

In the earlier STAD studies, a different system was used, in which the scores each student contributed to the team were based on the rank of the student's score among others of similar past performance (see Slavin, 1978c).

Team recognition. Team scores, the average number of points earned by the team members above their respective base scores, are recognized in a class newsletter or bulletin board.

Thus, STAD is designed to increase students' motivation to do academic work and to help and encourage one another academically by providing cooperative goals and cooperative tasks for students to achieve in small, face-to-face groups. Equality among students is emphasized both by the peer practice system, in which students work as equals, and by the scoring system that rewards individual improvement, which is within the reach of all students. STAD is constructed to improve relationships between students by having them work together as equals to accomplish something they value and to which they can all contribute meaningfully.

TEAMS-GAMES-TOURNAMENT

TGT is essentially the same as STAD in basic rationale and methodology. However, it replaces the quizzes and improvement score system used in STAD with a system of academic game tournaments, in which students from each team compete with students from other teams of the same level of past performance to try to contribute to their team scores. This competition with equals has the same rationale as the improvement score system of STAD; it gives every student an equal opportunity to contribute to the team score. The team assignments, lessons, team practice, and team recognition procedures are all the same for TGT as for STAD.

JIGSAW

In Jigsaw, students are assigned to heterogeneous teams as in STAD and TGT, except that each team has six members. Each team member receives a special topic on which he or she is to become the team's expert. For example, in a unit on Chile, one student might be appointed as an expert on Chile's history, another on its culture, another on its geography, and so on, for a total of five topics (two students share a topic unless someone on the team is absent). The students read their sections and then discuss them in "component groups" or "expert groups" made up of students from different teams who have the same topic. The "experts" then return to their teams to teach their teammates what they have learned. Students in Jigsaw are thus interdependent for information, which structures cooperative interaction among them, but, in contrast to STAD or TGT, there is no group feedback or reward.

OTHER COOPERATIVE METHODS

In addition to STAD, TGT, and Jigsaw, a few other cooperative learning methods have been developed and evaluated. Johnson and Johnson (1975) have developed techniques in which children work together in small groups to produce group reports or group worksheets and are evaluated based on their group product. The Johnsons and their colleagues have done several studies of their methods, but only one in a desegregated school (Cooper et al., 1980). Weigel et al. (1975) used a combination of cooperative techniques in desegregated junior and senior high schools. These methods involved various small-group activities, with information gathering, discussion, and interpretation of materials conducted by heterogeneous groups. Prizes were given to winning groups based on the quality of the group product. Other cooperative learning methods have also yielded interesting findings, but have not been studied in desegregated schools. These include methods researched by Sharan et al. (1980), Wheeler (1977), and Hamblin et al. (1971).

OUTCOMES OF COOPERATIVE LEARNING

RACE RELATIONS

Despite the warnings contained in the Social Science Statement, elaborated by Allport (1954), despite widespread agreement among social scientists since the *Brown* decision that conditions of interracial contact are important in determining outcomes of desegregation, and despite a body of experimental research that supports this contention (Cook, 1978), desegregated schools have tended to focus on trying to change teacher and student attitudes toward minorities by means of instruction in human relations rather than trying to change the conditions of contact between the races or ethnic groups. Many schools do provide human relations training for teachers, minority studies programs for students, student advisory committees to try to defuse racial tensions, and similar programs. These efforts are clearly not useless, but they just as clearly leave interracial contact between students as is — largely superficial, competitive, and often unequal. Under such conditions, it is unlikely that relationships between students of different ethnicities will grow.

Black, white, and Hispanic students typically live in different neighborhoods, ride different buses, like different activities, sit in different parts of the cafeteria, and in general find themselves with others like themselves much more often than with students of other ethnic backgrounds. To expect positive contact to arise under conditions of considerable ethnic separation, with or without programs designed to improve attitudes, is probably unrealistic. This is borne out by Slavin and Madden (1979), who studied questionnaire data from a national sample of integrated high schools. They found that assigning students of different races to work with one another was consistently related to positive racial attitudes and behaviors, but attempts at attitude change, such as teaching of minority history, workshops attempting to change teacher attitudes, and use of multiethnic texts, had inconsistent or no effects on these variables. Further, students who individually reported being on sports teams or having worked with students of another race were much more likely to have friends of another race and to have positive racial attitudes than were students who did not report such cooperative interactions. On the other hand, individual reports of having discussed race relations in class made few consistent differences in attitudes or behavior.

The experimental evidence on cooperative learning has generally supported the conclusions of the Social Science Statement and of Allport (1954), and has validated the findings of the correlational research (Slavin and Madden, 1979). With only a few exceptions, this research has demonstrated that when the conditions outlined by Allport are met in the classroom, students are more likely to have friends outside of their own race groups than they are in traditional classrooms, as measured by responses to such sociometric items as, "Who are your best friends in this class?"

DeVries et al. (1978) summarized data analyses from 4 studies of TGT in desegregated schools. In 3 of these, students who had been in classes that used TGT over periods of 9-12 weeks gained significantly more in friends outside of their own race groups than did control students. In a much shorter study (4 weeks), no differences were found, although there were positive effects on perceived cross-racial helping (DeVries and Edwards, 1974). The samples involved in the successful studies varied in grade levels from 7-12 and in percentage of minority students from 10 percent to 51 percent.

The evidence linking STAD to gains in cross-racial friendships is equally strong. In two studies, Slavin (1977a, 1979) found that students who had experienced STAD over periods of 10-12 weeks gained more in cross-racial friendships than did control students. Slavin and Oickle (1980) found significant gains in white friendships toward blacks as a consequence of STAD, but found no differences in black friendships toward whites. The Slavin (1979) study also included a follow-up into the next academic year, in which students who had been in the experimental and control classes were asked again to list their friends. Students who had been in the control group listed an average of less than one friend of another race, or 9.8 percent of all of their friendship choices; those who had been in the experimental group named an average of 2.4 friends outside of their own race groups, 37.9 percent of their friendship choices. Secondary analysis of the Slavin (1979) data showed that the effects of STAD on cross-racial friendships were equal for blacks and whites, boys and girls, and high and low achievers, and that the effects were strongest for close, mutual friendship choices, the ones most likely to be maintained and to be reflected in actual behavior in and out of school (Hansell and Slavin, 1979). The STAD research covered grades 6-8, and took place in schools ranging from 34 percent to 61 percent black.

Research on cooperative learning and race relations has generally been less successful outside of the Johns Hopkins tradition. Jigsaw has been evaluated in four desegregated settings. Of the Jigsaw studies, one presented no data on cross-racial friendship or other aspects of race relations (Lucker et al., 1976); two others used measures that cannot be seen as measures of race relations. Blaney et al. (1977) found that students who had experienced Jigsaw liked their groupmates better than they liked their other classmates. Since their groups were the same in racial composition as the class as a whole, this difference can hardly be taken as an indication of improved race relations. Geffner (1978) had students guess how classmates of other races would fill out a self-esteem measure, again hardly a measure of race relations. In the one Jigsaw study to actually measure intergroup attitudes, Gonzales (1979) found that Anglo and Asian students had better attitudes toward Mexican-Americans as a consequence of Jigsaw, but no differences were found in attitudes toward Anglos or toward Asians.

One study involving the Johnson techniques (Cooper et al., 1980) found greater friendship across race lines in a cooperative treatment than in an individualistic treatment.

One of the largest and longest studies of cooperative learning was conducted by Weigel et al. (1975) in triethnic (Mexican-American, Anglo, black) classrooms. They found positive effects of their cooperative methods on white attitudes toward Mexican-Americans, but not on white-black, black-white, black-Hispanic, Hispanic-black, or Hispanic-white attitudes. They also found positive effects of cooperative learning on teachers' reports of less interethnic conflict.

The effects of cooperative learning methods are thus not entirely consistent, but each of the cooperative learning studies showed positive effects on some aspect of race relations. Of the seven Johns Hopkins studies, six demonstrated that when the conditions of contact theory are fulfilled, friendships between black and white students increase.

The pattern of findings in studies in which all of the hypothesized effects were not found is an interesting one. In one case (DeVries and Edwards, 1974), the failure to find treatment effects on cross-racial friendships was probably due to the brief duration of the study. However, in three other studies (Slavin and Oickle, 1980; Weigel et al., 1975; Gonzalez, 1979), positive effects of cooperative learning were found for attitudes toward or friendships with one of the ethnic groups but not the other(s). In every case, the effects were found for majority group attitudes toward minority students, but not for minority-majority attitudes. This may be due to the fact that minority group members usually begin with better attitudes toward majority group individuals than the other way around (see, for example, Slavin and Madden, 1979), but this finding needs to be explored in greater depth before firm conclusions can be drawn.

The relatively strong and consistent effects of TGT and STAD, as compared to the other cooperative methods, may be due to any number of features unique to these two techniques. One possibility is that the scoring systems, which allow each student to excel if they do better than before, account for the particular success of these methods. The "equal opportunity" scoring systems put the teammates on an equal footing with regard to potential contribution to team success. This avoids the possibility that, because of either initial prejudice or actual achievement differences, the white students would see blacks on their teams as impediments to team success. STAD and TGT are also the most highly structured of the methods, and this may account for their success, or it may be because the dependent variables in the Johns Hopkins research have always been sociometric instead of attitudinal, and friendships are easier to change than attitudes.

ACHIEVEMENT

It is interesting to note, in light of the subsequent heavy research emphasis on achievement outcomes of desegregation, that the Social Science Statement made its argument against segregated schooling almost entirely on the basis of its psychological impact on minority children, not its impact on achievement. However, achievement for both minority and nonminority students is the most frequently studied outcome of desegregation, and is the outcome around which much of the current debate on this topic revolves.

Among the cooperative learning methods, TGT and STAD have been the most frequently studied in desegregated schools. There are two TGT studies which found significantly positive effects on mathematics achievement in desegregated junior high schools (Edwards et al., 1972; Edwards and DeVries, 1972), an additional study in desegregated seventh grades (Edwards and DeVries, 1974) which found positive TGT effects on math achievement, but not on social studies achievement, and a fourth study in a desegregated high school which found only marginal effects on social studies achievement. Unfortunately, the TGT studies did not break down the achievement results by race, so it is unclear whether the effects seen were due to equal gains for blacks and whites or whether students of one race or the other had outstanding gains.

There have been three studies of STAD conducted in desegregated schools. One (Slavin, 1979) showed no achievement differences; however, the other two had similar and quite interesting results. In both studies (Slavin, 1977b; Slavin and Oickle, 1980), the students who experienced STAD gained significantly more in language arts achievement than did control students. However, in both cases there were race × treatment interactions, and examination of the results separately by race revealed that, while white students in the experimental classes gained somewhat more than whites in the control classes, blacks in the experimental group gained far more than blacks in the control group. In both studies, control whites had higher achievement than control blacks on the pre- and posttests, but the significant initial race difference in achievement seen in the experimental group was gone by the time of the posttest.

The primary Jigsaw study designed to study the effects of this method on student social studies achievement also found this result; overall significant gains for the experimental group turned out to be due to small experimental-control differences for Anglos, but substantial differences for Mexican-Americans and blacks (analyzed together).

The race × treatment interactions for STAD were analyzed in detail by Slavin and Oickle (1980). They concluded that the effects were not due to ceiling effects or abnormal achievement distributions, and that they were only partially explained by pretest × treatment interactions, which did not approach significance within race groups.

Assuming that these race × treatment interactions are not artifactual, their potential importance is considerable. The continuing and persistent difference in measured academic achievement between minority and nonminority students (Coleman et al., 1966) is one of the most important problems in American education. It is, of course, impossible that a twelve-week experience in junior high school English class would overcome the cumulative effects of low socioeconomic status, prejudice, and early experiences of school failure characteristic of black students in our society. However, the fact that, in three of four studies of cooperative learning, minority students significantly narrowed the gap in achievement between themselves and their majority group classmates suggests something about the origin of that gap and, more importantly, points to a potential longer-term solution to reduce that gap.

One possible explanation advanced by Slavin and Oickle (1980) for the race × treatment interaction is that there is something in black and Hispanic psychology or culture that makes cooperation a more effective motivational system than competition for minority students. There is evidence to support this possibility. For blacks, the peer group is usually of greater importance than it is for whites. Black children's self-esteem depends more on how they see themselves getting along with their peer group than on how they are doing academically, while the reverse holds true for whites (Hare, 1977). When given a choice of competing or cooperating with a peer, blacks are more likely to cooperate than whites (DeVoe, 1977; Richmond and Weiner, 1973; Goodman, 1952). The same is true for Mexican-Americans, who are more cooperative than either blacks or Anglos (Kagan and Madsen, 1971; Madsen and Shapira, 1970).

In the traditional American classroom, students are in competition with one another for a limited supply of good grades, teacher praise, and other rewards. This competition can be disruptive to interpersonal bonds; when one individual's success requires that another fail, relations between those individuals suffer (see Johnson and Johnson, 1974). Students in the traditional classroom often express strong norms opposing academic success on the part of their peers, because it is in their interest to make sure that no one does too well academically and thereby reduces his or her peers' chances to succeed. Antiacademic norms are common in American secondary schools (Coleman, 1961). On the other hand, the school itself and students' parents strongly reward academic excellence.

Each student must choose between these opposing sets of standards. Those who choose the peer group, who choose not to compete to be the best, are unlikely to shine academically because to do so is to risk losing friends. In other words, too much of a peer group orientation is dysfunctional in terms of academic performance. Given that blacks are more cooperation oriented and more peer oriented than whites, they are more likely than whites to choose not to strive for academic excellence and risk exclusion by their peers.

In sharp contrast to the structure of the classroom is the structure of team sports. In sports, outstanding performance *helps* others. Peer norms unequivocally support sports achievement, because when an individual performs outstandingly, it helps the team win; when the team wins, the school wins (Coleman, 1961). In sports, there is little reason to expect that a strong, cooperative, peer orientation would interfere with performance; on the contrary, it might improve performance. In sports, black and Hispanic participation and performance is at least as high as that for whites.

Cooperative learning strategies significantly change the peer norms-school standards dilemma for all students. When students are encouraged to help one another with their school work and are rewarded on how much their group achieves, they are likely to care how their classmates are doing academically and to encourage them to do their best. Cooperative learning methods borrow from sports the "all for one, one for all" attitude created by a structure in which each student's academic performance in fact does benefit the peer group and the group's efforts in fact benefit the individual. Academic achievement becomes supported by the peer group. Changes in peer norms concerning classmates' achievement have been documented in three studies (Hulten and DeVries, 1976; Madden and Slavin, 1980; Slavin, 1978c), and two additional studies have shown that students in cooperative learning classes who were academically successful relative to their own past performance gained in sociometric status, while control students who were academically successful lost status (Slavin et al., 1975; Slavin, 1975).

Thus, if cooperative learning methods make academic achievement a peer-supported activity, and if peer support is more important to blacks and Mexican-Americans than to Anglos, then it is logical that the effects of cooperative learning on student achievement would be greatest for minority students. There is evidence that cooperatively oriented individuals learn best under cooperative conditions, while competitively oriented individuals learn best in competition (Wheeler, 1977). If blacks and Mexican-Americans are indeed more cooperatively oriented, then it makes sense that they would do best under a cooperative system.

If this explanation is correct, an argument could be made that one reason for the lower school performance of blacks as compared to whites could be that the traditional competitive structure of the classroom is inconsistent with the more cooperatively oriented black culture; that while the achievement of most white students is facilitated by the competitive structure, the achievement of many black students is not. If this is true, then it could be argued that educators should provide different kinds of instructional strategies that take into account the needs of both cooperatively and competitively oriented learners, perhaps by using both cooperative and traditional structures during different parts of the school day. This could provide students, regardless of race, who are cooperatively oriented or especially peer oriented with an instructional setting that meets their needs and allows them to enjoy the advantage of a match between their predisposition and the classroom structure now enjoyed only by competitive students, who are more tied to school and parental norms than to peer norms.

It should be noted that positive effects of cooperative learning are not limited to minority students or to desegregated schools. TGT studies in racially homogeneous white schools have found significantly positive effects on student achievement in junior high school math (Hulten and De Vries, 1976), in elementary language arts and reading (De Vries and Mescon, 1975; De Vries et al., 1975a, 1975b), and in junior high school language arts (De Vries et al., 1979). Similarly, STAD has had positive effects in racially homogeneous white classrooms on elementary language arts (Slavin, 1980b; Slavin and Karweit, 1979) and on elementary mathematics (Madden and Slavin, 1980). Sharan et al. (1980) and Wheeler (1977) found positive social studies achievement effects for cooperative learning strategies in all-white elementary schools, and Hamblin et al. (1971) documented positive effects on elementary mathematics achievement in an all-black school using a cooperative learning strategy related to behavior modification methods. Thus, while achievement effects of cooperative learning strategies are strongest for minority students in desegregated schools, there is considerable evidence that these methods are effective for most students in segregated as well as desegregated schools at all levels.

CONCLUSION

In summary, the cooperative learning strategies described in this chapter appear to be effective means of increasing positive race relations and achievement in desegregated schools. They meet the conditions outlined in the Social Science Statement that was part of *Brown* v. *Board of Education* for positive relationships to arise out of interracial contact: cooperative, face-to-face, equal-status contact between students of different races. As such, the research on cooperative learning strategies has shown that the social scientists writing in support of the *Brown* decision so long ago were right. They were right to be cautious about the effects of desegregation that did not meet their conditions, and they were right to predict that if programs that met them were devised, they would result in positive outcomes. If educators had paid attention to the Statement, perhaps we would not be in a position, more than 25 years after *Brown*, of having little to say about the effects of desegregation on racial attitudes and friendships.

For achievement, the research on cooperative learning has demonstrated that all students can benefit from working cooperatively in small groups. The research in desegregated schools has further suggested that if cooperative learning is incorporated as a major part of the school experience of students in desegregated schools, not only will all students gain, but the gap between minority and nonminority students in measured achievement may be reduced. Much work remains to be done to identify the limitations and further potential of cooperative learning for the desegregated school, but the research done to date justifies optimism that cooperative learning may be a significant step toward finally achieving the potential of integrated education.

REFERENCES

ALLPORT, G. (1954) The Nature of Prejudice. Cambridge, MA: Addison-Wesley.

ARONSON, E., N. BLANEY, C. STEPHAN, J. SIKES, and M. SNAPP (1978) The Jigsaw Classroom. Beverly Hills, CA: Sage.

BLANEY, N. T., C. STEPHAN, D. ROSENFIELD, E. ARONSON, and J. SIKES (1977) "Interdependence in the classroom: a field study." Journal of Educational Psychology 69, 2: 121-128.

BROWN v. BOARD OF EDUCATION (1954) 347 U.S. 483.

COHEN, (1975) "The effects of desegregation on race relations." Law and Contemporary Problems 39: 271-299.

―――― (1972) "Interracial interaction disability." Human Relations 25: 9-24.

COLEMAN, J.S. (1961) The Adolescent Society. New York: Macmillan.

―――――, E.Q. CAMPBELL, C.L. HOBSON, J.M. McPARTLAND, A.M. MOOD, F.D. WEINFELD, and R.L. YORK (1966) Equality of Educational Opportunity. Washington, DC: Government Printing Office.

COOK, S.W. (1979) "Social science and school desegregation: did we mislead the Supreme Court?" Personality and Social Psychology Bulletin 5: 420-437.

―――― (1978) "Interpersonal and attitudinal outcomes of cooperative interracial groups." Journal of Research and Development in Education 12: 97-113.

COOPER, L., D.W. JOHNSON, R. JOHNSON, and F. WILDERSON (1980) "Effects of cooperative, competitive, and individualistic experiences on interpersonal attraction among heterogeneous peers." Journal of Social Psychology 3: 243-252.

CRAIN, R. and R. MAHARD (1978) " Desegregation and black achievement: a review of the research." Law and Contemporary Problems 42, 3: 17-56.

DeVOE, M. V. (1977) "Cooperation as a function of self-concept, sex, and race." Educational Research Quarterly 2, 2: 1-8.

DeVRIES, D. L. and K. J. EDWARDS (1974) "Student teams and learning games: their effects on cross-race and cross-sex interaction." Journal of Educational Psychology 66: 741-749.

DeVRIES, D. L. and I. T. MESCON (1975) Teams-Games-Tournament: An Effective Task and Reward Structure in the Elementary Grades. Baltimore: Johns Hopkins University, Center for Social Organization of Schools.

DeVRIES, D. L. and R. E. SLAVIN (1978) "Teams-Games-Tournament (TGT): review of ten classroom experiments." Journal of Research and Development in Education 12: 28-38.

DeVRIES, D. L., K. J. EDWARDS, and R. E. SLAVIN (1978) "Biracial learning teams and race relations in the classroom: four field experiments on Teams-Games-Tournament." Journal of Educational Psychology 70: 356-362.

DeVRIES, D. L., P. LUCASSE, and S. SHACKMAN (1979) "Small group versus individualized instruction: a field test of their relative effectiveness." Presented at the annual convention of the American Psychological Association, New York.

DeVRIES, D. L., I. T. MESCON, and S. L. SHACKMAN (1975a) Teams-Games-Tournament in the Elementary Classroom: A Replication. Baltimore: Johns Hopkins University, Center for Social Organization of Schools.

—— (1975b) Teams-Games-Tournament (TGT) Effects on Reading Skills in the Elementary Grades. Baltimore: Johns Hopkins University, Center for Social Organization of Schools.

DORR, R. (1972) "Ordeal by desegregation." Integrated Education 10: 34-39.

EDWARDS, K. J. and D. L. DeVRIES (1974) The Effects of Teams-Games-Tournament and Two Structural Variations on Classroom Process, Student Attitudes, and Student Achievement. Baltimore: Johns Hopkins University, Center for Social Organization of Schools.

—— (1972) Learning Games and Student Teams: Their Effects on Student Attitudes and Achievement. Baltimore: Johns Hopkins University, Center for Social Organization of Schools.

—— and J. P. SNYDER (1972) " Games and teams: a winning combination." Simulation & Games 3: 247-269.

GEFFNER, R. (1978) "The effects of interdependent learning on self-esteem, interethnic relations, and intra-ethnic attitudes of elementary school children: a field experiment." Ph. D. dissertation, University of California — Santa Cruz.

GERARD, H. B. and N. MILLER (1975) School Desegregation: A Long-Range Study. New York: Plenum.

GONZALEZ, A. (1979) "Classroom cooperation and ethnic balance." Presented at the annual convention of the American Psychological Association, New York.

GOODMAN, M. (1952) Race Awareness in Young Children. Cambridge, MA: Addison-Wesley.

HAMBLIN, R. L., C. HATHAWAY, and J. S. WODARSKI (1971) " Group contingencies, peer tutoring, and accelerating academic achievement," in E. Ramp and W. Hopkins (eds.) A New Direction for Education: Behavior Analysis. Lawrence: University of Kansas, Department of Human Development.

HANSELL, S. and R. SLAVIN (1979) "Cooperative learning and interracial friendships." Presented at the annual convention of the American Psychological Association, New York.

HARE, B. R. (1977) "Racial and sociometric variations in preadolescent area-specific and general self-esteem." International Journal of Intercultural Relations 1: 31-51.

HULTEN, B. H. and D. L. DeVRIES (1976) Team Competition and Group Practice: Effects on Student Achievement and Attitudes. Baltimore: Johns Hopkins University, Center for Social Organization of Schools.

JOHNSON, D. W. and R. T. JOHNSON (1975) Learning Together and Alone. Englewood Cliffs, NJ: Prentice-Hall.

——— (1974) "Instructional goal structure: cooperative, competitive, or individualistic." Review of Educational Research 44: 213-240.

KAGAN, S. and M. C. MADSEN (1971) "Cooperation and competition of Mexican, Mexican-American, and Anglo-American children of two ages under four instructional sets." Developmental Psychology 5: 32-39.

LUCKER, G. W., D. ROSENFIELD, J. SIKES, and E. ARONSON (1976) "Performance in the interdependent classroom: a field study." American Educational Research Journal 13: 115-123.

MADDEN, N. A. and R. E. SLAVIN (1980) "Cooperative learning and social acceptance of mainstreamed academically handicapped students." Presented at the annual convention of the American Psychological Association, Montreal.

MADSEN, M. C. and A. SHAPIRA (1970) "Cooperative and competitive behavior of urban Afro-American, Anglo-American, Mexican-American, and Mexican village children." Developmental Psychology 3: 16-20.

Minnesota Law Review (1953) "The effects of segregation and the consequences of desegregation: a social science statement." Appendix to appellants' briefs: Brown v. Board of Education of Topeka, Kansas. Minnesota Law Review 37: 427-439.

RICHMOND, B. O. and G. P. WEINER (1973) "Cooperation and competition among young children as a function of ethnic grouping, grade, sex, and reward condition." Journal of Educational Psychology 64: 329-334.

ST. JOHN, N. H. (1975) School Desegregation: Outcomes for Children. New York: John Wiley.

SHARAN, S., R. HERTZ-LAZAROWITZ, and Z. ACKERMAN (1980) "Learning in cooperative small groups and academic achievement of elementary school children." Journal of Experimental Education.

SLAVIN, R. E. (1980a) "Effects of individual learning expectations on student achievement." Journal of Educational Psychology 72: 520-524.

——— (1980b) "Effects of student teams and peer tutoring on academic achievement and time on-task." Journal of Experimental Education 48: 252-257.

——— (1979) "Effects of biracial learning teams on cross-racial friendships." Journal of Educational Psychology 71: 381-387.

——— (1978a) "Student teams and achievement divisions." Journal of Research and Development in Education 12: 39-49.

——— (1978b) Using Student Team Learning. Baltimore: Johns Hopkins University, Center for Social Organization of Schools.

——— (1978c) "Student teams and comparison among equals: effects on academic performance and student attitudes." Journal of Educational Psychology 70: 532-538.

——— (1977a) "How student learning teams can integrate the desegregated classroom." Intergrated Education 15, 6: 56-58.

——— (1977b) Student Learning Team Techniques: Narrowing the Achievement Gap Between the Races. Baltimore: Johns Hopkins University, Center for Social Organization of Schools.

——— (1975) "Classroom reward structure: effects on academic performance, social connectedness, and peer norms." Ph. D. dissertation, Johns Hopkins University.

———— and N. L. KARWEIT (1979) "An extended cooperative learning experience in elementary school." Presented at the annual convention of the American Psychological Association, New York.

SLAVIN, R. E. and N. A. MADDEN (1979) "School practices that improve race relations." American Educational Research Journal 16, 2: 169-180.

SLAVIN, R. E. and E. OICKLE (1980) "Effects of learning teams on student achievement and race relations in a desegregated middle school." Presented at the annual meeting of the American Educational Research Association, Boston.

SLAVIN, R. E., D. L. DeVRIES, and B. H. HULTEN (1975) Individual vs. Team Competition: The Interpersonal Consequences of Academic Performance. Baltimore: Johns Hopkins University, Center for Social Organization of Schools.

STEPHAN, W. G. (1978) "School desegregation: an evaluation of predictions made in *Brown* v. *Board of Education*." Psychological Bulletin 85: 217-238.

WEIGEL, R. H., P. L. WISER, and S. W. COOK (1975) "Impact of cooperative learning experiences on cross-ethnic relations and attitudes." Journal of Social Issues 31, 1: 219-245.

WHEELER, R. (1977) "Predisposition toward cooperation and competition: cooperative and competitive classroom effects." Presented at the annual convention of the American Psychological Association, San Francisco.

10

IMPLEMENTING DESEGREGATION DECREES

MARK G. YUDOF

School desegregation litigation is perhaps the best example of what Chayes (1976: 1281) has described as public law litigation. In contrast to traditional damage suits in torts or contracts, the new litigation model involves many parties with diverse interests, continuing jurisdiction over complex organizations, and fact-finding and injunctive remedies that are forward-looking and involve broad issues of social change. In this context, as Kirp (1976b, 1977, 1979) and Clune (1979) have observed, the role of the judge becomes almost political in nature regardless of the doctrinal roots of a decision. If judges in desegregation cases are involved in politics and public policy, this suggests that they may encounter difficulties in managing social change akin to those encountered by legislatures and administrative agencies. The study of such encounters is generally lumped under the heading of "implementation" research.

In the present context, implementation research refers to the study of the "carrying out of an authoritative decision, i.e., a policy choice" (Berman, 1978; see also Pressman and Wildavsky, 1973). The premise is

AUTHOR'S NOTE: This chapter is a substantially revised version of an article entitled "Implementation Theories and Desegregation Realities," *Alabama Law Review* (Vol. 32, No. 2, Winter 1981), pp. 441-464. I am grateful to the Editorial Board of the *Alabama Law Review* for permission to reuse portions of that article in this book.

that things do not always work out as decision makers (such as judges) anticipate, that compliance with a legal norm is not necessary or automatic in a complex, institution-dominated, political environment, and that different implementation strategies may yield different outcomes. Desegregation decisions present a particularly compelling case for implementation analysis because, for more than 25 years, such decisions have sought to effectuate counter-majoritarian values. Clune (1979: 72) has put the matter well:

> There are no (or different) dilemmas to face if the object of a law is to benefit a well-represented majority . . . ; but if a legislative or administrative majority strongly disfavors a change, the implementation process becomes a universe of powerful constraints. Hence, the study of implementation is a product of the modern age of minority rights, usually enforced by the judiciary.

In this speculative essay, I propose to examine different ways of characterizing and grouping the processes by which the federal courts have sought to implement desegregation decrees. There is no pretense that prescient judges employed largely uninvented implementation constructs and strategies to move the nation toward desegregation. If the judges were guided by science, I suspect that, to borrow Lindblom's (1959) phrase, it was the "science of muddling through," that their decisions embodied a "succession of incremental changes" not informed by a single, overarching theory.

In the post-*Brown* period, judicial attempts to gain compliance with desegregation mandates, and indeed the identification of the goals for desegregation, varied significantly. Efforts to name these approaches and to ground them in implementation theory may bear fruit. Theory may expose suppositions and goals, and assist in evaluating their utility or futility. In this enterprise, guidance has been sought in the existing implementation literature. I have borrowed liberally from the works of such scholars as March (1978), McLaughlin (1975), Elmore (1978, 1979), and Bardach (1977). So too, from different perspectives, the historical processes of implementation in the desegregation field have been explored by Orfield (1969, 1978), Crain (1969), Radin (1977), and others. My purposes, however, lie in the application of theories to desegregation realities, and in the reformulation of legal remedies questions. In large measure, my hope is to play the role of translator, interpreting implementation theory for legal decision makers.

At the simplest level, implementation theory is concerned with the problem of examining organizational compliance with particular policy directives. The day is long gone when lawyers and social scientists could assume that court decisions and legislative and administrative rules would automatically be translated into the desired actions (Berman, 1978: 60). From school prayer (see Dolbeare and Hammond, 1971) to desegregation decisions, one cannot blithely assume compliance. The same is true for such federal programs as Title I of the Elementary and Secondary Education Act (see McLaughlin, 1975, 1976; Murphy, 1971). But the notion of compliance is beguiling. There is a tendency to treat policies as having single and unambiguous purposes, whereas in the real world purposes are often unclear and contradictory (Berman, 1978; March and Olsen, 1976). Indeed, a legislative body may wish to put into motion a process of defining goals, arguably what is occurring under the Education for All Handicapped Children Act. Even if objectives are clear, difficulties with measuring compliance may arise, and compliance with the letter of the law may be substituted for compliance with the spirit of a law (see Berman and McLaughlin, 1975). The physical mixing of bodies is no more the end-all of desegregation than additional contact with teachers is the goal of compensatory education programs. If some goals are not met, policy makers and implementers may carry out a "strategic retreat" on hard objectives, substituting process outcomes (see Wildavsky, 1976; Yudof, 1978a).

Implementation is complicated by still other factors. Lawyers frequently fail to distinguish between altering the behavior of an individual and altering the behavior of institutions (Stone, 1975; Ermann and Lundman, 1978). For example, criminal sanctions and damages may influence individual behavior, whereas they may be totally ineffective in the context of a public or private sector organization. The concept of individual fault may become attenuated as a large number of people, in varying capacities and over time, contribute to the formulation and implementation of policies (Stone, 1975). Resources allocated to the implementors may be insufficient to carry out the policy.

Those now in charge of large public sector organizations, be they school districts or other entities, may not be fully aware of earlier decisions, policies, and information-gathering efforts of their predecessors. In a strict sense, only people have memories; the abstractions we call institutions have no memories. Thus, much may turn on the flow of information within organizations — both horizontal and vertical — and among organizations, for instance, different levels of government. But most organizations are in a position of communications overload, and there will be a tendency to be selective about information dissemination, to distort threatening information, and to produce information, however inaccurate, which serves the purposes of the institution or persons within the institution.

Most important, since organizations are made up of individuals, implementation may well turn on systems of rewards and punishments addressed to specific individuals holding specific bureaucratic positions, on authority and influence differentials among key actors, and on the normative commitment of each actor or group of actors to the purposes of the policy (see Yale Law Journal, 1980; Gouldner, 1965; Allison, 1971; Kaufman, 1960). This means that an actor's position in the organization, previous experiences, professional orientation, and the like may be critical to successful implementation. Goal discrepancies may occur. So too, implementation theory raises questions about "top-down" strategies; for some measure of cooperation by those who execute policies will be necessary (see Elmore, 1978).[1] In its starkest form, the problem is one of the accommodation of discretion and control among those responsible for the day-to-day operations of an organization. Thus, Weatherly and Lipsky (1977) speak of teachers, social workers, police officers, and others as being "street-level" bureaucrats, and argue that grandiose policy schemes may well flounder unless they are persuaded or compelled to cooperate in reaching particular objectives. On the other hand, since the elimination of all discretion may defeat the policy, street-level bureaucrats must be encouraged to exercise independence in furthering that policy.

The conflict between discretion and compliance with policies embodied in rules has been long recognized in the law (see Shklar, 1964; Selznick, 1969; Lowi, 1969; Kirp, 1976a). There are many similarities between jurisprudence and implementation theory, as each seeks to unravel the complex relationship between coercive policies and rules and relatively autonomous decision making. Pound (1966) put the matter succinctly:

> Almost all of the problems of jurisprudence come down to a fundamental one of rule and discretion. . . . Suffice it to say that both are necessary elements in the administration of justice, and that instead of eliminating either we must partition the field between them.

The difficulties in partioning, however, are perhaps more treacherous than Pound imagined. One cannot partition discretion and rule for all time; rather, the boundaries must move as circumstances change. The boundaries may be different for different policies or particularized concepts of justice. Discretion may, in some circumstances, be a better method of achieving rule conformity than the application of rules in a coercive manner. Adjustment of discretion and rule to each other may lead to reformulations of the rule, as rule and discretion stand in a mutually affecting relationship.

Elmore (1978) has usefully divided implementation theory into four types: systems management, bureaucratic process, organizational development, and implementation as conflict and bargaining. These labels will be elaborated upon below. While there may be some overlapping of categories, one model may be more useful than another in achieving particular goals of desegregation.

The basic hypothesis is that the Supreme Court initially relied upon an organizational development model, and, finding it unavailing, resorted to management techniques supported by bureaucratic process. This change roughly coincided with the Civil Rights Act of 1964, and the Court's revised approaches were aided by the participation of the Office of Civil Rights and the Department of Justice. For a period, roughly from 1974-1978, Court pronouncements on the objectives and remedies for desegregation were clouded by divisions on the Court (Yudof, 1978), but in the recent *Columbus* (1979) and *Dayton* (1979) cases, the Court reaffirmed the objective of racial balance remedies for districts found to have engaged in racially discriminatory practices. Depending on one's definition of the goals of desegregation suits, a strong argument may be made that a management systems approach proved more efficacious for the actual mixing of black and white students, and much less so for the "second generation" problems, such as tracking, disciplinary policies, teacher transfer, and tenure policies (Levin and Moise, 1975). Indeed, as one moves beyond a narrow view of desegregation premised only on racially mixed student bodies and faculty and toward a learning perspective, the promise of the systems approach is substantially reduced (see Cohen, 1975, 1980). When the Court recently addressed the learning component of desegregation remedies, it rightly returned to an organization development strategy.

BROWN II AND ORGANIZATIONAL DEVELOPMENT

The implementation of the *Brown* (1954) decision was left largely to the discretion of lower court federal judges. Initiation of desegregation plans was to come in the first instance from school boards, and they were to take account of local concerns and problems in the desegregation process. This, in essence, was the message of *Brown II* (1955).

The effort was to achieve nondiscrimination by race by building a normative commitment and hence a consensus among those at the base of the organization responsible for carrying out the Court's directives. This is essentailly an organizational development approach. The Court did not so much coerce or directly restrain discretion as it committed itself to securing the cooperation of local federal judges, lawyers, law professors, interest groups, and local school districts. A psychological explanation is that organizations exist to satisfy psychological and social needs of people, and the way to do this is to minimize hierarchy and to maximize broad participation, community, mutual adaptation and agreement, and management of conflict (Elmore, 1978). The approach is essentially a grass-roots or bottom-up strategy. If the quality of interpersonal relations is high, if blacks and school officials and others are brought together and persuaded that they should observe desegregation rules and policies, the quality of decisions will improve and desegregation will be achieved.

To say that the Court chose this organizational development approach would be a gross distortion of the facts. But if the Court feared that it could not force compliance with the *Brown* decision, that topdown orders would be ignored, the most feasible strategy would be to coopt those responsible for implementation and to give them a shared sense of responsibility for it. In doing this, the Court relied on the highest traditions of the moral authority of the Supreme Court. Under an organizational development model, persuasion may take place through strong local training programs, the involvement of local experts and constituent groups, and mutual adaptation among highly motivated and voluntary participants. But the Court relied upon its ability, through moral suasion and by virtue of its position in the political order, to reach consensus by instilling new values among the hostile and uncommitted (see Rostow, 1967). The Court attempted to articulate the principles of nondiscrimination in such a way that people would internatlize those principles. Compliance would come out of a realization as to what was "right," and not out of a sense of coercion from a higher authority.

The Supreme Court's effort to gain cooperation at the grass-roots level is perhaps best exemplified, ironically, by *Cooper* v. *Aaron* (1958). In that case, in an opinion signed by all nine justices, the Court placed its imprimatur on the use of federal troops to enforce a desegregation order in Little Rock, Arkansas. For the first time, however, one of the justices wrote a separate concurring opinion in a desegregation case. Justice Frankfurter wrote that the success of desegregation depended upon "working together . . . in a common effort" to promote tolerance, understanding, and acceptance of desegregation orders. He was disturbed that "the process of the community's accommodation to new demands of law upon it," begun so "peacefully and promisingly," had been undermined by the interference of state authorities in Arkansas (*Cooper* v. *Aaron*, 1958: 20). Rather than threatening sanctions, he referred to Lincoln's phrase about the need to "appeal to 'the better angels of our nature' " (p. 26), and he specifically lectured public officials on their obligations in a democratic nation:

> The responsibility of those who exercise power in a democratic government is not to reflect inflamed public feelings but to help form its understanding [*Cooper* v. *Aaron*, 1958: 26].

Writing to his friend C. C. Burlingham at the time *Cooper* was decided, Frankfurter left no doubt about his reasons for writing separately:

> Why did I write and publish the concurring opinion? I should think anybody reading the two opinions would find the answer. My opinion, by its content and its atmosphere, was directed to a particular audience, to wit: the lawyers and the law professors of the South, and that is an audience which I was in a peculiarly qualified position to address in view of my rather extensive association, by virtue of my twenty-five years at the Harvard Law School, with a good many Southern lawyers and law professors. I myself am of the strong conviction that it is to the legal profession of the South on which our greatest reliance must be placed for a gradual thawing of the ice, not because they may not dislike termination of segregation but because the lawyers of the South will gradually realize that there is a transcending issue, namely, respect for law as determined so impressively by a unanimous Court in construing the Constitution of the United States [Hutchinson, 1979: 84].

Perhaps over the long run the Court has been successful in altering attitudes toward black Americans and in obtaining acceptance of the idea that racial discrimination is morally and constitutionally wrong. But in the short run the strategy failed. Consensus proved impossible, resistance to school desegregation was unflagging, and the processes of persuasion yielded important but only incremental results (Kirp and Yudof, 1974). As Orfield (1969) and others have noted, federal district judges were more inclined to yield to local prejudices and pressures than to insist on the enforcement of *Brown* (see Rodgers and Bullock, 1972; Peltason, 1961). Most did not attempt to persuade, but rather helped to maintain existing barriers. The Congress and the executive branch did not join in the crusade to create a new consensus against the dual school system. State legislatures and local school boards did not accept the new wisdom and, far from being drawn into a process of mutual consent and open communication, they actively resisted desegregation. Compliance with neither the letter nor the spirit of *Brown* occurred.

The experience in the early years after *Brown* demonstrates the circularity of the organizational development approach in many implementation contexts. Implementation is not perceived as a hierarchical process in which promulgators of rules and policies achieve adherence to their objectives whatever the hostilities and hesitations of those at the bottom of the hierarchy. To a great extent, implementation depends upon a prior consensus or at least acquiescence on the policies before they are imposed. This is more a model describing a social, political, and cultural unity than a prescription for strategies to achieve compliance.

On the other hand, values are not static. There is no timeless equilibrium. Processes of persuasion can work. While the law relies upon hierarchical controls and sanctions, it is a truism that most law compliance occurs because people are already predisposed to obey laws. Deterrence of murder and rape is not entirely a function of fear of sanctions for violating laws prohibiting them; rather the laws work to the extent they do largely because most persons agree with the values and judgments inherent in such statutes. Those who break murder and rape laws are deviant, atypical. Legislative bodies, by virtue of the electoral process, are more likely to reflect an existing consensus in their policy making. In the case of the Supreme Court, its success will frequently be a function of its capacity to ride the crest of a wave of changing mores and attitudes or to intrude where there is no already existent, deeply entrenched hostility. At the time of *Brown,* racial discrimination was not sufficiently deviant to bring forth an affirmative response to the decision, whatever the longer-term prospects for value inculcation and change.

SYSTEMS MANAGEMENT, BUREAUCRACY, AND THE CIVIL RIGHTS ACT OF 1964

After the enactment of the Civil Rights Act of 1964, the involvement of the federal executive branch in the enforcement of *Brown* (Radin, 1977), and the toughening of the judicial approach in the Fifth Circuit (*U.S.* v. *Jefferson County Board of Education,* 1966) and the Supreme Court (*Green* v. *New Kent County,* 1968), a systems management approach to the implementation of the desegregation cases began to unfold. School boards were described as obstinate, as engaging in delaying tactics (see, for example, *Green* v. *New Kent County,* 1968; *Swann* v. *Charlotte-Mecklenburg Board of Education,* 1971). No longer was the effort to create a consensus among district court judges, local school authorities, and interest groups around the *Brown* principles. Ambiguities as to what desegregation meant were reduced as the Office of Civil Rights in HEW and the courts began to embrace numerical formulas for deciding whether the dual school system had been eliminated

(Radin, 1977). As objectives were clarified, the emphasis was on obedience to rules emanating from hierarchical administrative and judicial authorities. Goal-directed behavior, accountability, strategic planning, and decisional rules were the hallmark of the *Greene* (1968) to *Keyes* (1973) era. The role of the Civil Rights Division of the Department of Justice in filing desegregaiton suits upon complaints of discrimination, the bureaucratic monitoring activities and guidelines of the Office of Civil Rights, and the rejection of freedom of choice plans that did not "work" by the Supreme Court are all examples of this new approach. Developmental processes were subservient to strategies that secured results — desegregated school systems. Sanctions, such as the threat of a cutoff of federal education funds, were utilized to alter the behavior of school officials (see U.S. Commission on Civil Rights, 1970). Lower federal courts were more severely instructed as to the rules they should follow in entertaining desegregation suits (see *Alexander* v. *Holmes County Board of Education,* 1969).

The conventional wisdom today, in the light of the alleged failure of so many federal programs enacted during the Johnson era, is that frequently the systems management approach does not work in a complicated federalist system, with semiautonomous local and state governments (Elmore, 1978, 1979). The problem is that there is no direct subordinate relationship between federal authorities and other levels of government — even if the basis of decision is the Constitution of the United States or duly enacted federal statutes. There are multiple and overlapping lines of authority, conflicting and ambiguous goals, and frequently a lack of normative commitment by those expected to execute federal policies. This has led some modern implementation theorists to redefine implementation in the most bizarre terms. Implementation does not describe a process of behavior change so much as a needed redefinition of what one means by compliance so that reality conforms to command.[2] Thus, it is unrealistic to expect school districts to obey desegregation orders, to adhere to Title I regulations, or to abide by the hearing requirements for the placement of handicapped students. Description becomes prescription. For fear that a program will be described as a failure, one simply changes the meanings of success and failure.

This concept of implementation is nonsense. If there is anything that the desegregation experience demonstrates, it is that hierarchically imposed rules can work. In the ten-year period of 1964-1974, the country did move closer to desegregation even if the world was far from perfect (Orfield, 1978). The amassing of federal resources and the clarification of goals and strategies did have an enormous impact. If anything, the notion of failure largely received attention because aspirations and goals had expanded. The courts began to move toward broader definitions of illegal segregative activities in the schools, and the remedy moved from nondiscrimination to one of racial balance (see Graglia, 1980; Yudof, 1978b; Wilkinson, 1974). Even in the context of these more difficult-to-achieve objectives, significant progress was made, particularly in the Deep South (Orfield, 1978).

This last point is worth emphasizing. If the goal of desegregation suits is to ensure nondiscrimination in the assignment of racial minorities, then, by any measure, enormous progress has been made. So, too, if the goal is to create integrated schools reflecting the proportions of the races in the school district, the achievement of the courts, utilizing a coercive approach, has been substantial (see *Milliken* v. *Bradley,* 1979). If, however, a unitary school system suggests the need for majority white schools and the elimination of all predominantly black schools, then the results of judicial intervention have been quite mixed (Armor, 1980). Most of America's largest cities have predominantly minority student populations, and intradistrict desegregation may contribute to the exodus of whites from the cities.[3] As Justice Powell recently stated, in his dissent from the dismissal of the writ of certiorari as improvidently granted in *Estes* v. *Metropolitan Branches of Dallas NAACP* (1980: 723):

> The pursuit of racial balance at any cost [within districts] . . . may encourage or set the stage for other evils. By acting against one-race schools, courts may produce one-race school systems.

Powell, like Frankfurter before him, worried about the lack of community support:

> A desegregation plan without community support, typically one with objectionable transportation requirements and continuing judicial oversight, accelerates the exodus to the suburbs of families able to move [p. 723].

Obviously, however, if the Court had pursued the systems management approach to its logical conclusion, that is, metropolitan remedies, this result probably would not have occurred (Orfield, 1978). The failure to endorse metropolitan desegregation plans may be consistent with other values, goals, and objectives, but it is not consistent with the majority white school remedy.[4]

Note a number of additional points about the systems management strategy after 1964. First, the strategy may have worked as well as it did because of the earlier devotion to organizational development. Perhaps the two models of implementation stand in a symbiotic relationship to each other. As a broader consensus was built around the proposition that racial discrimination was wrong, the ability to devise and succeed with a more coercive approach improved. Perhaps there is a basic threshold of agreement and acquiescence among portions of the population or among particular elites that is a prerequisite to more goal-directed implementation approaches. Second, the systems approach is consistent with a bureaucratic process approach (Elmore, 1978). The central attributes of this model are discretion and routine. The federal courts and the responsible administrative agencies sought to control the discretion of local and state school officials and to devise routines which would induce adherence to desegregation norms. New routines were substituted for old, and federal officials became increasingly concerned with the more mundane (but important) aspects of bureaucratic life (Radin, 1977).

Finally, the systems management approach worked reasonably well in the context of a relatively simple goal. The remedy was to mix black and white students and faculties in some designated proportions. Compliance could be measured with relative ease, for an integrated school stands on the input and not on the output side of the education production function. This suggests that the achievement of more complex and difficult-to-monitor objectives may not be as amenable to the systems management approach.

Compliance with the letter of the law may be more easily achieved than compliance with the spirit of the law. A natural parallel is the implementation process with respect to Title I of the Elementary and Secondary Education Act of 1965 (see McLaughlin, 1975). After it became clear that local and state school authorities were not providing the type of compensatory education envisioned in the statute, more detailed regulations were issued and various mechanisms, such as audit reports, data collection, policy evaluations, and lawsuits, were utilized to force compliance. These worked best where violations were blatant and easily discernable. Districts could not use Title I monies to purchase fire engines; they could not reduce expenditures on the poor and then substitute federal dollars; they could not make Title I programs available to all children regardless of poverty or educational disadvantage. In this regard, the enforcement effort has been something of a success, albeit there are still discrepancies. But if implementation means that poor children receive a truly compensatory education, that their cultural disadvantages are overcome, that their achievement levels rise dramatically, and that creative and innovative programs have been put into place, Title I must be judged to be, on the whole, a failure.

Systems management can achieve basic compliance with the letter of a compensatory education law, but its utility in reaching larger and more complex goals is more dubious. So, too, if desegregation is aimed at improving race relations, improving black achievement, and motivating black students to learn and to pursue higher education, a systems management approach may not be feasible (see Kalodner and Fishman, 1978). This does not necessarily mean that such goals will be forever beyond our grasp, but perhaps only that devices for control and monitoring and for accountability, for limiting discretion through hierarchically imposed rules, may not be the way to go about these tasks (see Yudof, 1979).

BUREAUCRATIC PROCESSES?

Overlapping the period of systems management implementation by courts and administrative agencies (1964 to present) is an interesting period in which the Court, on paper at least, appeared to move toward a bureaucratic process model. Elmore (1978: 199) describes the bureaucratic process model in the following terms:

> The two central attributes of organizations are discretion and routine; all important behavior in organizations can be explained by the irreducible discretion exercised by individual workers in their day-to-day decisions and the operating routines that they develop to maintain and enhance their position in the organization. . . . The dominance of discretion and routine means that power in organizations tends to be fragmented and dispersed among small units exercising relatively strong control over specific tasks within their sphere of authority.

For our purposes, we should think of judges as "workers" exercising discretion in desegregation cases in accordance with the discretionary principles laid down in *Swann* (1971). In the *Swann* case, the Court emphasized the need for prompt desegregation and affirmed the use of racial balance remedies, but, in doing so, it cast the decision in terms of the remedial discretion of lower court judges. On review, the issues were framed as if the only question was whether the judge had abused his or her discretion in approving a particular desegregation plan. Unlike *Brown II* (1955), discretion lay more with judges than with local school authorities.

This line of thinking was continued in *Keyes* (1973), at least superficially, and in a series of post-*Keyes* cases, in which it appeared that the Court might be backing off on broad racial balance remedies.[5] This occurred at roughly the same time that the Nixon Administration confusingly vacillated on executive enforcement of the Civil Rights Act of 1964. The emphasis on discretion, the notion that different local conditions might require different sorts of remedies, led to tremendous variations in remedies in factually indistinguishable circumstances (Yudof, 1978b). Ultimately, however, the emphasis on bureaucratic discretion was belied by the specific results reached by the Supreme Court in later cases. Invariably, the Court either permitted a racial balance remedy to go into effect or it remanded the case for further consideration (see *Dayton Board of Education* v. *Brinkman,* 1977; *Austin Independent School District* v. *U.S.,* 1976). The exception to this trend is the metropolitan desegregation case in Detroit, *Milliken* v. *Bradley* (1974). Thus, the Court affirmed a discretionary-bureaucratic approach in the language of its opinions, but sent a quite distinct message in terms of what it actually required of federal district court judges (Graglia, 1980). This was made even clearer in the *Columbus* (1979) and *Dayton II* (1979) cases, in which the Court reaffirmed that racial balance remedies were still the order of the day in the desegregation area.[6]

CONFLICT AND BARGAINING

In the 1970s the implementation as conflict and bargaining model also came to the fore. Under this model, organizations are viewed as arenas of conflict in which different groups at different times compete for power and control of scarce resources. Implementation is not so much compliance with top-down policies, as it is decision making among various groups where no consensus prevails. A series of complex bargains is a manifestation of the implementation processes, and no single set of purposes and no single definition of success is adopted. The process is one of mutual adjustment, as the parties bargain within legal constraints.

Successful implementation is relational, being dependent on the achievement of the goals of particular parties occupying particular places in the process. The distribution of power is unstable and changes over time (Elmore, 1978: 217-226). This political view of implementation can be seen in the desegregation context in terms of proposals for minority control of schools.[7] It can also be seen in those districts where some segment of the black community appears willing to exchange racial balance for opportunities for black educators, compensatory programs, and upgrading of facilities in black schools. While such bargaining sometimes has been approved by lower courts, the Supreme Court has never explicitly taken the position that the black community or portions of it may trade integration for other educational, political, and social goals. The recent rulings in *Estes* v. *Metropolitan Branches of Dallas NAACP* (1980), *Columbus Board of Education* v. *Penick* (1979), and *Dayton Board of Education* v. *Brinkman* (1979) would appear to indicate that the Court will not be receptive to a political implementation model that deviates in outcome so markedly from the racial balance remedies it desires to produce.

ORGANIZATIONAL DEVELOPMENT REVISITED

Finally, there have been some recent developments which indicate that the Court may be aware of the limitations on the systems management approach in the context of fulfilling the higher aspirations of desegregation. In a cyclical manner, the Court may be returning to a variation of the organizational development model that failed in the 1950s. After student bodies and faculties are racially integrated, myriad educational, disciplinary, and social decisions need to be made concerning student life and achievement in schools. The issues include such diverse matters as tracking, grade structure, bilingual education, compensatory education, availability of vocational programs, and student counseling. In the *Milliken II* (1977) decision, the Court affirmed a broad remedy which struck at the heart of such matters, and appeared to affirm the need to enlist the aid of local school authorities in devising the most efficacious desegregation order. The Court, in effect, affirmed a compact among the district judge, school authorities, and the plaintiffs (to a much lesser degree) about altering the quality and nature of education in the Detroit school district. The affirmation took place against the backdrop of schools that could not be integrated, in the sense of creating predominantly white schools, since Detroit is predominantly black and the Court had rejected a metropolitan remedy (see Yudof, 1979).

The *Milliken II* approach has much to commend it. If desegregation is to succeed in an educational sense, the cooperation of teachers and administrators must be secured. Learning takes place at the micro level, in the classroom, and cannot be settled by gross formulas for allocating students to different schools within the system. Systems management models applicable to racial balance remedies in relation to school districts are likely to be of little avail. Consider the relevant characteristics of school organizations outlined by March (1978). First, educational institutions are social institutions in the public sector with vague, contradictory, and often highly abstract objectives. Decisional rules are difficult to formulate, and discretion may be precisely what is needed to improve learning. In any event, one's view of good faith, compliance, efficacy, and related matters is likely to be a function of social values and ideology.

Second, education is labor intensive. This means that implementation in the learning context depends upon the cooperation of a large number of actors (teachers, principals) and not just those in the central administration charged with student and faculty school assignments. Further, the technology employed by these actors is one "of learning, development, and change in people" (March, 1978: 223). Such technologies are frequently elusive, so elusive that it is difficult to tie particular means to ends. Third, there is a tremendous amount of movement of personnel in and out of education positions:

> Most educational administrators attain the best job they will ever have at an early age and leave it considerably before normal retirement age; and most educational administrators will spend most of their working lives doing something else [March, 1978: 227].

This may pose severe problems of continuity of leadership. Further, since there are no profits to be appropriated privately, administrators may seek to maximize "profit in kind," for example, prestige, autonomy, and budgets (see Michaelson, 1977).

Fourth, "educational administration is only loosely coupled to educational activities in the classroom" (March, 1978: 224). Far from being a rigid hierarchy or typical bureaucracy, activities and components are only loosely coordinated and related to the formal structure of the school system. There are few rules regarding instructional practices, formal evaluations are infrequent or unused, and decision making tends to be decentralized (National Institute of Education, 1978). While this picture is oversimplified and not all organizational theorists would accept it, the "loose coupling" view would appear to make monitoring and implementation within school organizatons more difficult, particularly if the objective were to alter classroom regularities. Thus March (1978: 223) has come to think of educational organizations as "organized anarchies":

> The term [organized anarchies] is used to describe organizations in which technologies are unclear, goals ambiguous, and participation fluid. . . . Educational technology is poorly understood; assured educational objectives tend to be vague, contradictory, or not widely shared; participants in educational organizations include individuals and groups who move in and out of activity in the organization sporadically.

CONCLUSION

If the judicially defined goals of desegregation are to be met, the federal courts must continue along two lines of implementation. With respect to the physical mixing of the races, they should adhere to a coercive approach. Experience shows that racial balance remedies will not be abided without strong hierarchical constraints. With respect to learning, however, and after physical desegregation has taken place, the most productive path lies in the organizational development route. School systems should be encouraged to produce innovative programs, to provide in-service training for teachers, to exercise their discretionary powers to achieve the broader objectives of the process. One cannot order a teacher to provide a meaningful reading or social studies program for black children; rather the teacher must be normatively committed to the need for such programs, have sufficient resources, and be willing to work hard.

Ultimately, the success of the learning enterprise will be a function of local expertise, local talent, parental involvement, locally developed programs, and the participation of highly motivated school personnel. At best, the federal courts can seek to facilitate the processes of mutual agreement, communication, and consensus building. They will only fail if they seek to order changes in educational practices and routines within schools and classrooms.

NOTES

1. Elmore (1978: 215) notes:
    The result is that, in terms of the effective structure of organizations, the process of initiating and implementing new policy actually begins at the bottom and ends at the top. Unless organizations already have those properties that predispose them to change, they are not likely to respond to new policy.
See, generally, Berman et al. (1975), Bardach (1977), and Sarason (1971).

2. This version of implementation is reminiscent of Antoine de Saint Exupery's (1971: 41-42) story about the king of the planet whose vast ermine robe covered much of his domain. The planet was so cramped that the little prince could find no place to sit, and, since he was tired, he yawned:
    "It is contrary to etiquette to yawn in the presence of a king," the monarch said to him. "I forbid you to do so."
    "I can't help it. I can't stop myself," replied the little prince. . . . "I have come on a long journey, and I have had no sleep."
    "Ah, then," the king said, "I order you to yawn. It is years since I have seen anyone yawning. Yawns, to me, are objects of curiosity. Come now? Yawn again! It is an order."

3. The fact that some loss of white students is usually associated with school desegregation is not disputed (Armor, 1980). But scholars disagree over the extent, measurement, and conditions for white flight. See, for example, Armor (1980), Coleman

et al. (1975), Pettigrew and Green (1976), Rossell (1976), and Robin and Bosco (1976).

4. See Milliken v. Bradley (1974). But see Buchanan v. Evans (1977).

5. See, for example, Dayton Board of Education v. Brinkman (1977), Austin Independent School District v. U.S. (1976), and Pasadena City Board of Education v. Spangler (1976).

6. Graglia (1980: 96) notes: "The result of these latest Supreme Court decisions is to return the law to the position it was in at the time of *Keyes* and virtually to cancel all subsequent developments."

7. Atlanta, Georgia, is the most noteworthy example of this trend. For additional information, see Orfield (1978).

8. In addition, see Meyer and Rowan (1977) and Weick (1974).

CASES

ALEXANDER v. HOLMES COUNTY BOARD OF EDUCATION (1969) 396 U.S. 19
AUSTIN INDEPENDENT SCHOOL DISTRICT v. U.S. (1976) 429 U.S. 990
BROWN v. BOARD OF EDUCATION [BROWN I] (1954) 347 U.S. 483
BROWN v. BOARD OF EDUCATION [BROWN II] (1955) 349 U.S. 294
BUCHANAN v. EVANS (1977) 555 F.2d 373, cert. denied sub nom. Delaware State Board of Educaion v. Evans, 434 U.S. 880
COLUMBUS BOARD OF EDUCATION v. PENICK (1979) 99 S.Ct. 2941
COOPER v. AARON (1958) 358 U.S. 1
DAYTON BOARD OF EDUCATION v. BRINKMAN [DAYTON I] (1977) 433 U.S. 406
DAYTON BOARD OF EDUCATION v. BRINKMAN [DAYTON II] (1979) 99 S.Ct. 2971
ESTES v. METROPOLITAN BRANCHES OF DALLAS NAACP (1980) 100 S.Ct. 716
GOSS v. BOARD OF EDUCATION (1973) 482 F.2d 1044 (6th Cir.), cert. denied, 414 U.S. 1171 (1974)
GREEN v. SCHOOL BOARD OF NEW KENT COUNTY (1968) 391 U.S. 430
KEYES v. SCHOOL DISTRICT NO. 1, DENVER, COLORADO (1973) 413 U.S. 189
MEDLEY v. SCHOOL BOARD (1973) 482 F.2d 1061, cert. denied, 414 U.S. 1172 (1974)
MILLIKEN v. BRADLEY [MILLIKEN I] (1974) 418 U.S. 717
MILLIKEN v. BRADLEY [MILLIKEN II] (1977) 433 U.S. 276
MILLIKEN v. BRADLEY [MILLIKEN III] (1979) 476 F. Supp. 257 (E.D. Mich.)
PASADENA CITY BOARD OF EDUCATION v. SPANGLER (1976) 427 U.S. 424
SWANN v. CHARLOTTE-MECKLENBURG BOARD OF EDUCATION (1971) 402 U.S. 1
U.S. v. JEFFERSON COUNTY BOARD OF EDUCATION (1966) 372 F.2d 836, aff'd *en banc,* 380 F.2d 385 (1967), cert. denied, 389 U.S. 840 (1967)

REFERENCES

ALLISON, G. (1971) Essence of Decision: Explaining the Cuban Missle Crisis. Boston: Little, Brown.

ARMOR, D.J. (1980) "White flight and the future of school desegregation," in W. G. Stephan and J. R. Feagin (eds.) School Desegregation: Past, Present, and Future. New York: Plenum.

BARDACH, E. (1977) The Implementation Game: What Happens After a Bill Becomes a Law. Cambridge, MA: MIT Press.

BERMAN, P. (1978) "The study of macro- and micro-implementation." Public Policy 26: 157-184.

———— and M. McLAUGHLIN (1975) Federal Programs Supporting Educational Change, Volume IV: The Findings in Review. Santa Monica, CA: Rand Corporation.

————, D. MANN, P. GREENWOOD, and J. PINCUS (1975) Federal Programs Supporting Educational Change (5 Volumes). Santa Monica, CA: Rand Corporation.

BULLOCK, C. and H. RODGERS (1976) "Coercion to compliance: southern school districts and school desegregation guidelines." Journal of Politics 38: 987-1011.

CHAYES, A. (1976) "The roles of the judge in public law litigation." Harvard Law Review 89: 1281-1316.

CLUNE, W., II (1979) "Serrano and Robinson: studies in the implementation of fiscal equity and effective education in state public law litigation," in M. Feely et al. (eds.) Schools and the Courts. Eugene: ERIC Clearinghouse on Educational Management, University of Oregon.

COHEN, E. (1980) "Design and redesign of the desegregated school: problems of status, power, and conflict," in W. G. Stephan and J. R. Feagin (eds.) School Desegregation: Past, Present, and Future. New York: Plenum.

———— (1975) "The effects of desegregation on race relations." Law and Contemporary Problems 39, 2: 271-299.

COLEMAN, J. S., S. KELLY, and J. MOORE (1975) Trends in School Desegregation, 1968-1973. Washington, DC: Urban Institute.

CRAIN, R. L. (1969) The Politics of School Desegregation. Garden City, NJ: Anchor.

DOLBEARE, K. and P. HAMMOND (1971) The School Prayer Decisions. Chicago: University of Chicago Press.

ELMORE, R. (1979) "Backward mapping: implementation research and policy decisions." Political Science Quarterly 94: 601-616.

———— (1978) "Organizational models of social program implementation." Public Policy 26: 185-228.

ERMANN, M. D. and R. LUNDMAN [eds.] (1978) Corporate and Governmental Deviance: Problems of Organizational Behavior in Contemporary Society. New York: Oxford University Press.

GOULDNER, A. (1965) Patterns of Industrial Bureaucracy: A Case Study of Modern Factory Administration. New York: Macmillan.

GRAGLIA, L. (1980) "From prohibiting segregation to requiring integration," in W. G. Stephan and J. R. Feagin (eds.) School Desegregation: Past, Present, and Future. New York: Plenum.

———— (1976) Disaster by Decree: The Supreme Court Decisions on Race and the Schools. Ithaca, NY: Cornell University Press.

HUTCHINSON, D. (1979) "Unanimity and desegregation: decision making in the Supreme Court, 1948-1958." Georgetown Law Journal 68: 1-96.

KALODNER, H. and J. FISHMAN [eds.] (1978) Limits of Justice: Courts' Role in School Desegregation. Cambridge, MA: Ballinger.

KAUFMAN, H. (1960) The Forest Ranger: A Study in Administrative Behavior. Baltimore: Johns Hopkins University Press.

KIRP, D. (1979) "Race, schooling, and interest politics: the Oakland story." School Review 87: 355-397.

—— (1977) "School desegregation and the limits of legalism." Public Interest 47: 101-128.

—— (1976a) "Proceduralism and bureaucracy: due process in the school setting." Stanford Law Review 28: 841-876.

—— (1976b) "Race, politics, and the courts: school desegregation in San Francisco." Harvard Educational Review 46: 572-611.

—— and M. G. YUDOF (1974) Educational Policy and the Law. Berkeley, CA: McCutchan.

LEVIN, B. (1978) "School desegregation remedies and the role of social science research." Law and Contemporary Problems 42, 4: 1-36.

—— and P. MOISE (1975) "School desegregation litigation in the seventies and the use of social science evidence: an annotated guide." Law and Contemporary Problems 39: 50-133.

LINDBLOM, C. (1959) "The science of 'muddling through.'" Public Administration Review 19: 79-88.

LOWI, T. (1969) The End of Liberalism. New York: Norton.

McLAUGHLIN, M. W. (1976) "Implementation of ESEA Title I: a problem of compliance." Teachers College Record 77: 397-415.

—— (1975) Evaluation and Reform: The Elementary and Secondary Education Act of 1965, Title I. Santa Monica, CA: Rand Corporation.

MARCH, J. (1978) "American public school administration: a short analysis." School Review 86: 217-250.

—— and J. OLSEN (1976) Ambiguity and Choice in Organizations. Bergen, Norway: Universitatesforlaget.

MEYER, J. W. and B. ROWAN (1977) "Institutionalized organizations: formal structure as myth and ceremony." American Journal of Sociology 83: 340-363.

MICHAELSON, J. R. (1977) "Revision, bureaucracy, and school reform: a critique of Katz." School Review 85: 229-246.

MURPHY, J. (1971) "Title I of ESEA: the politics of implementing federal education reform." Harvard Educational Review 41, 1: 35-62.

National Institute of Education (1978) High School '77: A Survey of Public Secondary School Principals. Washington, DC: Government Printing Office.

ORFIELD, G. (1978) Must We Bus? Segregated Schools and National Policy. Washington DC: Brookings.

—— (1969) The Reconstruction of Southern Education: The Schools and the 1964 Civil Rights Act. New York: John Wiley.

PELTASON, J. (1961) 58 Lonely Men: Southern Federal Judges and School Desegregation. Urbana: University of Illinois Press.

PETTIGREW, T. F. and R. L. GREEN (1976) "School desegregation in large cities: a critique of the Coleman 'white flight' thesis." Harvard Educational Review 46: 1-53.

POUND, R. (1966) An Introduction to the Philosophy of Law. New Haven, CT: Yale University Press.

PRESSMAN, J. and A. WILDAVSKY (1973) Implementation. Berkeley: University of California Press.

RADIN, B. (1977) Implementation, Change, and the Federal Bureaucracy: School Desegregation Policy in HEW (1964-1968). New York: Teachers College Press.

ROBIN, S. and J. BOSCO (1976) "Coleman's desegregation research and policy recommendations." School Review 84: 352-363.

RODGERS, H. and C. BULLOCK (1972) Law and Social Change: Civil Rights Laws and Their Consequences. New York: McGraw-Hill.

ROSSELL, C.H. (1976) "School desegregation and white flight." Political Science Quarterly 90: 675-695.

ROSTOW,   (1967) "The democratic character of judicial review," in L. Levy (ed.) Judicial Review and the Supreme Court. New York: Harper & Row.

SAINT EXUPERY, A. de (1971) The Little Prince. New York: Harcourt Brace Jovanovich.

SARASON, S. (1971) The Culture of the School and the Problem of Change. Boston: Allyn & Bacon.

SELZNICK, P. (1969) Law, Society, and Industrial Justice. New York: Transaction.

SHKLAR, J. (1964) Legalism. Cambridge, MA: Harvard University Press.

STONE, C. (1975) Where the Law Ends: The Social Control of Corporate Behavior. New York: Harper & Row.

U.S. Commission on Civil Rights (1970) Federal Civil Rights Enforcement. Washington, DC: Government Printing Office.

WEATHERLY, R. and M. LIPSKY (1977) "Street-level bureaucrats and institutional innovation: implementing special education reform." Harvard Educational Review 47: 171-197.

WEICK, K. (1974) "Educational organizations as loosely coupled systems." Administrative Science Quarterly 21: 1-19.

WILDAVSKY, A. (1976) "The strategic retreat in objectives." Policy Analysis 2: 499-526.

WILKINSON, J.H. (1974) Serving Justice: A Supreme Court Clerk's View. New York: Charterhouse.

WILLIAMS, W. and R. ELMORE [eds.] (1976) Social Program Implementation. New York: Academic.

WISE, A. (1979) Legislated Learning: The Bureaucratization of the American Classroom. Berkeley: University of California Press.

Yale Law Journal (1980) "Judicial intervention and organization theory: changing bureaucratic behavior and policy." Yale Law Journal 89.

YUDOF, M.G. (1979) "Commentary on limits of justice." West New England Law Review 1.

——— (1978a) "An essay: federal child development programs and the helplessness of the helping professions." University of Texas Law Review 56.

——— (1978b) "School desegregation: legal realism, reasoned elaboration, and social science research in the Supreme Court." Law and Contemporary Problems 42, 4: 57-110.

11

IMPLEMENTING "ATTRACTIVE IDEAS": PROBLEMS AND PROSPECTS

JAMES E. CROWFOOT
MARK A. CHESLER

Effective school desegregation requires substantial changes in the organizational structure and operations of American schooling. Most attempts to press for racially equal access to educational opportunities have focused upon only a small portion of the changes required. It is no wonder, then, that our national experience with school desegregation is quite mixed. While there are clearly some gains, according to most scholars and practitioners desegregation has not led to all the hoped-for gains in achievement, race relations, or job mobility. Perhaps our hopes have been unrealistic; but perhaps we have failed to anticipate and analyze all the barriers to full implementation of desegregation.

At the very least, desegregation requires moving and mixing racial populations of students, and ending racial isolation in school attendance patterns. Even this step challenges prior patterns of separation, and the traditions and prejudices fostered thereby. To the extent that our efforts at school desegregation seek more than mere mixing but the realization of racial equality and justice in schooling, we encounter an even more difficult set of challenges.

As the society's agent for preparing and channeling a new generation of youth, schools have been primary conservators of racial separation, and more. They have been key elements in society's ability to maintain political and economic dominance in the hands of white and affluent groups. Access to resources, achievement outcomes, suspensions, curricula, tracking systems, cultural symbols, and staffing allocations all reflect patterns of white dominance of education, even when students of different races attend the same schools. The attempt to alter these patterns challenges whites' local and national economic and political interests, as well as the ideologies and operating processes of educators.

Current policy debates regarding desegregation center around the prospects of achieving: adequate student racial balance in the face of largely minority cities; more conspicuous student gains in achievement; control of conflict between students of different racial groups; reduction of the flight of white middle-class families to more racially separated suburban and exurban areas; and support for "busing" large numbers of white youth. Continuing controversy and struggle in these arenas obscures several underlying issues:

(1) the degree to which a variety of institutional reforms and innovative programs could be implemented to improve the quality and equality of schooling

(2) the degree to which failures to make such improvements are rooted in our history of racism and white domination of the economics, politics, and schooling of inequality

(3) the degree to which failures to make such improvements are rooted in a lack of technical and administrative skill in planning and carrying out complex processes of institutional change in education.

Such restatement of the agenda signifies the need for institutional change in education. Desegregation calls for changes which are difficult and complex to achieve and which inevitably require support from the wider political and economic community. In many instances, it requires restructuring of the power and roles of all groups involved, major changes in historic organizational patterns in schools, and changes in the schools' relations with community groups. Seldom do educators prepare for desegregation in ways that reflect these priorities and complexities. Seldom do court orders specify remedies, and ways of implementing remedies, that deal with these issues.

The cornerstone of our concern in this chapter is reflected in a concluding note to an earlier review: "We need to learn how to implement our best guesses, research findings, or praxis lessons, about what it is important to do in a desegregated school" (Chesler et al., 1979: 112). We are now prepared to discuss these problems of implementation, based upon a strong collection of guesses, findings, and lessons —

"attractive" ideas. In the attempt to create an operational agenda for meaningful racial change in schools, we have collected these ideas and organized them by their impact on the classroom, the local organization, the central administration, and the school community.

If, as suggested, we have failed to implement desegregation in ways that really deal with important issues and use new ideas, why is this so? What are the barriers to the spread of these attractive ideas, and to their actual utilization in desegregating schools and school systems? Codifying a number of attractive ideas, and understanding the barriers to effective implementation of desegregation, should permit more effective change plans for the future. There is little point to the generation of good research, or even of attractive ideas, unless we can help introduce them into the ongoing process of desegregated schooling. Furthermore, there is little point to such introduction unless we can figure out how these new plans and programs can be implemented and maintained over time.

WHAT ARE SOME "ATTRACTIVE" IDEAS?

There are several important components of a desegregation effort that are likely to increase its effectiveness. The standards for effectiveness, in the long run, should include the probability of gains in all students' achievement (but especially that of minority and poor students), in characteristic ways of thinking about and relating to members of other racial groups, and in expectations and realistic access to opportunities for future success in school and beyond.[1] Put another way, the standards for success should include increasing the school system's ability (at every level) to provide high quality educational services to everyone, and to increase the equality of its services to different social groups.

The ideas suggested here seem relevant to all components of success. Some are supported by considerable research; others are a product of careful reflection or even speculation by wise and informed scholars and practitioners and citizens.[2] Some of this knowledge has been retrieved from desegregation programs, but other attractive ideas are not necessarily unique to desegregated environments, nor should they be. We are concerned here with a dramatic need for the improvement of the entire educational scene.

We do not contend that these ideas are visionary or guaranteed, but they are an attractive and convenient summary and they set the stage for discussion of the problems of implementation. Obviously, successful implementation is not just a matter of doing these things, but of doing them in a spirit consistent with their potential for positive payoff.

IN THE CLASSROOM

The classroom is the primary locus of contact and learning in desegregated schools. As such, it is imperative for teachers to teach some new materials especially germane to an interracial situation, and to teach both old and new materials in different ways.

(1) Tests and instructional materials that are "culture-fair."

(2) Curricula that focus upon the history and cultures of various minority groups, including their traditions, music and literature, and heroes.

(3) Curricula that focus upon the local cultures and roles of different groups in the school and community.

(4) Curricula that focus explicitly on racism and race relations in America, including examination of current issues such as desegregation, unemployment, and affirmative action.

(5) Curricula that takes students into the community and that exposes them to the work and social situations of different racial groups.

(6) Organization of the classroom in ways that require students of different races to work with one another in interdependent task activities.

(7) A broad enough range of legitimate classroom tasks so that most students have expertise in some of them, so that task leadership can be shared throughout the class.

(8) Special preparation of youngsters for group skills required to work in interdependent task groups in and out of the class.

(9) Classroom reward systems that diminish the competitive press and academic status system, and that provide payoff for cooperative interracial endeavors.

(10) Teaching methods that respond to different and diverse racial and cultural styles, including linguistic and verbal/nonverbal preferences.

(11) Teaching methods that relate basic skills to the immediate life situations and needs of different student groups.

(12) Teacher attitudes, behaviors, and skills that make every child feel welcome and wanted in the classroom, and that stand as a model for students' behaviors with peers.

(13) Teaching approaches that invite student involvement in designing classroom tasks and other activities, and that seek feedback from students regarding their classroom experiences.

(14) Teaching methods that provide affirmative but critical feedback to students.

(15) Teachers, or teaching approaches, that are free of racism and invidious assumptions about the competence, probable success, or behavior problems of poor and minority students.

(16) Teacher attitudes, behaviors, and skills that can support and realize the above suggestions.

(17) Assistance to teachers so they can spend more time in individual or small-group instruction.

(18) The use of community (parent and other) resources in the form of citizens who have special skills or special information about the community, and who can share them in the classroom.

IN THE LOCAL BUILDING ORGANIZATION

The local school building is a secondary locus of student contact and a source of support for new classroom practices. Organizational policies and procedures must encourage and support innovative teacher activities in the classroom. In addition, the organization's structure and operating procedures, typically oriented to monocultural interests, must create a more pluralistic culture for the school and its inhabitants.

(1) Student assignment policies that promote an effective mix of students through all classrooms in the school, and in all activities, avoiding placement of solos.

(2) Development of school goals based on survival needs of a full range of students, and on the probable opportunities and constraints they will face in the future. These goals can be initiated by educators but should be verified or affirmed by community and student groups.

(3) Special teaching teams that are themselves interracial, and that stand as a working example of competence and positive racial relations.

(4) Development of equal-status working relations among staff members, and demonstration to students that the interracial staff can and does work together well, on an equal-status basis, and likes it!

(5) Vigorous searching and digging to discover any examples of racism. Passive postures or waiting for complaints are not adequate.

(6) Teacher involvement and, for some, co-control in major decisions about local desegregation efforts and local school policies and programs.

(7) Staff meetings that attend to school problems incidental to desegregation, and that seek to find solutions.

(8) Discussions among staff members that identify the warning signs of staff burnout and stress.

(9) Staff interaction patterns and helping relations that reduce feelings of isolation.

(10) Staff training sessions that help teachers relax and deal with the personal symptoms of stress and burnout.

(11) Rules and regulations for student behavior must be responsive to various cultural preferences, and administered in ways that are fair and consistent.

(12) Students must see rules and regulations as fair and administered fairly. This means special steps must be taken to promote perceptions of fairness, as well as fairness itself.

(13) Student participation, at some level of advice or influence, in setting policy for student behavior, cultural and social events, and so forth.

(14) Students, faculty, and community members also can play roles in co-governance of the local school, but there is little experience and much resistance regarding this option.

(15) Special vocational apprenticeship and preparation programs that might increase the economic payoff of school attendance for all students, especially for those from economically oppressed backgrounds.

(16) Principal and staff support for teacher reorganization of the classroom curriculum and new teaching approaches. This support must be public and vigorous, and include social as well as technical assistance.

(17) One way to make such support clear is for rewards to be provided to teachers who are either achieving gains with their students on agreed-upon outcomes or trying hard to develop and implement new classroom approaches. Peer esteem and affirmation, salary incentives, and public recognition are examples of relevant rewards.

(18) Counselor roles and styles that are not simply extensions of the school's disciplinary and social control mechanisms, but that seek to serve and respond to students' needs and interests. It is important not to stereotype or "track" youngsters into curricular, athletic, or social programs on race and class-based assumptions.

(19) Counselor activities that attempt to improve the entire community's services (recreational, economic, religious) to youth.

(20) Principal discussions with teachers regarding their contribution to student achievement and desegregation-related outcomes.

(21) Principal feedback to teachers on their pedagogical styles and methods.

(22) Development of a principal-staff team to provide leadership in desegregation programs.

(23) Administrative teams that are themselves interracial, and that stand as a working example of competence and positive racial relations.

(24) Staff support for minority administrators.

(25) Development of a norm of confrontation of obvious and subtle staff racism. (Confrontation does not mean brutality, but challenge to preexisting norms of racism.)

(26) Staff confrontation of other staff members who snipe or sabotage colleagues or administrators who are trying new ideas.

(27) The use of affirmative action criteria in hiring and placement of teachers and other staff members.

(28) Student and parent representation in staff selection.

(29) Orientation programs that acquaint new parents, especially those from distant neighborhoods, with school facilities, surroundings, programs and personnel, and vice versa.

(30) Use of parents as observers, data gatherers, and monitors of desegregation on buses, playgrounds, hallways, and in classrooms.

(31) Provision of incentives and rewards for parent participation in school activities.

(32) Development and use of parent resources in multicultural programs in and out of the school building.

(33) School programs that speak to community needs and interests and that draw the community into the school because it serves a variety of their local needs, not just because their children have to go.

(34) Establishment of bilingual bicultural programs for minority students.

(35) Alteration of school symbols (flags, songs, traditions) to reflect a multiracial multicultural student body.

(36) Development of a troubleshooter, ombudsperson, or other role that secures the trust of students, majority and minority, and is able to move in fast on growing problems and require others to attend to them. The role occupant must be provided protection so that she or he can challenge staff members or students.

(37) Provisions ensuring student safety on buses, at bus stops, on playgrounds, and so forth.

(38) A rumor control program that encourages parents to call a school staff member with any questions, concerns, or grievances.

(39) Development of self-assessment mechanisms whereby the entire school can have access to feedback on its operations by its staff and clientele.

(40) The establishment of mechanisms for securing input from the local community on matters pertinent to educational quality and equality.

(41) Periodic external evaluation of the school's operations in terms of preestablished criteria that specify indicators of racially just, high quality education.

IN THE CENTRAL ADMINISTRATION

In the offices of the school system administration there also are important innovations that can both support local programs and take the lead in encouraging changes that improve the impact of desegregation.

(1) Administrative support and new resources must be provided for local innovations. When Marcus Foster was superintendent of the Oakland schools, he told teachers he had a pot of $100,000 he would distribute to teachers and/or principals who came up with good ideas but needed a little extra money to make them go.

(2) The central board, superintendent, and staff must provide vigorous public leadership in support of desegregation in general, and in support of specific organizational changes required to make desegregation effective.

(3) Administrative support for desegregation also might provide extra resources for schools that voluntarily pair or desegregate their classes and services.

(4) Support might also take the form of providing expert help, either from inside the system or in the form of external consultants, for people trying to make changes.

(5) Similar leadership must be exercised to help develop active community groups in each school that can join with principals and staff members to co-plan local efforts, share community resources, monitor local activities, and help provide a push from above and below where local staffs are reluctant to move on their own.

(6) Support for local principals' staffing decisions when those decisions help serve the desegregation agenda. In particular, clear notification and support for the disciplining, relocation, and/or termination of teachers with histories of racist actions.

(7) Ability of principals to have upward influence in the system, to have impact on central staff policies and allocation of resources.

(8) Vigorous action to nonreward, remove, replace, or terminate a principal who is reluctant to move actively on the implementation of desegregation and/or who has a history of public racism in and out of school.

(9) A program of monitoring desegregation progress at the local school level, including evidence of any of the good ideas suggested earlier.

(10) Central office review of the quality of student achievement and race relations in student and student-staff interactions at various schools.

(11) Systemwide training programs in race relations for teachers, principals, and central office personnel, as well as freeing resources for such programs.

(12) An affirmative action program to increase the staff presence of minorities at all levels, especially in positions of authority. This is especially important for members of Hispanic groups.

(13) Here, as at the local school level, equal-status teams of educational leaders of various races and cultural groups, as well as sexes, need to visibly demonstrate their competence and their positive working relations.

(14) Invitations to groups of students to help create elements of a desegregation plan that will work for them and their peers.

(15) Employment of students as summer "aides" to help sell or build support for the plan in their own neighborhoods and schools.

(16) Engagement in efforts to cooperate with teachers' unions and associations in order to build professional support for, and commitment to, many of the good ideas above.

(17) The involvement of the local media in helping to carry out a public information and education program.

(18) Involvement of local police forces in planning desegregation programs and in spelling out interactions between police and school officials.

(19) Training programs for bus drivers and custodial staff in how to support desegregation.

(20) The mobilization of support from civic elites and leaders of the school-using sectors of the community to help guarantee jobs for students.

(21) Broad prodesegregation coalitions of municipal leaders can help mobilize public sentiment in support of desegregation, head off vigorous countermovements, help develop new resources to undergird innovative programs (such as foundation support for programs noted previously), and generate more good ideas.

(22) Special "orientation" programs that acquaint parents and community members, as well as newly reassigned staff and students, with the school and the sectors of the community from which they were previously isolated.

(23) Neighborhood meetings where public leadership is visible, new programs are explained, and input is sought from the community may help bridge the gap between the school hierarchy and concerned citizens.

(24) Central office initiative to involve parents in the regular review of principals' performances.

(25) The location of "magnets" in previously minority schools, as a way of encouraging majority student movement into those neighborhoods and schools.

(26) The development of special programs that act as "magnets" that are especially attractive to affluent and white students, and that may increase their retention in the system.

(27) A desegregation plan that immediately desegregates the youngest grade levels.

IN THE COMMUNITY

At the community leadership level there also are good ideas and resources relevant for increasing the effectiveness of school desegregation. In addition, at the grassroots or neighborhood level local parents and consumers can be helpful. Some of these options may be best implemented at the local building level, but others pertain to the entire community and the entire school system.

(1) Clear orders and pressure from the judiciary, if it has been active in the plan, will help, especially if the judiciary has done clear thinking about the good ideas and educational options available.

(2) Local grassroots coalitions can be encouraged to help support changes, and punish nonchanges, in local buildings. The possibility that local community groups might develop interracial memberships in support of innovative desegregation programming will place enormous pressure on the local school to get its act together.

(3) The development of active monitoring groups, whether officially appointed as blue-ribbon committees, or springing up as nascent local movements, can help pluralize knowledge about what is going on and prevent all knowledge, and therefore all power to act based upon knowledge, from resting in the hands of a small group of educators.

(4) Mobilization of local clergy to announce support for desegregation and values of racial equality during religious services.

(5) Establishment of connections with community groups working on social issues related to desegregation, such as urban transportation, housing discrimination, job discrimination, and tax policy.

(6) Community leaders also have the linkages that may make it possible to connect local desegregation efforts to other powerful figures in foundations or state and federal agencies. Thus, sources of support and resources to aid local programs may be facilitated.

(7) Efforts to bring together community groups who are ignorant or fearful of one another, but who might be able to share a common agenda of support for desegregation, or at least support for changes that might improve the quality of local schooling and ensure the safety of the children.

(8) Efforts to neutralize those community groups actively committed to sabotage or open resistance to desegregation itself, and/or to attempts to implement good ideas in desegregation.

(9) Establishment of a bureau of citizens and educators who can address local groups on the need to support desegregation (Kiwanis, Elks, Rotary, Masons, and so on).

(10) Establishment of parent-educator advisory boards for each school.

(11) Establishment of prodesegregation information displays in public buildings, including banks, businesses, and firehouses.

(12) Encouragement of local businesses to "adopt" and relate closely to particular schools. In this way external resources as well as job opportunities may be shared with students.

(13) Encouragement of local colleges and universities to "adopt" and relate closely with particular schools. In this way, external resources, as well as college information, may be made available to students.

(14) Support for political leaders who will push desegregation programs, even if their current constituency does not.

PROBLEMS OF IMPLEMENTATION

Our recent efforts at school desegregation are rife with examples of the nonimplementation of judicial orders and executive decisions, of the failure to carry out policies of effective desegregation at the community, school system, building, and classroom levels. Even the best administrative rhetoric and policy seldom is translated into effective programs at the local school level. We see examples of nonimplementation, and of resistance to racial and educational change, written in bold relief across the past 25 years of national history. They can be identified in the southern "massive resistance" of the 1950s and early 1960s and the northern "passive resistance" of the late 1960s and 1970s; in attempts at compliance with the letter but not the spirit of federal laws and judicial orders; in white flight, fright, and fight; in constant delay, dismay, and decay; and in the ways innovative desegregation programs and educational leaders have been ignored, sabotaged, coopted, or even fired and assassinated in character or person.

At the same time, we have many examples of truly innovative and attractive ideas and programs. Some schools and school systems have put them into effect and have even made them work over time. What makes the difference? Why are some policies and programs implemented and others not? Why do some schools and school systems move ahead effectively and others not? The reasons certainly may be various: overt resistance to the goals and value frameworks of new policies and programs; lack of power to enforce change, or lack of political will to risk new programs and behaviors; organizational inertia, lack of fit between policies and programs, or lack of support for change; and lack of knowledge or skill in teaching and managing in new ways.

The implementation process is not the same as the policy-making or decision-making process; however, policy making and implementation are deeply intertwined. The failure to plan for decision making and implementation together often results in substantial departures from the visions embodied in policy. In fact, the lack of congruence between policy making and policy implementation has led some observers to argue that what is really important to study is which policies are implemented, and not what decisions are made. Since the critical behaviors or activities affecting consumers, clients, or workers occur at the implementation stage, some scholars suggest that the study of policy processes should begin there:

> There are many contexts in which the latitude of those charged with carrying out policy is so substantial that studies of implementation should be turned on their heads. In these cases, policy is effectively "made" by the people who implement it [Pressman and Wildavsky, 1973: 174].

Unfortunately, the literature that studies only desegregation decision making by senior executives may be studying chimerical phenomena, abstract and distal processes. It is important to review post-decision-making problems, problems that prevent or delay implementation of ideas and programs that would comply with and actualize authoritative policies.

Part of what is problematic in understanding how social systems generate lower-level compliance with lawful orders of higher authorities is that simple compliance or noncompliance is not an adequate frame of analysis. Studies by Dolbeare and Hammond (1971) and Rodgers and Bullock (1972) indicate that there may be a wide variety of school leaders' responses to judicial orders, ranging from firm commitment to program objectives to lackadaisical carrying out of orders, to blind obedience, to subtle and even overt forms of resistance. Several studies of the implementation of authoritative decisions in organizations generate a similar range of responses. Merton (1940) and March and Simon (1958) discuss the dysfunctional aspects of each of these adaptations.

Following a design suggested by Terry (1980), we have organized the problems of implementing desegregation-related ideas into those of mission, power, structure, and resources. According to Terry (1980: 4):

> Mission refers to the purposes, directions, or visions of the future. Power is the expenditure of energy, the activity of making and keeping decisions over time. Structure points to a form, plan or regularized set of activities. Resources including anything that can be distributed.

These interdependent dimensions help us identify and map a series of problems in the organizational implementation of desegregation.[3]

PROBLEMS OF MISSION

Historic struggles over the mission of education are rooted in competing value frames regarding the American society. Some observers see our national educational system as an instrument of mass democracy, as a way of freeing all our people from the constraining limitations of social birth and background. Others see our educational institutions as instruments of continuing elite rule, as a covert way of channeling and maintaining inequities of birth across succeeding generations.[4] The ongoing struggle over the mission of mass public education is complicated by current social and economic conditions. Lack of clarity about the kind of adult world young people are being prepared for and what the dominant economic and social conditions will be in this future world further complicate any clear mission for our schools. Poverty and unemployment, especially the massive unemployment of young minority people, may render the question "Education for what?" quite futile. For these young people, education may not make any difference; and whether or not it is desegregated education may even be more irrelevant.

In the local school setting various professionals also may have different or contradictory goals: transmitting basic skills, orienting youth to citizenship, inculcating discipline and respect for authority, providing career and occupational preparation, keeping youth off the streets, operating as a public facility to the community, and generating commitment to a nonsectarian moral code. Elementary and secondary schools have different priorities with regard to these goals. When a school is desegregated and begins to serve a more heterogeneous student population, it may have to deal with competing cultural values regarding these goals; different racial or economic groups in the community may have different priorities. With such diffusion of goals, and confusion or even conflict about their priority, it is no wonder that the school has difficulty generating a clear mission. If school leaders do not analyze various groups' values or goals for schooling, they can scarcely understand, much less cope with, these alternative missions. Diffuse goals on controversial matters, or a lack of explicit priorities among goals, foster confusion and lack of commitment to sustained action for change. Moreover, it permits people opposed to official goals to question their legitimacy and relevance, and encourages evasion and resistance to implementation efforts.

Some form of desegregation has been our national policy since 1954, and many school systems have tried to act on the constitutional imperative and mix different racial groups in local schools. But early in the desegregation movement, some scholars and officials stressed the need to move beyond a concern for physical desegregation per se and to establish as policy the concept of "integration," "quality interracial education," or "effective desegregation." All these secondary symbols spoke to the problem of implementation once the legal or residential barriers to interracial education had been removed. However, all these terms have remained ambiguous, certainly more ambiguous than illegal segregation or racial imbalance, terms which have not been very clear over the years either.

For example, the Supreme Court has established equality of access to educational opportunity as the prevailing guide for desegregation. However, such access does not guarantee equal opportunity, and recent court decisions focusing on more specific remedies (such as remedial instruction and fair suspension policies) attempt to create more nearly equal opportunity as a goal for desegregation policies. Even such opportunity does not guarantee equal outcomes, certainly not in the midst of a racially unequal society. As a result, just what the long-term policy goal of desegregation *is* often is unclear. In this context, it is unclear what the mission of schools should or can be regarding racial inequality. The Myrdallian dilemma of American social values and mission is thus reenacted in the educational arena.

If one of the primary missions of all American schooling is to preserve and recreate the social order in succeeding generations, it is clear that maintaining racial distinctions and inequalities, with or without physical desegregation, is part of this priority. Institutional racism in American society acts as a subtle value commitment to affect all our public services, no less education. Hidden by alleged commitments to "merit" and "equal opportunity," institutional racism in schools covertly supports resistance to any "new" missions for an already overloaded school system and staff.

A lack of agreement regarding the values underlying any particular set of good ideas also may mitigate against their adoption. Reasonable people may disagree about the value of ideas such as student or community participation in school decisions, about new classroom curricula and task structures, or about alternative collegial relations. Without value agreement among implementers, and without clarity about where and how we disagree, how can we expect to gather the resources for commitment to change? The value problem in the organization is magnified when racial or other issues that divide the external community constitute the major lines of internal cleavage and conflict.

Since different groups are struggling to advocate their own senses of school mission, or at least their own priorities, those groups who have the most power in the community and the schools probably will have the greatest impact on the eventual mission. Thus, problems of mission and power interact with one another.

Examples of some of the attractive ideas mentioned above that pertain to the problem of mission in implementing effective desegregation include: (a) texts and instructional materials that are "culture fair" (Idea 1, in the Classroom); (b) development of a norm of confrontation of obvious and subtle staff racism (confrontation does not mean brutality, but challenge to preexisting norms of racism; Idea 25, in the Local Building); and (c) the development of special programs that act as "magnets" that are especially attractive to affluent and white students, and that may increase their retention in the system (Idea 26, in the Central Administration).

The development of an explicit statement of organizational values and goals can help articulate and command priorities among the many and often competing goals of education and of desegregated education. If persons from various interest groups can be involved in articulating and prioritizing these educational goals, they may help assess the impact of various options on their own needs, concerns, or traditions. Moreover, abstract and vague mission statements are harder to implement consistently and faithfully than more concrete and specific statements. Therefore, it may be useful for local school systems to evaluate their history of educational efforts and of racial equality and inequality in each district or building. Then, concrete and specific goal or mission statements can be developed for particular schools and communities, ones relevant to the particular needs or issues faced by students, citizens, and educators in that locale.

Another way to alter the mission of schools is to alter the beliefs and commitments of persons invested with policy-making or mission-setting responsibility. Value clarification and ideological "conversion" activities represent examples of such efforts. For instance, appeals may be made for all people to respect and act upon basic American values of "fair play" and "equal treatment." Consciousness-raising activities, which help people focus on the real sources and impacts of their actions and behavior, also may help effect such new visions and commitments. Activities that point out how old missions have failed to create equality, or even have backfired, may generate revision and reorientation.

Few Americans are racist by design and intent, and few consciously wish to deprive minority youth of equal educational opportunities. Much of the time value confusion, ignorance, and insensitivity to the implications of policy and program are involved, and mission-clarifying efforts can help address these issues. Of course, a subtle ideology of racism and deeply embedded institutional practices permit such confusion to exist; whether a frontal assault on these views will permit or provoke new understandings of the racial mission of schooling may depend on the power and resources available in the local community.

PROBLEMS OF POWER

Since desegregation is a process of racial as well as educational change, racism that maintains the power of white, male, affluent groups is a relevant barrier to change. Racial segregation is one means by which these groups exclude minorities from economic and educational privileges and opportunities. While the advance of desegregation challenges that power to exclude, it can be expected that ruling groups would either resist or try to control the pace and nature of the desegregation effort. Thus, it is important to consider what groups are involved in making major implementation decisions regarding school desegregation.

Several studies have emphasized the important role of local community elites in supporting or opposing school desegregation programs (U.S. Commission on Civil Rights, 1976; National Conference of Christians and Jews, 1976; Crain 1968). Most observers conclude that these persons and groups may not be very visible, but are potent nevertheless. Interestingly, at least one observer suggests that these elites may be quite vulnerable to shifting local politics and may follow rather than lead the mobilization of public opinion on controversial school issues (Rossell, 1976).

Whatever the causal chain, the consensus of scholars appears to be that local elites are an influential force in educational policy making, and therefore need to be involved in the implementation process. Community elites typically represent the dominant coalition in school boards and other groups that have substantial power to decide on school policies. Clearly, the interests of these elites are not necessarily the same as those of other community members and groups. Minority parents and students, or those from less affluent or powerful groups, may have different conceptions of the organization's mission, as well as different roles in the school organization and its decision-making processes.

School superintendents are, of course, primarily responsive to local power structures. To the extent they can satisfy elite parties, superintendents can probably maximize their discretionary power, and have greater personal latitude as well as security. For instance, in trying to understand superintendents' lack of forthright actions in encouraging principals' and teachers' compliance with court rulings on prayer in school, Dolbeare and Hammond (1971: 117) discovered that:

> superintendents uniformly defended their inaction by pointing to their many important priorities and emphasizing the need to conserve their political capital for such purposes.

With particular regard to civil rights and desegregation issues, Rodgers and Bullock (1972) noted that local political leaders provided a series of cues to school system leaders and members of other community groups regarding their desires. In attempting to understand why otherwise law-respecting and law-abiding influentials encouraged noncompliance with judicial orders, Rodgers and Bullock suggest the following factors: (1) disagreement with the law itself, (2) personal payoff (power and prestige) gained from defying the law, and (3) need to conform and avoid conflict with friends. Thus, the need to conserve one's power base, primarily by satisfying a powerful and affluent white constituency, may help explain nonimplementation. The power that sustains the current educational system can be expected to maintain it against incursions to alter it. If externally powerful groups try to contain the desegregation effort, to keep it impotent, they can do so by lending support to the implicit racism within the professional system of the schools.

Crain (1968) indicates that elites might support desegregation efforts for a series of reasons related to their legitimacy or desire for stability in the community (and of their status): (1) peace in the community, (2) a sense of charity or altruism for deprived groups, (3) maintenance of a stable economic environment and profitability, and (4) maintenance of an image of a progressive community. If these interests are not challenged, there may be little reason for the powerful to act in ways that meet other groups' needs or desires.

Suppose key power figures did act, and act positively, on desegregation plans and programs. What would be the effect of their actions? Johnson (1967) has developed an interesting analytic frame, paying careful attention to the mobilization of several different forms of social power as a means of gaining compliance with authoritative orders for change. He suggests that members throughout an organization will comply with such decisions to the extent that they attribute coercive, legitimate, and expert powers to the power holder. Coercive power is defined as the expectation of severe sanctions if compliance is not produced. Recognition of legitimate power is the conviction that one has a moral duty to accept the influence of an appropriate decision maker. Finally, attribution of expert power is the perception that the decision maker has superior knowledge by which policy is made. To the extent that judges, school boards, or other decision makers are reluctant to apply sanctions (or reluctant to imply that they will apply sanctions), their coercive power is weakened. To the extent they appear to be making decisions they have no right to make (intruding on local control of schools), their legitimate power is weakened. To the extent they appear to be making decisions on the basis of inadequate knowledge of the law or of education fact (suggesting innovative classroom practices, recommending "infeasible" programs), their expert power is weakened. In addition, no civil authority can "require" parents to continue living in a desegregated school system, "mandate" teachers to care for their students, or "order" students to learn. All power is limited.

School boards and superintendents are not the only key actors, however. Although many studies of school system change ignore or overlook other power figures, House (1974: 47) indicates quite clearly that "both the Central Office Staff (COS) and the superintendent act as gatekeepers through which innovations must pass. By controlling information, the COS manages initiative." Moreover, he notes:

> Organizations are controlled at the top by an informal elite. And in the school district, this elite consists of elements of the central office staff. The initiatory power of innovation adoption resides there, though not necessarily the power to implement the innovation. One must deal with this organizational elite in some way to effect educational innovation [House, 1974: 50].

The local school principal also has power. Berman and McLaughlin (1980: 67) point out the central role of the principal in helping all kinds of educational innovations and changes come about and be maintained over time.

> The principal's unique contribution to implementation lies not in "how to do it" advice better offered by project directors, but in giving moral support to the staff and in creating an organizational climate that gives the project legitimacy.

Metz's studies (1978) of the actions of principals in desegregated junior high schools provide some examples of this complex behavior set. She notes that the principals she studied were "keenly aware that they were responsible both for imaginative academic education and for safety and order in every part of the school. They were also aware that this double responsibility entailed practical contradictions and the necessity for choice" (Metz, 1978: 189).

In human services systems, as in voluntary agencies, the commitment and energy of lower-level participants (teachers, parents, and students) are essential for effective desegregation. This requirement gives lower-level personnel significant power to affect the course of the entire desegregation effort. In some cases, teachers' unions have resisted efforts to transfer teachers, and individual teachers have sabotaged efforts with minority youth. In other cases, students and teachers have taken the lead in making sure new programs work. In a similar vein, cooperation from parents and other low-power community members is likely to be essential at critical stages in the implementation process. Their lack of potent involvement or commitment to change deprives educators of important sources of power.

One theme of this section is that we often lack power to overcome other resistances and barriers to implementation, such as inertia, racism, nonrewards, and overt powers supporting nonchange. Without the power, or access to the power, to reassign faculties, remove principals, mobilize parents, promote innovative educators, develop new programs, reallocate system resources, or create and capture coalitions, it is very difficult to implement desegregation strategies. Thus, power is a key to actualizing mission as well as to altering structure, and to gathering and using new resources.

Examples of some of the attractive ideas outlined above that pertain to the problem of power in implementing effective desegregation include: (a) teaching approaches that invite student involvement in designing classroom tasks and other activities, and that seek feedback from students regarding their classroom experiences (Idea 13, in the Classroom); (b) teacher involvement and, for some, co-control in major decisions about local desegregation efforts and local school policies and programs (Idea 6, in the Local Building); and (c) ability of principals to have upward influence in the system, to have impact on central staff policies and allocation of resources (Idea 7, in the Central Administration).

Segregation has resulted from well-organized groups exerting their will on school policies, and any change to this tradition will require challenges to this will. Thus, the redirection of existing power, or the mobilization of new sources of power, may be keys to solving implementation problems. One way to proceed is for concerned groups to try to influence or capture the support of regional political or economic leaders. These influentials may be able to mobilize public support for a mission of more equal schooling, or they may be able to free private, state, or foundation funds.

Administrative and professional leaders also can develop new powers, or simply exert old ones, by creating mandates requiring other organizational members to implement new policies and programs. The use of official power can be very helpful in directing the efforts of school system employees. However, as we previously indicated, all executive power, even that of the federal judiciary, can be muted by the power of teachers and other educators to operate autonomously in their classrooms, by the power of parents and students to leave a desegregated school system, and by the power of higher level officials to mobilize resistance or to subtly and covertly fail to comply with the spirit as well as the letter of an authoritative decision. Thus, decisions must be backed up with clear sanctions.

Professionals committed to effective desegregation also can organize among their peers. Teachers' unions and associations of supervisors often can play a potent role in articulating the need for change and in leading the way to more imaginative and effective programs. In so doing, they can create peer pressure for change that may complement administrative pressures or sanctions.

If such leadership groups are not prepared to create and implement more effective programs for school desegregation, challenges to these people or their interests may have to occur. The history of local decision making with regard to desegregation bears this possibility out; it should be relevant to the process of implementation as well.[5] How are changes brought about in established centers of power? How are new centers of power generated? The mobilization of people throughout the community to support desegregation usually calls for action on the part of various constituencies. Students and parents can exert significant power to alter school operations if they can organize in large groups, articulate their own interests in new plans and programs, and mobilize others to challenge the power of school officials and structures. Attempts to exert such influence have sometimes required the development of new forms or pathways of power, including disruption of traditional educational operations. Strikes, boycotts, and demonstrations have been effective in helping many previously excluded groups gain substantial influence on local school and school system programs. One student or parent group generally cannot generate enough power to make a difference by itself; several groups may need to form a coalition (interracial, citizen-educator, student-adult) to work for change. Minorities, along with whites committed to effective desegregation, must be mobilized and organized to pressure decision makers and to monitor new programs over long periods of time.

While the development of leadership groups in schools and in the external community are both essential, more informal groups play important roles. Sometimes organizational development programs have been tried in school systems undergoing desegregation.[6] These efforts may create more open influence patterns among participants at various levels of the organization. Informal persuasion and influence often work where more overt and formal challenges or dictates fail or cannot be used. Moreover, such programs permit insiders and outsiders, educators and citizens to work together for change. Since the resources and the structures required for effective desegregation involve a wide variety of people in a wide variety of situations, change efforts that bring many of these people together may be quite effective.

PROBLEMS OF STRUCTURE

Some unique aspects of the common structure of school systems may contribute to the problem of nonimplementation of desegregation-related decisions and innovations. For instance, Nakamura and Smallwood (1980) make it clear that there is a wide range of implementation structures for court decisions regarding desegregation. They compare, for example, the orders of Judge Weigel in San Francisco and Judge Garrity in Boston. According to their quote of Kirp's report, Weigel "left implementation in the hands of those formally charged with the responsibility for running the school system" (Nakamura and Smallwood, 1980: 99). Garrity, in contrast, dealt with overt resistance by creating a special Department of Implementation in the Boston school system, and making that department directly accountable to the court: "In effect, Judge Garrity and his appointees became both the desegregation policy-makers and implementers for the Boston schools" (Nakamura and Smallwood, 1980: 100). Garrity himself did not become the actual implementor, but his order(s) specified implementation roles and programs, indicated his concern that new programs be carried out, and demonstrated his intent to monitor these processes. Weigel's order did not specify implementation programs or roles.

The school organization is a highly complex and differentiated structure, with many different hierarchical levels. In the case of authoritative decisions, for instance, the decision must pass from the school board to the local superintendent, to central office staffs, to principals, to teachers, to its final impact on students. At each step a policy decision may be reinterpreted and modified, implemented or not implemented. Furthermore, the number of steps in this command system blurs the responsibility for carrying out official orders. According to Nakamura and Smallwood (1980: 93):

> When court decisions should affect the behavior of large numbers of people who are not direct parties to a case, there still can be uncertainty about which other actors should obey the decision. Since the court's communication with these parties is not direct, there are opportunities for these parties to misperceive or selectively perceive their newly formulated legal obligations.

At various levels the school organization can be characterized as a "loosely coupled" system. That is, educational organizations lack close internal coordination. Curriculum is minimally integrated over years and subjects, task-oriented peer relations seldom occur among teachers of autonomous classes, outcomes often are uncontrolled and uninspected, and key implementers, such as teachers and principals, often operate without much direct supervision of their activities. While individual teachers and principals may not feel their roles are "loosely coupled," or minimally controlled, they are much less tightly integrated than similar organizations engaged in production or primary transformation tasks (Meyer and Rowan, 1978).

Various studies of the process of implementing educational innovations help us identify other aspects of this diffuse organizational structure. Gross and his colleagues (1971), as well as other scholars (Van Horn and Van Meter, 1977; Sabatier and Mazmanian, 1979; Monti, 1979) indicate that implementation will be more difficult under the following structural conditions: (1) when there is a lack of organizational motivators, including incentives and constraints; (2) when work arrangements require people to act in ways that are incompatible with the innovation; (3) when there is not an effective communication system between managers and subordinates; and (4) when there is no monitoring system that develops feedback. All these conditions reflect aspects of a loosely coordinated and monitored system.

When the loosely coupled character of school organizations is combined with the ideology of professional competence and autonomy, it often leads to patterns of staff relations and work that are quite atomistic. Many staff members work alone in their solitary classrooms, only vaguely aware of their colleagues' acts. Their work is not coordinated with other staff members and their interdependence is low. The outcomes of this organizational structure include loneliness and isolation in the face of pressures from students. When desegregation places added pressure on staff members, and when relations between staff members and their clients are not going smoothly, this lack of staff interdependence often can lead to extreme stress and burnout. The experience of teacher stress in desegregated schools is even more obvious when professionals and their clients exist in a mutual "war zone," bound to each other involuntarily, with mutual suspicion and distrust. Since asking for help is often shunned as a sign of weakness, and giving help is often seen as arrogance and presumption, teachers experiencing stress may have nowhere and no one to go to.

The large size and independent character of classroom and school structures often make it difficult for staff members to communicate effectively with one another and with students. Without effective interpersonal communications and social relationships, the school structure may be held together by the force of coercion — the fact that students must attend, and that they must abide by the directives and actions of school personnel. When these conditions are complemented by racial conflict or staff-student distrust, many students may feel frustrated and restless or alienated in their school experience. High rates of absenteeism, discipline problems, and low commitment to the learning process all may be organizational indications of this student stress and alienation.

As a result of loose coupling at the organizational level, tight controls and standardization of tasks often exist elsewhere in the school. The use of a single mode of instruction and vast numbers of rules for student behaviors weave a tight bureaucratic web over this diffuse professional system. Teachers' and students' apparent freedom is constrained severely by the limited options for interaction available and practiced in school. The diversity in goals and styles brought about by desegregation places severe strain on the ability of these structures to respond to all students' needs.

Although these strains may be most apparent in racial terms, societal divisions among persons of different ages, sexes, and socioeconomic status also are reflected in the internal structures of schools. School programs usually demonstrate how males and females and affluent and poor youngsters are expected to behave differently, to have different school goals, different friends and friendship patterns, and to be interested and competent in different educational activities. Tracking of various kinds maintains these societal divisions in the life of the school. Moreover, sharp status divisions between students and staff reinforce age separation, as does the organization of student academic and social life by seniority by grade level in the system. All these divisions help keep student groups separated from one another, divided in experience and interaction, and atomized in the face of a somewhat more coherently organized faculty and staff. Without cross-cutting associations, they are easy prey to external ideologies of racism, and to the influences of various groups and social forces resistant to more effective desegregation.

Examples of some of the attractive ideas discussed earlier that pertain to the problems of structure in implementing effective desegregation include: (a) organization of the classroom in ways that require students of different races to work together with one another in interdependent task activities (Idea 6, in the Classroom); (b) development of a troubleshooter, ombudsperson, or other role that secures the trust of students, majority and minority, and is able to move in fast on growing problems and require others to attend to them (Idea 36, in the Local Building); and (c) here, as at the local school level, equal-status teams of educational leaders of various races and cultural groups, as well as sexes, need to visibly demonstrate their competence and their positive working relations (Idea 13, in the Central Administration).

The attempt to "tighten" a loosely coupled school structure somehow also must "loosen" the standardization experienced at lower levels of the organization. Some of these efforts may proceed from the top, via administrative mandate and direction. Greater educator accountability can be instituted, as can procedures for monitoring instructional practices. Specific rewards can be made available to educators who can create student outcomes consistent with the desegregation agenda (greater achievement especially for minority youth, more positive racial interactions and attitudes, and so forth). Moreover, administrative directives can encourage teachers and counselors to depart from standard instructional practices and regimented rules and rule enforcement. The relaxation of control over students' school and classroom behavior may permit greater voluntary engagement of students of all races in the life of the school. Clearly, however, loosening control at this level requires greater coordination among staff members and between principals and educators, as well as among students.

Other efforts to alter the school structure may proceed from the "bottom up," from the efforts of newly involved students and parents. The development of client self-help groups is a phenomenon sweeping many human service systems; they could be part of school structures seeking to utilize all school and community participants in making the system operate more effectively. The development of more permeable school boundaries could permit parents and other community members more consistent access to the school, as well as engaging more educators in the ongoing problems and activities of the community. Through these new school-community structures, the resources of all concerned citizens could be made available to the school through regular forms of coordination and exchange.

Alterations in the structure of the school organization must be reflected in the nature of classroom organization as well. The use of collective tasks and rewards for students, small group work, and mobile desks and architectural arrangements all involve destandardization of classroom instructional technologies. Teachers may be encouraged to adopt these innovative approaches through the provision of special rewards and resources for change. Training programs that provide assistance and support in generating new behaviors and practices are also needed.

A number of organizational development programs also speak to these issues in desegregated schooling. They often attempt to develop new kinds of relations among staff members and more effective networks of social and professional support within the staff. Moreover, better communication patterns, both vertical and horizontal, often are a focus of such programs. Such efforts may help create informal structures that can dampen or alleviate stress and burnout. They provide teachers with an ideology and networks of help and colleagueship. These examples also debureaucratize the formal organization of schooling, and leaven it with multicultural and cross-status relationships among various participants.

PROBLEMS OF RESOURCES

Many observers of school desegregation processes indicate that educators and communities do not have the requisite resources to make a success of desegregation. Money, goodwill, energy, materials, personnel, and skill are all part of the resource base that often is lacking. Without them, even a clear mission cannot be enacted and power cannot be exercised effectively. In a resource vacuum the structure has nothing to work with.

Information or ideas, such as those presented in this and other articles, are a resource. The lack of public availability of useful ideas has been one force maintaining schools much as they have always been, regardless of the entrance of new and different groups of students. Without adequate information about possible programs, and without existing visions of the future, how could we expect anything but the status quo?

Another important kind of information is knowledge about the local community and school, its population, personnel, structure, power base, and resources. If staff members do not have this information base they cannot do a very good job planning for change. Moreover, without it they cannot fine tune or adapt these good ideas to the reality of their local situations.

A lack of skill on the part of educators generally interested in trying out good ideas represents another resource problem. Even people who are informed about and who share positive values toward desegregation, or who guess right about some useful components, may lack the skills to carry them off. Sometimes these skills may be technical in character, as in gathering data and organizing material; sometimes they may be social-relational in character, as in teaching differently, aiding students in group work, administering fairly, developing an interracial team, acting in nonracist ways, running a meeting, organizing parents, or manning a picket line.

Often school systems do not have funds to pay for developing and implementing new programs. Money may not always be the critical factor, however, and other resources, such as energy and commitment and voluntary time, may suffice. But, in some times and places, money for extra programs is quite important, and its absence represents a substantial barrier to change and more effective desegregation. In depression-ravaged urban and suburban areas, money may become an increasingly scarce resource for schooling.

Often the energy, political capital, time, and other resources that could aid the desegregation process are tied up in competing agendas. For instance, competent and committed educators must deal with demands to defend teachers from attack, maintain the school board's control over policy and program, prevent vandalism, please the white community, raise teachers' salaries, and maintain order in the school. In order to satisfy the demands of various groups and, at the same time, not leave personal and organizational resources so depleted as to be "burnt out," new managerial structures and procedures will be necessary.

In the same vein, the full utilization of even those resources that are available is made problematic by structural barriers to staff sharing and support. Specialization and separation may facilitate certain educational operations, but they also diminish the collective resources and energy available for implementing new programs during desegregation. Moreover, the staff's typical distance or isolation (or even defense) from minority youth and parents deprives them of the resources these groups may have. Thus, the problem of resource availability and utilization cannot be separated from the need for structural change in the school organization.

Examples of other attractive ideas discussed earlier that pertain to the problems of resources in implementing effective desegregation include (a) the use of community (parent and other) resources in the form of citizens who have special skills or special information about the community, and who can share them in the classroom (Idea 18, in the Classroom); (b) administrative support and new resources must be provided for local innovations (Idea 1, in the Central Administration); and (c) support might also take the form of providing expert help, either from inside the system or in the form of external consultants, for people trying to make changes (Idea 4, in the Central Administration).

The mission of implementing effective desegregation requires some new tasks to be performed; in turn, some resources become more critical than others. Moreover, resources formerly deployed for certain activities may need to be directed toward new priorities. For instance, hiring minority staff members may become a critical priority, as may improving educators' skills in race relations. Other standard components of educational operations may become less important. If obvious reallocation patterns do not appear feasible, the need to generate additional monetary or human resources becomes even more critical.

One obvious approach is to engineer new financial packages that can sustain innovation at the district or local school level. Sources of such support include the federal government (Title III and IV funds, as well as ESEA funds earmarked directly for desegregation-related projects), various foundations, and local businesses. In several urban areas, major corporations have "adopted" local schools, providing financial and personnel resources, as well as establishing a channel for future student employment.

Key practitioners' information and skills are other important resources, and materials or retraining programs directed at teachers and principals represent a popular form of resource development. Sometimes the focus of these efforts is on cognitive skills of educators; at other times it is on their behavioral or pedagogical skills. Clearly, the improvement of teachers' repertoires of classroom management skills is a necessity in dealing with new and different mixes of students with varied needs, orientations, behaviors, and learning styles.

In a labor-intensive operation such as the school, efforts to maximize human resource development and use are a basic managerial concern. In fact, the ability to convert "slack" or "underdeveloped" resources into actual energy, skill, and commitment is a basic managerial resource. Often, however, the structure and power relations of schools simply do not permit the full use of students' and teachers' energy, skills, and commitments. Being "free to teach" and "free to learn" cannot occur without support from new missions, power centers, and organizational structures of the school.

SOME THOUGHTS ABOUT LIMITS

The "attractive ideas" suggested in this chapter cannot be implemented successfully without changes in the mission, power patterns, structures, and resources currently available and operative in schools. Moreover, these changes in the organization of schooling will not be possible without substantial change in other aspects of the local or regional environment. For instance, it is unlikley that we can implement effective desegregation programs in schools while:

(1) racism in the society at large supports white beliefs and values that degrade or fear minorities, and that obscure the realities of racial oppression and privilege in America;

(2) allocations of political power deprive minorities of meaningful control of public goods and services;

(3) allocations of economic resources disproportionately create and sustain poverty for racial minorities and offer little in terms of economic mobility or payoff for minority youth;

(4) control of the school's mission and operation is in the hands of affluent white groups, and their commitment to the needs and interests of minorities is suspect (at best);

(5) political boundaries and ideologies create cities that cannot tap the human and material resources of the broader metropolitan areas in which they are located;

(6) jobs and housing patterns are segregated by race; and

(7) many whites and minority members lack the skills and experience to enable them to interact on an equal-status basis.

Unless these other aspects of the national and local racial environments surrounding schools can be altered, it will be impossible to realize fully the promise of desegregation.

The civil rights movement and the desegregation agenda must be tied to changes in these other aspects of our society. Racism is at the root of segregation, and it is at the root of the unequal division of political and economic opportunities and resources throughout America. Plant closings and corporate flight, rampant inflation and unemployment, escalating energy costs, the location of political power in major economic institutions, and the transfer of political power to "sun belt" areas penalize minority people most severely. Reform and eradication of racism in this society, and in its schools, is no doubt a lifelong endeavor, requiring concerted action on many fronts.

Failure to alter these societal forces does not mean that all work on the implementation of desegregation is futile. Indeed, the attempt to "nibble away" at the process of school change is imperative: Too many lives hang in the balance for us to wait for a more supportive society. Moreover, on occasion, real victories will be won at the local level and in schools that can deviate from surrounding forces. However, unless we broaden our agenda successfully, we will need to admit the limits of desegregation's potential. Major changes in our schools will not be implemented fully without changes in our society.

NOTES

1. Excellent reviews of the research on each of these standards and components of effective desegregation can be found in Crain and Mahard (1978), McConahay (1978), and McPartland (1978).

2. Some especially useful summaries or syntheses of research that have practical value for practitioners and citizens include Chesler et al. (1978, 1981), Forehand and Ragosta (1976), Orfield (1975), St. John (1975), and Weinberg (1977). In addition, reviews or presentations of practitioners' efforts that have practical value for others with these concerns include Burges (1978), Dennis (1976), Hylton (1976), and the Texas Advisory Board Committee (1977).

3. Although these are common characteristics in all organizations and all theories of organizations, different theories may order these features differently. Structural-functionalists often see structure as the key organizational characteristic, guiding power and mission. Marxists, and other power-conflict theorists, often see power as the dominant characteristic, providing guidance to mission and structure as well as resources. As a theologian and philosopher, Terry (1980) sees mission as having priority, and these ideologies or cultural ideals generating the framework within which power and structure operate. Since it is Terry's scheme, we have tried to reflect his sense of priorities. Obviously others may disagree, but his fourfold characterization is provocative and dynamic enough to be useful regardless of the priority or ordering of its elements.

4. Contrasting consensus and conflict ideologies or paradigms of schooling have been reviewed in Chesler et al. (1978, 1979), as well as many other sources.

5. Rothenberg and Chesler (1980) indicate how often it takes a court order to force a school system to act positively on the desegregation agenda. In many cases, a local community group had to create challenge after challenge, and finally to undertake litigation to achieve such a policy decision. Even then, official delays, evasion and appeals resulted in the need to undertake more litigation in order to force local implementation of judicial orders.

6. A variety of organizational development efforts in schools have been described in Schmuck and Miles (1971) and Milstein (1980).

REFERENCES

BERMAN, P. and M. McLAUGHLIN (1980) "Factors affecting the process of change," in M. Milstein (ed.) Schools, Conflict and Change. New York: Teachers College Press.

BURGES, W. (1978) Good Things Can Happen: Your Community Organization and School Desegregation. Cleveland: Federation for Community Planning.

CHESLER, M., B. BRYANT, and J. CROWFOOT (1981) Making Desegregation Work: A Professional Guide to Effecting Change. Beverly Hills, CA: Sage.

CHESLER, M., J. CROWFOOT, and B. BRYANT (1979) The Institutional Contexts of School Desegregation: Contrasting Models of Research and Practice. Ann Arbor: University of Michigan, Center for Research on Social Organizations.

——— (1978) "Institutional changes to support school desegregation: alternative models underlying research and implementation." Law and Contemporary Problems 42, 4: 174-213.

CRAIN, R. L. (1968) The Politics of School Desegregation. Chicago: Aldine.

——— and R. MAHARD (1978) "Desegregation and black achievement: a review of the research." Law and Contemporary Problems 42, 3: 17-56.

DENNIS, E. (1976) Human Relations: A Guide to Intergroup Relations in the Denver Public Schools. Denver: Denver Public Schools, Office of Community Affairs.

DOLBEARE, K. and P. HAMMOND (1971) The School Prayer Decisions. Chicago: University of Chicago Press.

FOREHAND, G. and M. RAGOSTA (1976) A Handbook for Integrated Schooling. Princeton, NJ: Educational Testing Service.

GROSS, N., J. GIACQUINTA, and M. BERNSTEIN (1971) Implementing Organizational Innovations. New York: Basic Books.

HOUSE, E. (1974) The Politics of Educational Innovation. Berkeley, CA: McCutchan.

HYLTON, W. (1976) School Community Relations: A Guide to Interaction Between the School and the Community. Richmond, VA: State Department of Education, Office of School Integration.

JOHNSON, R. (1967) The Dynamics of Compliance. Evanston, IL: Northwestern University Press.

McCONAHAY, J. (1978) "The effects of school desegregation upon students' racial attitudes and behavior: a critical review of the literature and a prolegomenon to future research." Law and Contemporary Problems 42, 3: 77-107.

McPARTLAND, M. (1978) "Desegregation and equity in higher education and employment: is progress related to the desegregation of elementary and secondary schools?" Law and Contemporary Problems 42, 3: 108-132.

MARCH, J. and H. SIMON (1958) Organizations. New York: John Wiley.

MERTON, R. (1940) "Bureaucratic structure and personality." Social Forces 18: 560-568.

METZ, M. H. (1978) Classrooms and Corridors: The Crisis of Authority in Desegregated Secondary Schools. Berkeley: University of California Press.

MEYER, J. and B. ROWAN (1978) "The structure of educational organizations," in J. M. Meyer (ed.) Environments and Organizations. San Francisco: Jossey-Bass.

MILSTEIN, M. [ed.] (1980) Schools, Conflict and Change. New York: Teachers College Press.

MONTI, D. (1979) "Administrative discrimination in the implementation of desegregation policies." Education Evaluation and Policy Analysis 1, 4.

NAKAMURA, R. and F. SMALLWOOD (1980) The Politics of Policy Implementation. New York: St. Martin's.

National Conference of Christians and Jews (1976) Desegregation Without Turmoil: The Role of the Multiracial Community Coalition in Preparing for Smooth Transition. New York: Author.

ORFIELD, G. (1975) "How to make desegregation work: the adaptation of schools to their newly integrated student bodies." Law and Contmeporary Problems 39, 2: 314-340.

PRESSMAN, J. and A. WILDAVSKY (1973) Implementation. Berkeley: University of California Press.

RODGERS, H. and C. BULLOCK (1972) Law and Social Change: Civil Rights Laws and Their Consequences. New York: McGraw-Hill.

ROSSELL, C. H. (1976) "Assessing the unintended impacts of public policy: school desegregation and resegregation." (unpublished)

ROTHENBERG, J. and M. CHESLER (1980) "Authorities' responses to community challenge during desegregation." Presented at meetings of the Society for the Study of Social Problems, New York.

SABATIER, P. and D. MAZMANIAN (1979) "The conditions of effective implementation." Policy Analysis 5, 4: 481-504.

ST. JOHN, N. (1975) School Desegregation: Outcomes for Children. New York: John Wiley.

SCHMUCK, R. and M. MILES [ed.] (1971) Organizational Development in Schools. Palo Alto, CA: National Press.

TERRY, R. (1980) "Impact of white racism on white values and actions." Presented at the Conference on the Impact of Racism on White Americans, Gaithersberg, Maryland, April 18-19.

Texas Advisory Board Committee (1977) Working with Your School. Washington, DC: U.S. Commission on Civil Rights.

U.S. Commission on Civil Rights (1976) Fulfilling the Letter and Spirit of the Law. Washington, DC: Government Printing Office.

VAN HORN, C. and C. VAN METER (1977) "The implementation of intergovernmental policy." Policy Studies Annual Review 1: 97-120.

WEINBERG, M. (1977) Minority Students: A Research Appraisal. Washington, DC: National Institute of Education.

12

EQUITY AND QUALITY IN EDUCATION: CHARACTERISTICS OF EFFECTIVE DESEGREGATED SCHOOLS

WILLIS D. HAWLEY

It seems reasonable to assert that no domestic social policy in the last 25 years has been as divisive as school desegregation. Moreover, it would appear that school desegregation has few ardent proponents left. While most Americans endorse desegregation in principle, most oppose busing and, therefore, oppose the only way substantial reductions in racial isolation can be achieved in most school systems with significant proportions of minority students. Perhaps the most pervasive belief about school desegregation is that it can be achieved only at the expense of quality education.

While former advocates of desegregation are apparently losing faith and members of Congress stampede to support antibusing legislation that creates hardships on desegregating school systems, evidence mounts that desegregation often has had positive consequences for students and is correlated with improved race relations in the society. More important, there is growing evidence that certain practices can

AUTHOR'S NOTE: This chapter is a revised version of the conclusions of a study by the author synthesizing the available research on school desegregation. This study relies heavily on the work of the National Review Panel on School Desegregation Research and was supported by the Ford Foundation and the National Institute of Education (Grant 77-0066).

result in both equal educational opportunity and quality education for children of all races and ethnic backgrounds.

To say that school desegregation has often benefited students, especially minority students, is not, of course, to say that it always has. Nor would it be proper to argue that because we can identify several policies and practices that will increase the effectiveness of desegregation that these are readily brought about. Nonetheless, it seems surprising that the characteristics of effective desegregated school systems are so unsurprising.

This chapter, then, identifies several generalizations that together constitute the essentials of effective desegregation. No attempt is made to list all the good ideas one might derive from the preceding chapters or from other research (see Hawley et al., 1981). My purpose here is to focus on a few key things *school systems* can do to enhance the effectiveness of desegregation. I will not document all of these assertions here. My coauthors in this volume provide much of the evidence, and the interested reader may wish to turn to another recent synthesis of research and expert opinion (Hawley et al., 1981). In addition, this chapter briefly considers two continuing controversies: the alleged hardship that busing imposes on children and the argument that we should be strengthening minority schools rather than emphasizing desegregation.

Let me be clear that the issue dealt with here is not whether desegregation is justified. That is a fundamental constitutional question. The concern of this chapter is with what can be done to enhance the effectiveness of desegregation at the levels of the school district, the school, and the classroom once the desegregation process begins. This focus excludes some significant issues, such as how community conflict can be minimized or what states or the federal government might do to facilitate effective desegregation.

KEY STRATEGIES FOR MORE
EFFECTIVE SCHOOL DESEGREGATION

Desegregated schools seem most likely to improve race relations and to enhance achievement, increase self-esteem, and improve the "life chances" of students if, in addition to having those characteristics that generally foster school effectiveness, they take the several actions listed below. Too often schools seem to focus on only one goal or one strategy to achieve effective desegregation. It seems important to stress the need to develop comprehensive plans and strategies. Generally speaking, the attainment of one goal will enhance the possibilities of achieving another. The actions described here should, therefore, be implemented simultaneously, if possible.

Desegregate students early, in kindergarten if possible. If there is one thing about desegregation that can be said with certainty, it is that the younger the student is when first desegregated, the better the outcome. Paradoxically, parents often fear most for their youngest children and resist plans to desegregate primary grades. Thus, we have desegregated many school systems first and, in some cases, only at the junior high and high school levels where the difficulty of achieving effective desegregation is greatest. It is reasonable to expect desegregation to pose greatest problems at the junior high level.

Encourage substantial interaction among races both in academic settings and in extracurricular activities. There is simply no better way to improve race relations than to increase interracial contact. Such contact is not the automatic result of desegregation; it requires careful structuring and encouragement by teachers and administrators. Moreover, such contact is most effective when students of different races are placed in cooperative, interdependent, and mutually supportive situations. Several strategies have been developed to foster such interaction. These strategies not only improve race relations, they often enhance achievement. These strategies are not financially costly and they are not difficult to learn.

Avoid academic competition, rigid forms of tracking, and ability grouping that draw attention to individual and group achievement differences that are correlated with race. Students should be encouraged to compete with goals rather than with each other. Evidence on the effects of inflexible "ability grouping" suggests that it is most harmful to younger children. School practices that draw attention to racial differences in performance will probably retard race relations and undermine the self-esteem of low achievers. This does not mean that when achievement is correlated with race ability grouping should never be used, but rather that it should be limited to those special cases where it is educationally necessary. Student movement among groups should be possible and should be determined largely by objective criteria. If ability grouping is used in certain classes, special efforts should be made to provide for interracial contact in other settings, such as other classes and extracurricular activities.

If possible, organize so that schools and classrooms have a "critical mass" of each racial group being desegregated. When children of any race find themselves in a distinct minority, they may withdraw or be excluded so that little racial contact occurs. Moreover, if the minority has special needs, teachers and faculties may not be responsive to those needs. The number of students necessary to create this "critical mass" is unknown, but it probably is between 10 and 20 percent depending on the needs and backgrounds of the numerical minority and the predisposition of the dominant racial group and the school staff to interact across racial lines. This proposition has important implications for pupil assignment plans and raises questions about the difficulty of achieving the potential benefits of desegregation through interdistrict and other voluntary plans that involve small numbers of children being moved to predominantly one-race schools.

Minimize the scale of the students' educational experience and decrease the number of students with whom a given teacher has contact. Two ways to do this are to have smaller schools and classes within schools. Another is to avoid overspecializing teacher and administrator roles so that, for example, teachers also act as counselors and outreach workers. The basic idea is to create a more personal sense of community within schools, making it easier to identify and enforce common values, develop friendships, and decrease the uncertainty with which students and teachers must deal. These conditions will probably foster learning, assist in breaking down stereotypes, reduce anxiety, and facilitate the maintenance of a positive sense of order and continuity.

Develop rules and procedures for governing schools that are clear, fair, and consistent and administer them with persistence and equity. This admonition, like almost all others here, applies to all schools. But in desegregating schools there is uncertainty inherent in adapting to new situations and an increase in the variety of the values and behaviors that must be reconciled and adapted to. This requires good government and the elimination of disruptions that threaten effective learning and a sense of personal security. This does not mean that a heavy-handed police state is desirable. On the contrary, desegregated schools must be democratic environments, where rights are protected and due process is ensured. The development of a positive environment in desegregating schools must ultimately rest on a sense among students, and between students and teachers, that the school is a community of shared goals in which mutual respect and support is expected and rewarded.

Maintain a relatively stable student body over time. One aspect of school desegregation that poses problems for achieving most desegregation goals is the fact that it requires many students to adjust to unfamiliar environments. The more often students are moved, the more difficult it will be to make desegregation effective. Some school systems have designed plans which require excessive movement for individual children in order to mollify parents about busing. Other systems have adopted strict racial balance requirements that necessitate the frequent redrawing of pupil assignment plans. There are a number of reasons that frequent movement may be necessary, but the bias should be, once racial isolation is largely ended, toward stability of student-student and student-teacher relationships.

Recruit and retain a racially diverse staff of teachers who are unprejudiced, supportive, and insistent on high performance and racial equality. What teachers do in classrooms is the single most important determinant of effective education. Teachers who are racially biased cannot be good teachers of the children against whom they are prejudiced. Few school systems have strategies for detecting teacher bias or identifying and rewarding positive teacher behaviors that foster desegregation. Moreover, efforts to deal with teacher bias, where they do exist, usually are limited to teacher workshops on "cross-cultural differences" and similar efforts to sensitize teachers to the need for better "human relations" attitudes. It is more effective to focus training efforts on teacher behavior, rather than on attitudes, and to demonstrate to teachers how they can structure classrooms, provide evaluation and feedback, and deal with discipline so as to improve race ralations and their effectiveness as teachers.

Recruit or retrain principals and other administrators who are supportive of desegregation and exert leadership to that effect. All students of desegregation agree that principals play a key role in the effectiveness of desegregated schools, though there are no systematic studies of how variations in the actual behavior of principals account for variations in the results of desegregation. Few school systems, however, provide much desegregation-related training to principals or other administrators, and the topic of desegregation gets short shrift in most college and university educational administration training programs. Among the things administrators can do are to foster cooperation within a multiracial teaching staff and ensure that persons of different races share positions of status and power within the school.

Develop ongoing programs of staff development that emphasize the problems relating to successful desegregation. A continuing staff development effort focused on desegregation is important and should be designed and, when possible, conducted by teachers and principals themselves. Too often, staff development is planned and determined in the central office and is seen as a two-day-a-year enterprise orchestrated by outside consultants. Such programs are probably a waste of time and money. Because of the importance of teacher commitment to the desegregation process, it is critical that teachers be involved in planning for and evaluating desegregation. Few school systems have involved teachers in a meaningful way in the design of such strategies and practices.

Involve parents at the classroom level in actual instructional and/or learning activities. School desegregation often increases the discontinuity between home and school environments for some children while it makes it more difficult for some parents to participate in school activities. Communitywide parent advisory committees are no answer to these problems. Parent committees at the school level, while potentially useful, seem insufficient. Involving parents in the education of their own children so that the responsibility for defining and meeting needs is shared by home and school seems to hold the greatest promise of increasing the effectiveness of desegregated schools. This will require active outreach efforts by the school and especially by teachers whose time would be well spent in such activities as visiting homes and/or holding parent-teacher conferences in neighborhood facilities such as churches.

When a district has sizable proportions of minority students, incentives for voluntary desegregation should be accompanied by mandatory requirements. Magnet schools, open enrollment, "jawboning," and other strategies to encourage voluntary desegregation may be effective when the amount of student relocation required to achieve desegregation is low. But when the minority population is a third or more of the population, voluntary action must be encouraged by the prospect of mandatory assignment of students if any sizable reductions in segregation are to occur.

School systems should take positive steps to involve and interest the community, especially parents, in the desegregation process and its benefits. Community and parent involvement will probably enhance the general acceptability of the desegregation plan and the specific attractiveness of its provisions. Opposition to desegregation is most likely from those who have had no firsthand experience with it. But simply providing opportunities to participate is not enough. Districts should recruit participants, provide information, and, in general, try to sell the school system to parents. Teachers may be the most effective representatives of the school system's message. Some school systems have set up communitywide citizen advisory committees or "blue-ribbon panels." These strategies are no substitute for school level person-to-person efforts to involve and inform.

Obviously, this prescription for effective desegregation is not a definitive or complete set of strategies and tactics. More research and experimentation is needed to understand how the effects of these actions vary in different school contexts, to increase the specificity of these proposals, and to increase the certainty with which one might adopt and implement the policies and practices they imply.

RECURRENT ISSUES: BUSING AND
QUALITY EDUCATION IN MINORITY SCHOOLS

BUSING

Millions of Americans claim not to oppose desegregation but to oppose busing. There are two main points that can be made from the research dealing with busing. First, the available evidence gives one reason to be skeptical that the bus ride is really the *major* reason that most whites who resist desegregation do so (see McConahay and Hawley, 1977; Pride and Woodard, 1978; and Rossell, 1980). As some black leaders have said, "It's not the bus, it's us." The extent of busing to achieve desegregation is not as great as most people believe it is. Estimates vary, but at most 5-7 percent of the children who ride buses to school do so because of desegregation. In Los Angeles, for example, where "forced busing" was a symbol used to successfully amend the state constitution, only 4 percent of all the district's students were bused as a result of the desegregation plan. If opposition to desegregation is related to beliefs that desegregation will lead to negative social and educational experiences for students, and such concern often appears to be a large part of the explanation, reducing the length of the bus ride, increasing bus safety, or eliminating busing altogether will not reduce opposition by whites to sending their children to what was previously a predominantly minority school or to a school in a minority neighborhood, or to a school with large numbers of minority students.

Second, busing itself appears to have little effect on students. In many cases, when parents are confronted with the possibility that their children will be bused in order to attain desegregation they genuinely worry that such busing will be a hardship. Studies that have addressed this concern generally indicate that riding the bus to a school outside of one's neighborhood has no adverse effects on learning. Davis (1973: 119), after looking at data from a large number of desegregated southern school districts, concludes that "there is no evidence that busing per se . . . [or] attending one's own neighborhood school has any effects, positive or negative, on school achievement or social climate." Natkin (1980) studied the effects of busing on desegregated second-grade students in Jefferson County (Louisville) during the 1978-1979 school year. He found no impact of busing on the scores of either black or white students. Zoloth (1976) examined data on the effects on children of the amount of time spent riding the bus and concluded that it has no relationship to achievement. To be sure, some desegregation plans require some students to spend considerably more time getting to school than they did before desegregation. It seems reasonable to assume that riding buses for extended periods of time would be tiring and would take children away from other activities from which they could benefit, and this possibility warrants further study. Nonetheless, it also seems likely that we have romanticized the virtues of the neighborhood school. And, riding the bus is safer for students than walking to school.

WHY NOT MINORITY SCHOOLS?

As we learn more about how to help minority children learn and become more frustrated about the possibilities of effectively desegregating schools, especially in central-city districts with larger minority student enrollments, we will no doubt hear that improving minority schools, *rather than desegregation,* should be our first priority. Some advocates of limiting desegregation go further, to argue that giving priority to desegregation is a form of reverse racism because such advocacy implies that minorities can only learn in the presence of whites (Coleman, 1978). What can be said to the charge that desegregation should not be pushed if it saps energy and resources from efforts to strengthen minority schools?

First, improving minority schools and desegregation are not mutually exclusive objectives.

Second, it is clear that all-minority schools that employ appropriate instructional methods and have teachers and administrators who want minority children to learn, and believe that they can, can be very effective in fostering academic achievement (Bloom, 1976; Coulson and MacQueen, 1978; Edmonds, 1979; Brookover and Lezotte, 1979).

Third, if it is true that the enhancement of the academic achievement of minorities can be as great in segregated as in desegregated schools, it seems unlikely that segregated schools will be as effective as desegregated ones in fostering greater postschool income and occupational status or in developing among minorities a sense of confidence that they can be effective in a society which is (and is likely for the foreseeable future to be) dominated by whites. Also, it is surely the case that segregated schools will be less effective in promoting racial tolerance among both whites and minorities.

Fourth, teachers appear to be less demanding of and responsive to minority children in segregated classrooms than in desegregated classrooms. Presumably this situation can be corrected without desegregation, but we cannot know by looking at evidence from studies of exemplary minority schools or educational innovations.

Finally, the case can be made that desegregation, in general, increases the equity with which the educational resources necessary to foster minority achievement are allocated. This case for the benefits of desegregation is based on three assumptions:

(1) Resources, particularly physical facilities and quality of teaching, make a difference to the quality of education and opportunities minority students have.

(2) Economic resources and control over these allocations are usually in the hands of whites. This is true even where communities are politically "controlled" by minorities, because a significant proportion of the resources available derive from an economic system which is white-dominated and from state and federal agencies dominated by whites.

(3) Whites will discriminate against racially isolated schools in the allocation of resources.

There is growing evidence that financial resources applied intelligently to the needs of students will bring about improved learning (see, for example, Coulson et al., 1977; and Glass and Smith, 1979). This does not mean, of course, that spending more money on schools will necessarily have positive effects.

It is also clear that, in most cases, whites control the economic resources available to public education. It can be reasonably argued, and many minority leaders believe it to be the case, that whites generally will discriminate against minorities in the allocation of funds and that this propensity is held in check when whites go to school with minority students. If the resource allocation theory is correct, its negative consequences might be remedied either by school desegregation or by school finance laws that assign resources to public schools with regard to learning needs that are tied to objective indicators, thus reducing the opportunities whites have to discriminate against minorities. (It is not surprising, then, that minorities have sought increased federal and state support of public schools, since such support is invariably tied to funding formulas which, if they had negative consequences for minorities, might be subject to constitutional challenge.)

One response to the idea that whites will discriminate against minorities in the allocation of resources if schools are segregated is that whites will be willing to pay the bill for minority schools as long as doing so reduces the contact whites must have with minorities. There is no evidence that speaks clearly to this possibility, except, perhaps, a recent study by Noboa (1980) which finds that Hispanics are more likely to have access to a broad range of special programs — including bilingual funds — in racially mixed school districts than in segregated school districts.

Let me reemphasize the point that quality minority schools can be pursued at the same time we desegregate. In many big cities, where most minorities live, almost all schools will have more minority students than white students. They will be, in effect, minority schools. Moreover, judges have been willing to tolerate, in the context of a desegregation plan, the existence of some schools where almost all students are of one color. It seems reasonable, as the minority plaintiffs argued in the Los Angeles case, that more effective minority schools should be preserved when the logistics and demography of desegregation place limits on the elimination of racially identifiable schools.

CONCLUSION

A careful review of the research indicates that cynicism about the past and future consequences of school desegregation is unsupported by the available evidence. To be sure, desegregation often has fallen short of the goals it advocates have held for it. And, 25 years after the U.S. Supreme Court's decision to end legally sanctioned racial isolation in the public schools, many children, especially outside the South, attend racially identifiable schools.

But, wherever school systems have been purposively desegregated, interracial contact has increased. More often than not, desegregation has resulted in benefits for the children involved. Moreover, research and experience provide the basis for enhancing the positive effects of school desegregation, reducing its costs, and developing further knowledge. The most difficult aspect of desegregation clearly is the impact it has on residential white flight in some cities. It is hard to believe that more knowledge, commitment, and imagination would not lead to more satisfactory resolutions of this vexing problem.

More effective desegregation will require that old myths and ideologies be put aside; we must see desegregation involving a range of strategies, and realize that the appropriateness of these strategies will vary with local conditions. This should allow more atteniton to be focused on the objectives that most people of all races share. Desegregation is not a game in which some must lose so that others can win.

REFERENCES

BLOOM, B. (1976) Human Characteristics and School Learning. New York: McGraw-Hill.
BROOKOVER, W. B. and L. W. LEZOTTE (1979) Changes in School Characteristics Coincident with Changes in Student Achievement. East Lansing: Michigan State University, Institute for Research on Teaching.

COLEMAN, J.S. (1978) "Can we integrate our public schools without busing?" Chicago Tribune (September 17).

COULSON, J.E. and A.H. MacQUEEN (1978) Emergency School Aid Act (ESAA) Evaluation: Overview of Findings from Supplemental Analyses. Santa Moncia, CA: System Development Corporation.

COULSON, J.E. and S.D. HANES, D.G. OZENE, C. BRADFORD, W.J. DOHERTY, and J.A. HEMENWAY (1977) The Third Year of Emergency School Aid Act (ESAA) Implementation. Santa Monica, CA: System Development Corporation.

DAVIS, J. (1973) "Busing," in Southern Schools: An Evaluation of the Emergency School Assistance Program and of Desegregation. Chicago: National Opinion Research Center.

EDMONDS, R. (1979) "Effective schools for the urban poor." Educational Leadership 37: 15-24.

GLASS, G.J. and M.L. SMITH (1979) "Meta-analysis of research on class size and achievement." Educational Evaluation and Policy Analysis 1: 2-16.

HAWLEY, W.D., R.L. CRAIN, C.H. ROSSELL, R.R. FERNANDEZ, J.W. SCHOFIELD, M.A. SMYLIE, R. TOMPKINS, W.T. TRENT, M.S. ZLOTNIK, J.B. McCONAHAY, M. WEINBERG, C.A. BROH, C.B. VERGON, B. WILLIAMS, and C. ANDERSEN (1981) Assessment of Current Knowledge About the Effectiveness of School Desegregation Strategies, Volumes 1-9. Nashville, TN: Vanderbilt University, Institute for Public Policy Studies, Center for Education and Human Development Policy.

McCONAHAY, J.B. and W.D. HAWLEY (1977) Is It the Buses or the Blacks: Self-Interest Versus Symbolic Racism as Predictors of Opposition to Busing in Louisville. Durham, NC: Duke University, Institute of Policy Sciences and Public Affairs, Center for Educational Policy.

NATKIN, G.L. (1980) "The effects of busing on second grade students' achievement test scores (Jefferson County, Kentucky)." Presented at the annual meeting of the American Educational Research Association, Boston, April.

NOBOA, A. (1980) An Overview of Trends in Segregation of Hispanic Students in Major School Districts Having Large Hispanic Enrollment (Final Report). Washington, DC: National Institute of Education.

PRIDE, R.A. and J.D. WOODARD (1978) "Busing plans, media agenda, and white flight." Presented at the annual meeting of the Southwestern Political Science Association, Houston, April.

ROSSELL, C.H. (1980) "The effectiveness of desegregation plans in reducing racial isolation, white flight, and achieving a positive community response," in W.D. Hawley (ed.) An Assessment of Effective Desegregation Strategies: Preliminary Report. Durham, NC: Duke University, Institute of Policy Sciences and Public Affairs, Center for Educational Policy.

ZOLOTH, B. (1976) "The impact of busing on student achievement: a reanalysis." Growth and Change 7, 7: 43-52.

ABOUT THE AUTHORS

JOMILLS HENRY BRADDOCK II is Research Scientist at the Center for Social Organization of Schools of Johns Hopkins University. He has written numerous articles on the long-term effects of school desegregation on social mobility outcomes of minority young adults. He received his Ph.D. in sociology from Florida State University.

MARK A. CHESLER is Associate Professor of Sociology at the University of Michigan and Executive Director of Community Resources, Ltd., in Ann Arbor. He was formerly Project Director and Program Coordinator of the Center for Research on the Utilization of Scientific Knowledge of the Institute for Social Research at the University of Michigan. He has also served as consultant to schools and community groups regarding problems of school desegregation, institutional discrimination, organizational change, and community development. He received his Ph.D. in social psychology from the University of Michigan and has published widely in the areas of educational and institutional change, teaching in desegregated classrooms, and postimplementation classroom strategies in desegregated schools. His most recent book deals with the issue of access to power and privilege as a component of the sociology of education.

ROBERT L. CRAIN is Senior Social Scientist for the Rand Corporation and Principal Research Investigator at the Center for the Social Organization of Schools of Johns Hopkins University. He has coauthored four books on the politics of school desegregation and effective desegregation strategies, and has also published a number of articles on desegregation and minority academic achievement. He holds a Ph.D. in sociology from the University of Chicago.

JAMES E. CROWFOOT is Associate Professor of Urban and Regional Planning and Natural Resources at the University of Michigan and serves as Project Director of Community Resources, Ltd., in Ann Arbor. He was formerly Project Director and Lecturer in the School of Education and Program Associate for the Center for Research on the Utilization of Scientific Knowledge of the Institute for Social Research at the University of Michigan. He has coauthored several articles on institutional changes to support school desegregation, institutional conflict and change, and the use and allocation of resources for social change, and has also written on negotiation as a tactical tool for citizen organizations. He has served as consultant to citizen groups, public interest organizations, and democratically managed enterprises concerning problems of organization effectiveness and social change strategy. He received his Ph.D. in organizational psychology from the University of Michigan.

EDGAR G. EPPS is Marshall Field IV Professor of Urban Education at the University of Chicago. He has served as Associate Editor of the American Sociological Review and President of the Association of Social and Behavioral Scientists. His writing deals primarily with the impact of school desegregation on aspirations, self-concepts, achievement orientation, and other aspects of personality, and includes works on interdistrict desegregation and students in historically black colleges. He holds a Ph.D. in sociology from Washington State University.

RICARDO R. FERNANDEZ is Associate Professor in the Department of Cultural Foundations of Education of the University of Wisconsin at Milwaukee and is Director of the Midwest National Origin Desegregation Assistance Center. He currently serves as Past President of the National Association for Bilingual Education and is a member of the Monitoring Board for the Desegregation of Milwaukee Public Schools and of the Board of Directors for the Puerto Rican Legal Defense and Education Fund. His research and writing emphasize the status of education for Hispanic students and desegregation and Hispanics. He received his Ph.D. in Romance languages and literatures from Princeton University.

JUDITH T. GUSKIN is an Adjunct Associate Professor of Anthropology at the University of Wisconsin at Parkside and Senior Researcher for the National Institute of Education Bilingual Education Community Study. She was formerly Senior Program Associate for the Midwest National Origin Desegregation Assistance Center, Assistant Professor at Clark University, and Research Associate in the School of Education at the University of Michigan. She has also been affiliated with the Bilingual Education Service Center in Illinois. She received her Ph.D. from the University of Michigan. Her publications deal with bilingual education and desegregation, and planning educational change.

WILLIS D. HAWLEY is Dean of Peabody College, Vanderbilt University's School of Education and Human Development, and Professor of Education and Political Science at Vanderbilt. Before coming to Vanderbilt, he was Director of the Center for Educational Policy at Duke University. He served as Director of the Education Department Study of the President's Reorganization Project from 1977-1978. He has been a consultant to the Office of Management and Budget, the U.S. Department of Education, and numerous state and local agencies. From 1979 to 1981 he was director of the U.S. Department of Education's Educational Policy Development Center for Desegregation. His writings deal with educational policy, educational research and development, organizational change, and the learning of political and social values. He received his Ph.D. in political science from the University of California at Berkeley, and he holds a teaching certificate in California.

JOHN B. McCONAHAY is Associate Professor of Public Policy and Psychology at Duke University. He has served as Associate Director of the Institute of Policy Sciences and Public Affairs at Duke University and as Director of the Psychology and Politics Program at Yale University. His research has included issues of psychology and urban dilemmas, symbolic racism, and effects of school desegregation on students racial attitudes and behavior. He holds a Ph.D. in social psychology from the University of California, Los Angeles.

JAMES M. McPARTLAND is Co-Director of the Center for Social Organization of Schools of Johns Hopkins University, and has served as consultant to the U.S. Commission on Civil Rights. He has authored a variety of articles on the sociology of education and has coauthored books on violence in schools and the equality of educational opportunity. He has also written on racial isolation in public schools. He received his Ph. D. in sociology from Johns Hopkins University.

RITA E. MAHARD is currently a doctoral student in social psychology at the University of Michigan and serves as Consultant to the Rand Corporation. She has coauthored a variety of publications on such topics as school racial composition and black college attendance and achievement, and desegregation and minority achievement. She received her M. A. in sociology from the University of Michigan.

GARY ORFIELD is Professor of Political Science at the University of Illinois and chairs the National Institute of Education's Desegregation Study Group. He also served as a court-appointed expert for the St. Louis and Los Angeles desegregation cases. He has written widely on school desegregation issues, including segregation and national policy, schools and the Civil Rights Act of 1964, demographic and housing trends and desegregation policy, and desegregation in metropolitan areas. He received his Ph. D. in political science from the University of Chicago.

CHRISTINE H. ROSSELL is Assistant Professor of Political Science at Boston University. She has served as Consultant to the Rand Corporation, the U.S. Office of Education, and the U.S. Department of Justice. Her primary research areas include white flight and school desegregation, desegregation and community social change, and the use of social science research in education equity cases. She received her Ph. D. in political science from the University of Southern California.

ROBERT E. SLAVIN received his Ph. D. in social relations in 1975 from Johns Hopkins University. Since that time he has been an Associate Research Scientist and Research Scientist at the Center for Social Organization of Schools at Johns Hopkins University. His research is primarily concerned with classroom interventions involving student learning teams and their effects on student achievement, intergroup relations, mainstreaming, and other outcomes, but he has also conducted other research in desegregation, motivation, field research methodologies, and energy conservation.

WILLIAM L. TAYLOR currently serves as Director of the Center for National Policy Review at Catholic University School of Law. He is also a member of the National Board and Executive Committee of Americans for Democratic Action, and of the Executive Committee of the Leadership Conference on Civil Rights. He was formerly Staff Director for the U.S. Commission on Civil Rights and Secretary of the President's Sub-Cabinet Group on Civil Rights. His research deals with a variety of legal and social issues, including equality and urbanization, legal issues in school desegregation, school busing, and metropolitan desegregation. He received his LL.B. from Yale University School of Law.

MARK G. YUDOF is Marrs McLean Professor of Law and Associate Dean for Academic Affiars at the University of Texas School of Law. He also chairs the National Study Group on Legal and Governmental Studies of the National Institute of Education. He has written on educational policy and the law, international human rights and school desegregation in the United States, and government expression and the First Amendment. He received his LL.B. from the University of Pennsylvania School of Law.